FAVORITE BRAND NAME™
Asian

Publications International, Ltd.

Favorite Brand Name Recipes at www.fbnr.com

ISBN-13: 978-1-4127-2287-2
ISBN-10: 1-4127-2287-X

Library of Congress Control Number: 2005925714

Manufactured in China.

8 7 6 5 4 3 2 1

Microwave Cooking: Microwave ovens vary in wattage. Use the cooking times as guidelines and check for doneness before adding more time.

Preparation/Cooking Times: Preparation times are based on the approximate amount of time required to assemble the recipe before cooking, baking, chilling or serving. These times include preparation steps such as measuring, chopping and mixing. The fact that some preparations and cooking can be done simultaneously is taken into account. Preparation of optional ingredients and serving suggestions is not included.

CONTENTS

Introduction

If you love Asian cuisine, you've chosen an exciting cookbook that includes the spicy zing of Thai cooking, the wonderful mysteries of Indian dishes, authentic tastes from China, the exotic appeal of Vietnamese dishes and more. You'll quickly discover just how easy it is to add these dishes to your everyday meals. From appetizers to main dishes, this cookbook provides many opportunities to exercise your creativity while providing recipes that are simply beautiful without all the fuss.

While some Asian dishes require common ingredients like long-grain rice, soy sauce and cabbage, others call for unfamiliar ingredients. Always check the glossary on the following pages for a brief description before looking for these items in a local ethnic market or international sections of your supermarket. Shopping for the Asian staples for your kitchen may seem overwhelming, but a lot of the ingredients are used in many dishes.

Whether you're trying your hand at cooking Asian dishes for the first time or you have already had some practice, these recipes will provide a flavorful overview of what the region has to offer. So start exploring Asian cuisine and you will find an exciting path to new culinary experiences!

BAMBOO SHOOTS: These young shoots from an edible species of bamboo are plucked as soon as they poke through the ground. They are crunchy, slightly sweet and mild tasting. Fresh bamboo shoots are rarely available in the United States. Sliced bamboo shoots are available in cans; they should be drained and rinsed well before using.

BEAN PASTE: Also known as brown or yellow bean sauce and miso in Japan, bean paste is a thick sauce made from fermented soybeans, flour, water and salt. It may be smooth or contain whole beans. Hot bean paste, which gets its heat from chilies, is also available.

BEAN SPROUTS: Small white shoots of the mung bean, bean sprouts are one of the few sprouts that are sturdy enough to stand up to cooking. Both fresh and canned bean sprouts are available and should be thoroughly rinsed in cold water and drained before using.

BEAN THREADS: Also called transparent or cellophane noodles, these dry, fine white noodles are made from powdered mung beans. They have little flavor, but readily absorb the flavors of other foods. Bean threads are available in packets or bundles.

BLACK FUNGUS: This fungus, also called cloud ears or wood ears, can be found growing on various woods, such as mango or kapok woods. It is also available dried. On one side, it is greyish black and the other side is either grey or beige. Black fungus should be added at the end of cooking so that its crunchy texture may be retained. It has no flavor of its own but absorbs the seasonings of the dish.

BOK CHOY: A member of the cabbage family, bok choy has 8- to 10-inch-long white or greenish-white stalks and large dark green leaves. Both the stalks and leaves are used in cooking, but cooked separately.

CARDAMOM: Cardamom seeds grow in pods, about 15 seeds to a pod. An aromatic spice often used in Indian cooking, cardamom is available most often as seeds or ground into a powder, but the edible seed-filled pods are sometimes available.

CHILI OIL: This reddish-colored oil is made from peanut oil infused with dried red chili peppers. Use it sparingly as it is blazing hot.

CHILI PASTE: Chili paste and garlic chili paste are used extensively in Chinese, Thai, Vietnamese and other Asian cuisines. Made from mashed chili peppers, soy beans, vinegar, seasonings and often garlic, chili paste is extremely hot.

CHILI PEPPERS: Green and red Thai chili peppers are 1 to 1½ inches long and very narrow. Jalapeño and serrano chili peppers may be substituted for most other Asian chili peppers.

CHINESE CHILI SAUCE: A thick, fiery sauce of ground chilies and salt, Chinese chili sauce should be used sparingly.

CHUTNEY: A spicy fruit-based relish served as a refreshing accompaniment to certain Indian dishes, chutney can be raw or cooked. Prepared chutneys can be purchased in most supermarkets.

COCONUT MILK/COCONUT CREAM: A creamy unsweetened liquid made from the grated meat of mature coconuts, coconut milk should not be confused with the thin liquid that is drained from a fresh coconut. A richer coconut cream is also available. Both coconut milk and coconut cream are readily available in most supermarkets.

CORIANDER SEEDS: This aromatic spice comes from the parsleylike plant of the same name. Many Americans know the green leaves of the coriander plant as cilantro. The seeds are used in Indian cooking. The leaves are used in Thai, Vietnamese and Indian cuisines as well as in Latin and Caribbean cooking.

CORN, BABY: The edible cobs of baby corn are 2 to 3 inches long with rows of tiny yellow kernels. They are slightly sweet and crunchy. Available in cans or jars packed in salted water, baby corn should be drained and rinsed with cold water to remove brine before using.

CURRY PASTE: A mixture of clarified butter, curry powder, vinegar and other seasonings, this paste is usually only found canned. Fresh curry paste is rarely seen outside the Asian countries.

DAIKON: This long, white radish with a sweet flavor is used extensively in Japan. Daikons are most often grated and eaten raw as a condiment. They are also cooked in some simmered or braised dishes. Slender white icicle radishes may be substituted.

EGG NOODLES, CHINESE–STYLE: Made of flour, eggs, water and salt, Chinese egg noodles can be purchased fresh, frozen or dried. They may be eaten hot or cold. The common cooking methods include steaming, stir-frying and deep frying.

EGG ROLL WRAPPERS: These thin sheets of noodlelike dough are available in 7- and 8-inch squares or circles. Wonton wrappers are also available, but are cut into 3- and 4-inch squares. Both are sold refrigerated or frozen. Keep wrappers tightly wrapped in plastic to prevent drying during storage.

FERMENTED, SALTED BLACK BEANS: These pungent, salty black soybeans are used in Chinese cooking. Fermented black beans are available in Asian markets. They need to be rinsed under cold running water before using to reduce their saltiness.

FISH SAUCE: A salty brown liquid extract of fermented fish, fish sauce is used as a flavoring in several Southeast Asian cuisines. It is called nuoc nam in Vietnam, nam pla in Thailand and shottsuru in Japan. In American supermarkets it is most often labeled as fish sauce. The strong aroma disappears during cooking.

FIVE–SPICE POWDER: This blend of five ground spices has a pungent, slightly sweet flavor. Generally made of anise seed, fennel, cloves, cinnamon and ginger or pepper, five-spice powder is readily available in most supermarkets.

GINGER, FRESH: This knobby root with light brown skin is available fresh in the produce section. Always remove the tough outer skin before using ginger. Wrapped in plastic, ginger will keep for several weeks in the refrigerator. Peeled ginger can also be kept in salted water or dry sherry in the refrigerator for several months.

HOISIN SAUCE: This dark brown sauce is made of soybeans, flour, sugar, spices, garlic, chilies and salt. It has a sweet, spicy flavor and is used in many Chinese recipes. Once opened, canned hoisin sauce should be transferred to a glass container, sealed and refrigerated.

KIMCHEE: Kimchee, or kimchi, is a hot and spicy pickled vegetable mixture served as a condiment with many Korean meals. It is most often made of cabbage. Available in jars in the produce sections of some supermarkets and in Asian markets, kimchee must be kept refrigerated.

LEMONGRASS: A stiff, pale green grasslike plant, lemongrass is an essential part of Southeast Asian cooking. It has a lemony aroma. To use, remove the outer leaves and chop or slice it across the stem from the base up to where the leaves begin to separate.

MUSHROOMS, DRIED ASIAN: Dehydrated black or brown mushrooms from Asia are available packaged or by the ounce. They are often labeled as Chinese or Asian mushrooms. Dried mushrooms must be soaked in warm or hot water until they are softened.

MUSHROOMS, SHIITAKE: These wild Japanese mushrooms are readily available both fresh and dried in most supermarkets. They are also called Chinese black mushrooms.

MUSHROOMS, STRAW: These small mushrooms with a deep umbrella shape are most commonly found canned. Used in Chinese cuisine, they have a mild flavor.

NAPA CABBAGE: Also known as Chinese cabbage, napa is a loosely packed elongated head of light green stalks that are slightly crinkled. It has a mild flavor.

OYSTER SAUCE: This thick, brown Chinese sauce is made from oysters that have been boiled with soy sauce and seasonings and then strained. Oyster sauce adds a surprisingly delicate taste to meat and vegetable dishes. Its salty, fishy flavor disappears when cooked.

PLUM SAUCE: A thick, piquant, chutney-like sauce, plum sauce is frequently served with duck or pork dishes.

RICE, BASMATI: This long-grain aromatic rice is grown in the foothills of the Himalaya Mountains, where the soil and climate contribute to its special taste. It has a perfumy aroma and nutlike flavor. Look for it in large supermarkets and Indian markets.

RICE, JASMINE: A long-grain aromatic rice, jasmine rice is grown in Thailand. It has a subtle aroma and a slightly nutty taste.

RICE STICK NOODLES: Also called rice noodles, these dried flat noodles are made from rice flour. They are available in several widths. Soften the noodles in warm water before using, unless they will be fried in oil.

RICE VERMICELLI: Available in several widths in packets or small bundles, rice vermicelli are dried round noodles made from rice flour. They look similar to bean threads.

RICE VINEGAR: Mellow and tangy in flavor, this vinegar is made from fermented rice. Chinese rice vinegar is pale yellow in color and is generally more readily available than the almost colorless Japanese rice vinegar.

RICE WINE: Made from fermented rice, rice wines are sweet and usually low in alcohol. Japanese versions are sake and mirin.

SAKE: see Rice Wine.

SATAY: Satay is the Indonesian version of marinated meat that is cubed, threaded on a skewer and either grilled or baked. Shish kebabs and shashi are similar to satay except that they include vegetables along with the meat, fish or poultry.

SESAME OIL: Dark or Asian sesame oil is an amber-colored oil pressed from toasted sesame seeds. It has a strong nutty taste that if used sparingly adds a unique flavor to Asian dishes. Do not confuse it with the pale-colored sesame oil made from untoasted sesame seeds.

SOBA: Grayish brown in color, Japanese soba noodles are made of buckwheat flour. Unlike other dried noodles, soba must be used within two or three months.

SOY SAUCE: This dark, salty liquid is made from fermented soybeans and wheat or barley. Although there are different varieties available, such as dark and light, the major brands found in supermarkets are all-purpose. A reduced-sodium version is available as well.

SZECHUAN PEPPER: A reddish-brown pepper, szechuan pepper has a strong, pungent aroma and a flavor with a time-delayed action—its numbing effect may not be noticed immediately. It should be used sparingly. The pepper can be found either whole or crushed, but never ground.

TAHINI: A thick and mild Middle Eastern paste made from ground sesame seeds, tahini has a rich, nutty flavor. It is a key ingredient in such preparations as hummus and baba ghanouj. It should not be confused with Asian sesame seed paste, which is made from roasted sesame seeds, resulting in a more pronounced flavor.

TAMARI: A dark liquid made from soybeans, tamari is similar to soy sauce but is thicker and stronger in flavor.

TANDOORI: A term used to describe Indian food that is cooked over a very hot, smoky fire in a tandoor oven. Chicken or meat is often threaded onto skewers before baking. The oven is also used to cook the traditional bread of India, naan.

TERIYAKI SAUCE: Used as a marinade, the sauce is made of soy sauce, sake, sugar, ginger and seasonings. The sugar gives cooked food a slightly glazed look.

TOFU: Also known as bean curd, tofu is made from soy milk. It is white or creamy in color with a smooth texture. Tofu, which is high in protein, has a bland, slightly nutty flavor but readily takes on the flavor of foods it is cooked with. Firm and extra-firm tofu can be cut into pieces and used in cooking. Tofu is available fresh in the refrigerated section of some supermarkets. It is also found in aseptic packages (a form of vacuum packaging); store these packages at room temperature.

UDON NOODLES: These noodles are made of wheat flour, salt and water. They come round or flat and vary in length and thickness.

WASABI: This Japanese horseradish comes from the root of an Asian plant. It has a sharp, hot flavor and is made into a green-colored condiment by adding water, either to its paste or powder form.

WATER CHESTNUTS: Water chestnuts are the fruit of an Asian aquatic plant. They add crunchiness to stir-fries, salads and rice dishes. Water chestnuts are readily available canned, both whole and sliced.

WONTON WRAPPERS: see Eggroll Wrappers.

Enticing Appetizers

SESAME CHICKEN SALAD WONTON CUPS

Nonstick cooking spray
20 (3-inch) wonton wrappers
1 tablespoon sesame seeds
2 cups water
2 small boneless skinless chicken breasts (about 8 ounces)
1 cup fresh green beans, cut diagonally into ½-inch pieces
¼ cup reduced-fat mayonnaise
1 tablespoon chopped fresh cilantro (optional)
2 teaspoons honey
1 teaspoon reduced-sodium soy sauce
⅛ teaspoon ground red pepper

1. Preheat oven to 350°F. Spray miniature muffin pan with cooking spray. Press 1 wonton wrapper into each muffin cup; spray with cooking spray. Bake 8 to 10 minutes or until golden brown. Cool in pan on wire rack before filling.

2. Place sesame seeds in shallow baking pan. Bake 5 minutes or until lightly toasted, stirring occasionally. Set aside to cool.

3. Meanwhile, bring water to a boil in medium saucepan. Add chicken. Reduce heat to low; cover. Simmer 10 minutes or until chicken is no longer pink in center, adding green beans after 7 minutes. Drain.

4. Finely chop chicken. Place in medium bowl. Add green beans and remaining ingredients; mix lightly. Spoon lightly rounded tablespoonful chicken mixture into each wonton cup. Garnish, if desired.

Makes 10 servings

SESAME CHICKEN SALAD WONTON CUPS

THAI LAMB & COUSCOUS ROLLS

5 cups water, divided
16 large napa or Chinese cabbage
    leaves, stems trimmed
2 tablespoons minced fresh ginger
1 teaspoon red pepper flakes
⅔ cup uncooked quick-cooking
    couscous
    Nonstick cooking spray
½ pound ground lean lamb
½ cup chopped green onions
3 cloves garlic, minced
¼ cup plus 2 tablespoons minced
    fresh cilantro or mint, divided
2 tablespoons reduced-sodium soy
    sauce
1 tablespoon lime juice
1 teaspoon dark sesame oil
1 cup plain nonfat yogurt

1. Place 4 cups water in medium saucepan; bring to a boil over high heat. Drop cabbage leaves into water; cook 30 seconds. Drain. Rinse under cold water until cool; pat dry with paper towels.

2. Place 1 cup water, ginger and red pepper in medium saucepan; bring to a boil over high heat. Stir in couscous; cover. Remove saucepan from heat; let stand 5 minutes.

3. Spray large saucepan with cooking spray; add lamb, onions and garlic. Cook and stir over medium-high heat 5 minutes or until lamb is no longer pink. Remove lamb from skillet; drain in colander.

4. Combine couscous, lamb, ¼ cup cilantro, soy sauce, lime juice and oil in medium bowl. Spoon evenly down centers of cabbage leaves. Fold ends of cabbage leaves over filling; roll up. Combine yogurt and remaining 2 tablespoons cilantro in small bowl; spoon evenly over rolls. Serve warm. Garnish, if desired.
Makes 16 appetizers

Tip

Fresh unpeeled ginger, tightly wrapped, may be refrigerated for three weeks. It may be frozen up to six months wrapped in plastic wrap and sealed in a resealable plastic freezer bag. To use, slice off what is needed and return the remaining ginger to the freezer.

THAI LAMB & COUSCOUS ROLLS

CRISP FISH CAKES

Ginger Dipping Sauce (recipe follows)
1 pound boneless catfish, halibut or cod fillets, cut into 1-inch pieces
1 tablespoon fish sauce
3 cloves garlic, minced
1 tablespoon chopped fresh cilantro
2 teaspoons grated lemon peel
1 teaspoon finely chopped fresh ginger
⅛ teaspoon ground red pepper
Peanut oil for frying
1 head curly leaf lettuce
1 medium green or red apple, cut into thin strips or 1 ripe mango, diced
½ cup fresh cilantro leaves
⅓ cup fresh mint leaves

1. Prepare Ginger Dipping Sauce; set aside.

2. Process fish pieces in food processor 10 to 20 seconds or just until coarsely chopped. *Do not purée.* Add fish sauce, garlic, chopped cilantro, lemon peel, ginger and red pepper; process 5 seconds or until combined.

3. Rub cutting board with 1 to 2 teaspoons oil. Place fish mixture on board; pat evenly into 7-inch square. Cut into 16 squares; shape each square into 2-inch patty.

4. Heat 1 to 1½ inches oil in Dutch oven or large skillet over medium-high heat until oil registers 360°F to 375°F on deep-fry thermometer. Place 4 patties on slotted spoon and lower into hot oil.

5. Fry patties 2 to 3 minutes or until golden and fish is opaque in center. (Overcooking will dry fish and cause patties to shrink.) Remove with slotted spoon to paper towels; drain. Repeat with remaining patties, returning oil to 360°F to 375°F before adding new batch.

6. Pile fish cakes on serving platter with lettuce leaves, apple, cilantro leaves, mint and Ginger Dipping Sauce. To eat, stack 1 fish cake, apple strips, cilantro and mint in center of lettuce leaf. Drizzle with sauce; enclose filling in lettuce leaf and eat out of hand.

Makes 6 to 8 servings

GINGER DIPPING SAUCE

¼ cup rice vinegar
2 tablespoons water
1 teaspoon sugar
1 teaspoon finely chopped fresh ginger
½ teaspoon red pepper flakes
½ teaspoon fish sauce

Combine all ingredients in small bowl; stir until sugar dissolves.

Makes about ⅓ cup sauce

CRISP FISH CAKES

PORTOBELLO MUSHROOMS SESAME

4 large portobello mushrooms
2 tablespoons sweet rice wine
2 tablespoons reduced-sodium soy sauce
2 cloves garlic, minced
1 teaspoon dark sesame oil

1. Remove and discard stems from mushrooms; set caps aside. Combine remaining ingredients in small bowl.

2. Brush both sides of mushrooms with soy sauce mixture. Grill mushrooms top side up on covered grill over medium coals 3 to 4 minutes. Brush tops with soy sauce mixture and turn over; grill 2 minutes more or until mushrooms are lightly browned. Turn again and grill, basting frequently, 4 to 5 minutes or until tender when pressed with back of spatula. Remove mushrooms and cut diagonally into ½-inch-thick slices.

Makes 4 servings

MINIATURE TERIYAKI PORK KABOBS

1 pound boneless pork, cut into 4×1×½-inch strips
1 small green bell pepper, cut into 1×¼×¼-inch strips
1 can (11 ounces) mandarin oranges, drained
¼ cup teriyaki sauce
1 tablespoon honey
1 tablespoon vinegar
⅛ teaspoon garlic powder

Soak 24 (8-inch) bamboo skewers in water about 10 minutes. Thread 1 pepper strip, then pork strips accordion-style with mandarin oranges on skewers. Place 1 pepper strip on end of each skewer. Arrange skewers on broiler pan.

For sauce, combine teriyaki sauce, honey, vinegar and garlic powder in small bowl; mix well. Brush sauce over kabobs. Broil, 6 inches from heat, about 15 minutes or until pork is done, turning and basting with sauce occasionally.

Makes about 24 appetizers

Favorite recipe from **National Pork Board**

PORTOBELLO MUSHROOMS SESAME

CHICKEN KABOBS WITH THAI DIPPING SAUCE

1 pound boneless skinless chicken breasts, cut into 1-inch cubes
1 small cucumber, seeded and cut into small chunks
1 cup cherry tomatoes
2 green onions, cut into 1-inch pieces
⅔ cup teriyaki baste & glaze sauce
⅓ cup *Frank's® RedHot®* Original Cayenne Pepper Sauce
⅓ cup peanut butter
3 tablespoons frozen orange juice concentrate, undiluted
2 cloves garlic, minced

Thread chicken, cucumber, tomatoes and onions alternately onto metal skewers; set aside.

To prepare Thai Dipping Sauce, combine teriyaki baste & glaze sauce, **Frank's RedHot** Sauce, peanut butter, orange juice concentrate and garlic; mix well. Reserve ⅔ cup sauce for dipping.

Brush skewers with some of remaining sauce. Place skewers on oiled grid. Grill over hot coals 10 minutes or until chicken is no longer pink in center, turning and basting often with remaining sauce. Serve skewers with reserved Thai Dipping Sauce. Garnish as desired.

Makes 6 appetizer servings

CREAMY HONEY SESAME DIP FOR VEGETABLES

¾ cup nonfat mayonnaise
¼ cup rice vinegar
¼ cup honey
3 tablespoons toasted sesame seeds
1 to 2 tablespoons grated fresh gingerroot
1 small clove garlic, minced
¾ teaspoon Oriental sesame oil
⅛ teaspoon crushed red pepper flakes
Salt to taste

Whisk together mayonnaise, vinegar and honey in small bowl. Add remaining ingredients; mix thoroughly. Dip may be stored tightly covered in refrigerator up to 1 week. Serve with assorted fresh vegetables.

Makes 1⅓ cups dip

*Favorite recipe from **National Honey Board***

CHICKEN KABOBS WITH THAI DIPPING SAUCE

POT STICKERS

2 cups all-purpose flour
¾ cup plus 2 tablespoons boiling water
½ cup very finely chopped napa cabbage
8 ounces lean ground pork
2 tablespoons finely chopped water chestnuts
1 green onion with top, finely chopped
1½ teaspoons cornstarch
1½ teaspoons soy sauce
1½ teaspoons dry sherry
½ teaspoon minced fresh ginger
½ teaspoon dark sesame oil
¼ teaspoon sugar
2 tablespoons vegetable oil, divided
⅔ cup chicken broth, divided
Soy sauce, vinegar and chili oil

1. Place flour in large bowl; make well in center. Add boiling water; stir until mixture forms dough. Knead dough on lightly floured surface until smooth, about 5 minutes. Cover dough; let rest 30 minutes.

2. For filling, squeeze cabbage to remove as much moisture as possible; place in large bowl. Add pork, water chestnuts, onion, cornstarch, soy sauce, sherry, ginger, sesame oil and sugar; mix well.

3. Divide dough into two equal portions; cover one portion with plastic wrap or clean towel while working with other portion. On lightly floured surface, roll out dough to ⅛-inch thickness. Cut out 3-inch circles with round cookie cutter or top of clean empty can.

4. Place 1 rounded teaspoon filling in center of each dough circle. To shape each pot sticker, lightly moisten edges of one dough circle with water; fold in half.

5. Starting at one end, pinch curled edges together making four pleats along edge; set dumpling down firmly, seam side up. Cover finished dumplings while shaping remaining dumplings. (Cook dumplings immediately, refrigerate for up to 4 hours or freeze in resealable plastic food storage bag.)

6. To cook dumplings, heat 1 tablespoon vegetable oil in large nonstick skillet over medium heat. Place ½ of pot stickers in skillet, seam side up. (If cooking frozen dumplings, do not thaw.) Cook until bottoms are golden brown, 5 to 6 minutes.

7. Add ⅓ cup chicken broth; cover tightly. Reduce heat to low. Simmer until all liquid is absorbed, about 10 minutes (15 minutes if frozen). Repeat with remaining vegetable oil, dumplings and chicken broth.

8. Place pot stickers, browned side up, on serving platter. Serve with soy sauce, vinegar and chili oil for dipping. *Makes about 3 dozen pot stickers*

POT STICKERS

SHRIMP TOAST

12 large shrimp, shelled and
    deveined, leaving tails intact
1 egg
2 tablespoons plus 1½ teaspoons
    cornstarch
¼ teaspoon salt
    Dash pepper
3 slices white sandwich bread,
    crusts removed, quartered
1 hard-cooked egg yolk, cut into
    ½-inch pieces
1 slice (1 ounce) cooked ham, cut
    into ½-inch pieces
1 green onion with top, finely
    chopped
    Vegetable oil for frying
    Hard-cooked egg half and green
    onion for garnish

1. Cut deep slit down back of each shrimp; press gently with fingers to flatten.

2. Beat one egg, cornstarch, salt and pepper in large bowl until blended. Add shrimp; toss to coat well.

3. Place one shrimp, cut side down, on each bread piece; press shrimp gently into bread.

4. Brush or rub small amount of egg mixture over each shrimp.

5. Place one piece each of egg yolk and ham and scant ¼ teaspoon onion on top of each shrimp.

6. Heat oil in wok or large skillet over medium-high heat to 375°F. Add three or four bread pieces at a time; cook 1 to 2 minutes on each side or until golden. Drain on paper towels. Garnish, if desired.

Makes 1 dozen appetizers

TANGY PLUM SHORT RIBS

2 tablespoons vegetable oil
1 teaspoon chopped garlic
¾ pound cooked short ribs, cut into
    small pieces
3 tablespoons LEE KUM KEE® Plum
    Sauce
1 tablespoon LEE KUM KEE® Panda
    Brand Oyster Flavored Sauce

Heat skillet over medium heat. Add oil. Sauté garlic. Add short ribs and stir-fry until heated through. Add Plum Sauce and Oyster Flavored Sauce. Stir well and serve.

Makes 4 servings

SHRIMP TOAST

MICROWAVE ORIENTAL RELISH DIP

1 cup peeled, chopped tomatoes
¼ cup soy sauce
¼ cup drained canned crushed
    pineapple
1 tablespoon sugar
1 tablespoon finely chopped red
    bell pepper
1 tablespoon finely chopped green
    onion
1 tablespoon minced garlic
2 teaspoons fresh lemon juice
1½ teaspoons grated fresh ginger
2 teaspoons rice wine vinegar
1 teaspoon dark sesame oil
2 teaspoons cold water
1 teaspoon arrowroot *or*
    1½ teaspoons cornstarch
4 cups plain low-fat yogurt
1 cup creamy peanut butter
8 cups assorted fresh vegetables for
    serving

1. Combine tomatoes, soy sauce, pineapple, sugar, bell pepper, onion, garlic, lemon juice and ginger in 1-quart glass measuring cup.

2. Microwave at HIGH (100% power) 8 minutes, stirring every 2 minutes. Stir in vinegar and oil. Microwave 5 to 6 minutes until tomato mixture is reduced to 1 cup.

3. Combine water and arrowroot in small dish; stir until well blended. Add to tomato mixture; stir well. Let stand at room temperature to cool slightly. Store relish, covered, in glass container in refrigerator.

4. To make dip, combine relish with yogurt and peanut butter in large bowl; mix until well blended.* Serve with assorted vegetables.

Makes 16 servings

To make one serving of dip, combine ¼ cup plain low-fat yogurt, 1 tablespoon peanut butter and 1 tablespoon relish in small bowl. Serve with ½ cup assorted vegetables.

NOTE: Relish is also great mixed with reduced-calorie mayonnaise and used as a sandwich spread or salad dressing.

MICROWAVE ORIENTAL RELISH DIP

BEAN AND VEGETABLE EGG ROLLS

1 tablespoon sesame seeds
1 tablespoon dark sesame oil
2 green onions with tops, sliced
1 tablespoon minced fresh ginger
2 cloves garlic, minced
2 cups shredded napa cabbage
1 cup shredded carrots
½ cup chopped celery
½ cup chopped mushrooms
4 ounces fresh or canned bean
   sprouts, rinsed
1 can (15 ounces) chick-peas,
   rinsed and drained
1½ teaspoons reduced-sodium soy
   sauce
   Black pepper (optional)
1 egg, beaten
12 egg roll wrappers
   Peanut or vegetable oil
   Plum Dipping Sauce (recipe
   follows)

⅔ cup plum sauce
2 green onions with tops, sliced
3 tablespoons reduced-sodium soy
   sauce
2 tablespoons rice wine vinegar or
   cider vinegar
1 tablespoon grated fresh ginger
1 tablespoon honey
3 to 4 drops hot chili oil (optional)

1. Combine sesame seeds and sesame oil in large skillet. Cook and stir over low heat 2 to 3 minutes or until sesame seeds begin to brown. Add green onions, ginger and garlic; cook and stir 1 to 2 minutes. Add cabbage, carrots, celery, mushrooms and bean sprouts; cover. Cook 8 minutes or until cabbage is wilted. Stir in chick-peas and soy sauce; season to taste with pepper, if desired. Cool 10 minutes; stir in egg.

2. Place ⅓ cup vegetable mixture near one corner of egg roll wrapper. Brush edges of egg roll wrapper with water. Fold bottom corner of egg roll wrapper up over filling; fold sides in and roll up. Repeat with remaining filling and egg roll wrappers.

3. Heat 1 inch peanut oil in large, heavy saucepan over medium-high heat until oil is 375°F; adjust heat to maintain temperature. Fry egg rolls 3 to 5 minutes or until golden. Drain on paper towels; serve hot with Plum Dipping Sauce. Garnish, if desired. *Makes 12 servings*

NOTE: While preparing egg rolls, keep unused egg roll wrappers covered with a damp towel to prevent them from drying out.

PLUM DIPPING SAUCE

Combine all ingredients in medium bowl; mix well. Cover; refrigerate until ready to serve. *Makes about 1 cup sauce*

BEAN AND VEGETABLE EGG ROLL

CRAB CAKES CANTON

7 ounces thawed frozen cooked crabmeat or imitation crabmeat, drained and flaked
1½ cups fresh whole wheat bread crumbs (about 3 slices)
¼ cup thinly sliced green onions
1 clove garlic, minced
1 teaspoon minced fresh ginger
2 egg whites, lightly beaten
1 tablespoon teriyaki sauce
2 teaspoons vegetable oil, divided Prepared sweet and sour sauce (optional)

Combine crabmeat, bread crumbs, onions, garlic and ginger in medium bowl; mix well. Add egg whites and teriyaki sauce; mix well. Shape into patties about ½ inch thick and 2 inches in diameter.*

Heat 1 teaspoon oil in large nonstick skillet over medium heat until hot. Add about half of crab cakes to skillet. Cook 2 minutes per side or until golden brown. Remove to warm serving plate; keep warm. Repeat with remaining 1 teaspoon oil and crab cakes. Serve with sweet and sour sauce, if desired. *Makes 6 servings (12 cakes)*

*Crab cakes may be made ahead to this point; cover and refrigerate up to 24 hours before cooking.

LETTUCE WRAP

1½ tablespoons LEE KUM KEE® Hoisin Sauce
1 tablespoon LEE KUM KEE® Panda Brand Oyster Flavored Sauce
1 tablespoon vegetable oil
3 ounces diced onion
½ pound ground chicken or turkey
⅔ cup diced cucumber Large lettuce leaves Additional LEE KUM KEE® Hoisin Sauce

Combine 1½ tablespoons Hoisin Sauce and Oyster Sauce in small bowl; set aside. Heat skillet over medium heat. Add oil. Sauté onion. Add chicken, cucumber and sauce mixture. Cook until chicken is no longer pink. To serve, wrap chicken mixture in lettuce leaves. Serve with additional Hoisin Sauce for dipping. *Makes 4 servings*

CRAB CAKES CANTON

CHICKEN SATAY

1 pound boneless skinless chicken breast halves
1 recipe Peanut Dip (recipe follows), divided
Cucumber slices
Chopped fresh cilantro

1. Soak 8 (6-inch) bamboo skewers in hot water 20 minutes. Cut chicken lengthwise into 1-inch-wide strips; thread onto skewers.

2. Place skewers in large shallow glass dish. Pour ½ cup Peanut Dip over chicken, turning to coat evenly. Cover and marinate in refrigerator 30 minutes.

3. Place skewers on oiled grid and discard any remaining marinade. Grill over high heat 5 to 8 minutes or until chicken is no longer pink, turning once. Place on serving platter. Serve with cucumber, cilantro and remaining Peanut Dip. *Makes 8 appetizer or 4 main-dish servings*

Prep Time: 15 minutes
Marinate Time: 30 minutes
Cook Time: 5 minutes

PEANUT DIP

⅓ cup peanut butter
⅓ cup *French's*® Napa Valley Style Dijon Mustard
⅓ cup orange juice
1 tablespoon chopped peeled fresh ginger
1 tablespoon honey
1 tablespoon *Frank's*® *RedHot*® Original Cayenne Pepper Sauce
1 tablespoon teriyaki baste and glaze sauce
2 cloves garlic, minced

Combine peanut butter, mustard, juice, ginger, honey, *Frank's RedHot* Sauce, teriyaki baste and glaze sauce and garlic in large bowl. Refrigerate until ready to serve. *Makes 1 cup dip*

Prep Time: 10 minutes

SERVING SUGGESTION: Serve with Chicken Satay or as a dip for assorted cut-up fresh vegetables. It is also great as a spread on grilled French bread with grilled vegetables.

CHICKEN SATAY AND PEANUT DIP

ORIENTAL SALSA

1 cup diced unpeeled cucumber
½ cup chopped red bell pepper
½ cup thinly sliced green onions
⅓ cup coarsely chopped fresh
    cilantro
2 tablespoons reduced-sodium soy
    sauce
1 tablespoon rice vinegar
1 clove garlic, minced
½ teaspoon dark sesame oil
¼ teaspoon red pepper flakes
    Easy Wonton Chips (recipe
    follows) or assorted fresh
    vegetables for dipping

1. Combine cucumber, bell pepper, onions, cilantro, soy sauce, rice vinegar, garlic, oil and red pepper flakes in medium bowl until well blended.

2. Cover and refrigerate until serving time. Serve with Easy Wonton Chips or assorted fresh vegetables for dipping. Or, use as an accompaniment to broiled fish, chicken or pork. *Makes 4 servings*

EASY WONTON CHIPS

1 tablespoon reduced-sodium soy
    sauce
2 teaspoons peanut or vegetable oil
½ teaspoon sugar
¼ teaspoon garlic salt
12 wonton wrappers
    Nonstick cooking spray

1. Preheat oven to 375°F. Combine soy sauce, oil, sugar and garlic salt in small bowl; mix well.

2. Cut each wonton wrapper diagonally in half. Place on 15×10-inch jelly-roll pan coated with nonstick cooking spray. Brush soy mixture lightly over both sides of skins.

3. Bake 4 to 6 minutes or until crisp and lightly browned, turning after 3 minutes. Transfer to cooling rack; cool completely.

Makes 2 dozen chips

ORIENTAL SALSA AND EASY WONTON CHIPS

STUFFED
MUSHROOMS

**24 fresh medium mushrooms (about
    1 pound)**
6 ounces boneless lean pork
**¼ cup whole water chestnuts (¼ of
    8-ounce can)**
3 green onions with tops
½ small red or green bell pepper
1 small rib celery
2 teaspoons dry sherry
1 teaspoon cornstarch
1 teaspoon minced fresh ginger
1 teaspoon soy sauce
½ teaspoon hoisin sauce
1 egg white, lightly beaten
    Vegetable oil for frying
½ cup all-purpose flour
    Batter (recipe follows)
    Fresh thyme leaves for garnish

1. Remove stems from mushrooms; set caps aside. Chop stems finely and transfer to large bowl.

2. Finely chop pork, water chestnuts, onions, bell pepper and celery. Add to chopped mushroom stems. Add sherry, cornstarch, ginger, soy sauce, hoisin sauce and egg white; mix well.

3. Spoon pork mixture into mushroom caps, mounding slightly in center.

4. Heat oil in wok or large skillet over high heat to 375°F. Meanwhile, prepare batter.

5. Dip mushrooms into ½ cup flour, then into batter, coating completely.

6. Add six to eight mushrooms to hot oil; cook about 5 minutes or until golden brown on all sides. Drain on paper towels. Repeat with remaining mushrooms. Garnish, if desired. *Makes 2 dozen*

BATTER

½ cup cornstarch
½ cup all-purpose flour
1½ teaspoons baking powder
¾ teaspoon salt
⅓ cup water
⅓ cup milk

Combine cornstarch, flour, baking powder and salt in medium bowl. Add water and milk; stir until well blended.

STUFFED MUSHROOMS

STEAMED PORK AND SHRIMP DUMPLINGS

1 package (5 ounces) frozen cooked tiny shrimp, thawed and rinsed
1 pound lean ground pork
½ cup finely chopped water chestnuts
2 green onions with tops, finely chopped
1 tablespoon soy sauce
1 tablespoon dry sherry
2 teaspoons cornstarch
1 teaspoon minced fresh ginger
½ teaspoon dark sesame oil
¼ teaspoon sugar
1 egg, separated
1 tablespoon water
36 wonton wrappers (3 inches in diameter)*
36 fresh green peas (5 or 6 pods)
Additional soy sauce (optional)
Chili oil (optional)
Fresh tarragon sprig for garnish

*Most markets carry square wrappers. In some markets, 3-inch round wrappers are available; omit step 3 if using round wrappers.

1. Drain shrimp on paper towels. Set aside 36 shrimp. Place remaining shrimp in large bowl. Add pork, water chestnuts, onions, 1 tablespoon soy sauce, sherry, cornstarch, ginger, sesame oil and sugar; mix well.

2. Stir egg white into pork mixture until well blended; set aside. Place egg yolk in cup. Whisk water into egg yolk; set aside.

3. To trim square wrappers into circles, stack 12 wrappers on top of each other, keeping remaining wrappers covered with plastic wrap to prevent drying. Cut into 3-inch circles with tip of paring knife using round cookie cutter as guide. Repeat procedure 2 more times, keeping trimmed wrappers covered with plastic wrap.

4. Brush each wrapper with egg yolk mixture. Spoon 1½ tablespoons pork mixture onto center of each wrapper. Bring edge of wrapper up around filling in small pleats, leaving top of filling exposed. Press wrapper around filling in middle to form pinched "waist." Place on tray and cover with plastic wrap. Repeat with remaining wrappers and filling.

5. To steam dumplings, place 12-inch bamboo steamer in wok. Add water to ½ inch *below* steamer. (Water should not touch steamer.) Remove steamer. Cover wok; bring water to a boil over high heat.

6. Oil bottom of bamboo steamer. Arrange ½ of dumplings about ½ inch apart in steamer. Brush tops lightly with egg yolk mixture; place 1 pea and 1 reserved shrimp on top of each dumpling, pressing to secure.

7. Place steamer in wok over boiling water; reduce heat to medium. Cover and steam dumplings about 12 minutes or until pork is firm to the touch. Remove wok from heat. Transfer dumplings to serving plate.

8. Repeat steps 6 and 7 with remaining dumplings. Serve immediately with soy sauce and chili oil for dipping, if desired. Garnish, if desired.

Makes 3 dozen dumplings

STEAMED PORK AND SHRIMP DUMPLINGS

DIM SUM
BAKED BUNS

9 (18 ounces) frozen bread dough
    rolls
6 to 8 dried shiitake mushrooms
3 green onions, minced
2 tablespoons plum sauce
1 tablespoon hoisin sauce
    Nonstick cooking spray
8 ounces ground chicken
4 cloves garlic, minced
1 tablespoon minced fresh ginger
2 tablespoons cholesterol-free egg
    substitute
¾ teaspoon sesame seeds

1. Thaw frozen rolls according to package directions.

2. Place mushrooms in small bowl. Cover with warm water; let stand 30 minutes. Rinse well and drain, squeezing out excess water. Cut off and discard stems. Finely chop caps. Combine mushrooms, green onions, plum sauce and hoisin sauce in large bowl.

3. Spray medium nonstick skillet with cooking spray; heat over high heat. Add chicken; cook without stirring 1 to 2 minutes or until no longer pink. Add garlic and ginger; cook and stir 2 minutes more. Add mushroom mixture; mix well.

4. Spray 2 baking sheets with cooking spray. Lightly flour hands and work surface. Cut each roll in half; roll each piece into a ball. Shape each piece between hands to form disk. Press edge of disk between thumb and forefinger, working in circular motion to form circle 3 to 3½ inches in diameter (center of disk should be thicker than edges.)

5. Place disk flat on work surface. Place 1 generous tablespoon filling in center. Lift edges of dough up and around filling; pinch edges of dough together to seal. Place seam side down on baking sheet. Repeat with remaining dough and filling.

6. Cover buns with towel; let rise in warm place 45 minutes or until buns have doubled in size. Meanwhile, preheat oven to 375°F. Brush buns with egg, then sprinkle with sesame seeds. Bake 16 to 18 minutes or until buns are golden brown.

Makes 18 buns

CRISPY SHRIMP WONTONS

1 pound raw large shrimp, shelled and deveined
½ cup sliced water chestnuts
1 green onion, coarsely chopped
¼ cup *Frank's® RedHot®* Original Cayenne Pepper Sauce
2 tablespoons minced fresh cilantro
1 package (16 ounces) wonton wrappers
Nonstick olive-oil-flavored cooking spray
Sesame seeds
Dipping Sauce (recipe follows)

1. Preheat oven to 350°F. Line baking sheets with foil; grease foil. Place shrimp in food processor; process until fairly smooth. Add water chestnuts, green onion, *Frank's RedHot* Sauce and cilantro. Pulse processor on and off until water chestnuts are finely chopped and mixture is almost smooth.

2. Spoon 1 tablespoon shrimp mixture into center of 1 wonton wrapper. Moisten edges of wrapper with water. Fold wrapper into triangle; press to seal edges. Repeat with remaining wrappers and filling.

3. Arrange wontons, 2 inches apart, on prepared baking sheets. Generously spray wontons with nonstick cooking spray; sprinkle with sesame seeds. Bake 15 to 20 minutes or until golden. Prepare Dipping Sauce. Serve wontons warm with sauce.   *Makes 3½ dozen wontons*

DIPPING SAUCE

¼ cup teriyaki sauce
2 tablespoons *Frank's® RedHot®* Original Cayenne Pepper Sauce
2 tablespoons rice wine vinegar
1 tablespoon minced green onion
1 teaspoon Oriental sesame oil

Combine teriyaki sauce, *Frank's RedHot* Sauce, rice wine vinegar, green onion and sesame oil in medium serving bowl. Mix until well blended.

Makes ½ cup sauce

Prep Time: 30 minutes
Cook Time: 15 minutes

THAI CHICKEN SKEWERS

¼ cup creamy peanut butter
2 tablespoons finely chopped onion
2 tablespoons finely chopped parsley
2 tablespoons fresh lemon juice
1½ teaspoons soy sauce
1 clove garlic, finely chopped
1 teaspoon TABASCO® brand Pepper Sauce
½ teaspoon ground coriander
1 pound boneless, skinless chicken breasts, cut into 1-inch pieces
Wooden skewers

Combine all ingredients except chicken and skewers in medium bowl. Add chicken; toss to coat. Cover and refrigerate 6 to 8 hours or overnight.

Preheat broiler or grill. Thread marinated chicken on skewers. Broil or grill 6 to 8 minutes, turning frequently. (Do not overcook.) Serve warm on skewers.

Makes 30 to 35 pieces

INDIAN-SPICED WALNUTS

2 egg whites, lightly beaten
1½ teaspoons curry powder
1 tablespoon ground cumin
1½ teaspoons salt
½ teaspoon sugar
4 cups California walnuts, halves and pieces

Preheat oven to 350°F. Coat large, shallow baking pan with nonstick cooking spray. In a large bowl, mix egg whites with spices, salt and sugar. Stir in walnuts and coat thoroughly. Spread in prepared pan. Bake 15 to 18 minutes or until dry and crisp. Cool completely before serving.

Makes 4 cups

Favorite recipe from **Walnut Marketing Board**

THAI CHICKEN SKEWERS

SHRIMP IN PEA COATS

Chinese Dipping Sauce (recipe follows)
½ pound large fresh snow peas (about 40)
1 piece fresh ginger, peeled
2 teaspoons dark sesame oil
2 teaspoons vegetable oil
¼ teaspoon hot chili oil
1 pound raw medium shrimp (about 40), peeled and deveined

1. Prepare Chinese Dipping Sauce; set aside.

2. Snap ends off snow peas; remove and discard strings.

3. Bring 4 cups water to a boil in medium saucepan over high heat. Add snow peas; cook 2 to 3 minutes or until snow peas turn bright green and are crisp-tender. Immediately plunge into ice water; drain and set aside.

4. Grate enough ginger to measure 1 tablespoon.

5. Heat sesame oil, vegetable oil and hot chili oil in wok or medium skillet over medium-high heat. Add ginger; stir-fry about 1 minute. Add shrimp; stir-fry 2 to 3 minutes or until shrimp turn pink and opaque. Set shrimp aside; cool.

6. To assemble appetizers, make small slit in snow pea seam with paring knife. Pull apart with fingers; insert 1 cooked shrimp. Secure with toothpick. Serve immediately with Chinese Dipping Sauce or refrigerate until serving.
Makes about 40 appetizers

CHINESE DIPPING SAUCE

¼ cup reduced-sodium soy sauce
1 tablespoon rice vinegar
1 teaspoon dark roasted sesame oil

Combine soy sauce, rice vinegar and sesame oil in small bowl.
Makes about ¼ cup sauce

SHRIMP IN PEA COATS

Delicious Soups

SZECHUAN VEGETABLE LO MEIN

2 cans (about 14 ounces each) vegetable or chicken broth
2 teaspoons minced garlic
1 teaspoon minced fresh ginger
¼ teaspoon red pepper flakes
1 package (16 ounces) frozen vegetable medley, such as broccoli, carrots, water chestnuts and red bell peppers
1 package (5 ounces) Asian curly noodles or 5 ounces angel hair pasta, broken in half
3 tablespoons soy sauce
1 tablespoon dark sesame oil
¼ cup thinly sliced green onion tops

1. Combine broth, garlic, ginger and red pepper flakes in large deep skillet. Cover and bring to a boil over high heat.

2. Add vegetables and noodles to skillet; cover and return to a boil. Reduce heat to medium-low; simmer, uncovered, 5 to 6 minutes or until noodles and vegetables are tender, stirring occasionally.

3. Stir soy sauce and sesame oil into broth mixture; cook 3 minutes. Stir in green onions; ladle into bowls.   *Makes 4 servings*

Prep and Cook Time: 20 minutes

NOTE: For a heartier, protein-packed main dish, add 1 package (10½ ounces) extra-firm tofu, cut into ¾-inch pieces, to the broth mixture with the soy sauce and sesame oil.

SZECHUAN VEGETABLE LO MEIN

SIMMERING HOT & SOUR SOUP

2 cans (about 14 ounces each) chicken broth
1 cup chopped cooked chicken or pork
4 ounces fresh shiitake mushroom caps, thinly sliced
½ cup sliced bamboo shoots, cut into thin strips
3 tablespoons rice vinegar or rice wine vinegar
2 tablespoons soy sauce
1½ teaspoons chili paste *or* 1 teaspoon hot chili oil
4 ounces firm tofu, well drained and cut into ½-inch pieces
2 teaspoons Asian sesame oil
2 tablespoons cornstarch
2 tablespoons cold water
Chopped cilantro or sliced green onions

Slow Cooker Directions

1. Combine chicken broth, chicken, mushrooms, bamboo shoots, vinegar, soy sauce and chili paste in slow cooker. Cover; cook on LOW 3 to 4 hours.

2. Stir in tofu and sesame oil. Combine cornstarch with water; mix well. Stir into soup. Cover; cook on HIGH 10 minutes or until soup is thickened.

3. Serve hot; garnish with cilantro. *Makes 4 servings*

Prep Time: 15 minutes
Cook Time: 3 to 4 hours

SIMMERING HOT & SOUR SOUP

ASIAN RAMEN NOODLE SOUP

2 cans (about 14 ounces each) fat-free reduced-sodium chicken broth
4 ounces boneless pork loin, cut into thin strips
¾ cup thinly sliced mushrooms
½ cup firm tofu, cut into ¼-inch cubes (optional)
3 tablespoons white vinegar
3 tablespoons sherry
1 tablespoon reduced-sodium soy sauce
½ teaspoon ground red pepper
2 ounces uncooked low-fat ramen noodles
1 egg, beaten
¼ cup finely chopped green onions, green tops only

1. Bring chicken broth to a boil in large saucepan over high heat; add pork, mushrooms and tofu, if desired. Reduce heat to medium-low; simmer, covered, 5 minutes. Stir in vinegar, sherry, soy sauce and pepper.

2. Return broth mixture to a boil over high heat; stir in ramen noodles. Cook, stirring occasionally, 5 to 7 minutes or until noodles are tender. Slowly stir in beaten egg and green onions; remove from heat. Ladle soup into individual bowls.

Makes 4 servings

Tip ■ ■ ■

Tofu must be drained before being stir-fried or deep-fried. Remove any remaining water by placing the block of tofu on several layers of paper towels and covering it with additional paper towels weighted down with a heavy plate. Let it stand for 15 to 20 minutes before slicing or cubing.

ASIAN RAMEN NOODLE SOUP

WONTON SOUP

¼ **pound ground pork, chicken or turkey**
¼ **cup finely chopped water chestnuts**
2 **tablespoons soy sauce, divided**
1 **egg white, lightly beaten**
1 **teaspoon minced fresh ginger**
12 **wonton wrappers**
1 **can (46 ounces) chicken broth**
1½ **cups sliced fresh spinach leaves**
1 **cup thinly sliced cooked pork (optional)**
½ **cup diagonally sliced green onions**
1 **tablespoon dark sesame oil**
   Shredded carrot for garnish

1. Combine ground pork, water chestnuts, 1 tablespoon soy sauce, egg white and ginger in small bowl; mix well.

2. Place 1 wonton wrapper with a point toward edge of counter. Mound 1 teaspoon filling toward bottom point. Fold bottom point over filling, then roll wrapper over once. Moisten inside points with water. Bring side points together below the filling, overlapping slightly; press together firmly to seal. Repeat with remaining wrappers and filling.* Keep finished wontons covered with plastic wrap, while filling remaining wrappers.

3. Combine broth and remaining 1 tablespoon soy sauce in large saucepan. Bring to a boil over high heat. Reduce heat to medium; add wontons. Simmer, uncovered, 4 minutes.

4. Stir in spinach, cooked pork, if desired and onions; remove from heat. Stir in sesame oil. Ladle into soup bowls. Garnish with shredded carrot.

Makes 2 servings

*Wontons may be made ahead to this point; cover and refrigerate up to 8 hours or freeze up to 3 months. Proceed as above, if using refrigerated wontons. Increase simmer time to 6 minutes, if using frozen wontons.

PORK & MISO SOUP

Fresh ginger
4 cups fish stock
4 ounces lean boneless pork, cut into very thin ½-inch-wide strips
½ cup miso*
2 to 3 large green onions, cut into ½-inch slices

*If miso is quite salty, decrease amount to 3 tablespoons.

1. Cut, peel and grate 1-inch piece of ginger. Squeeze grated ginger between thumb and fingers to extract juice. Repeat as necessary to get 2 teaspoons ginger juice. Discard ginger pulp, reserving juice.

2. Place fish stock in large saucepan; bring to a boil over medium-high heat. Add pork strips; cook 2 minutes.

3. Place miso in large bowl; gradually add about 1 cup hot soup to miso, stirring constantly until miso is dissolved. Stir miso mixture into soup.

4. Add onions to soup. Return to a boil and remove from heat. Ladle soup into individual serving bowls. Stir ½ teaspoon reserved ginger juice into each serving. *Makes 4 servings*

INDONESIAN CURRIED SOUP

1 can (14 ounces) coconut milk*
1 can (10¾ ounces) condensed tomato soup
¾ cup milk
3 tablespoons *Frank's® RedHot®* Original Cayenne Pepper Sauce
1½ teaspoons curry powder

*You can substitute 1 cup half-and-half for coconut milk BUT increase milk to 1½ cups.

1. Combine all ingredients in medium saucepan; stir until smooth.

2. Cook, over low heat, about 5 minutes or until heated through, stirring occasionally. *Makes 6 servings (4 cups)*

Prep Time: 5 minutes
Cook Time: 5 minutes

HOT AND SOUR SOUP

3 cans (about 14 ounces each) chicken broth
8 ounces boneless skinless chicken breasts, cut into ¼-inch-thick strips
1 cup shredded carrots
1 cup thinly sliced mushrooms
½ cup bamboo shoots, cut into matchstick-size strips
2 tablespoons rice vinegar or white wine vinegar
½ to ¾ teaspoon white pepper
¼ to ½ teaspoon hot pepper sauce
2 tablespoons cornstarch
2 tablespoons soy sauce
1 tablespoon dry sherry
2 medium green onions, sliced
1 egg, lightly beaten

Combine chicken broth, chicken, carrots, mushrooms, bamboo shoots, vinegar, pepper and hot pepper sauce in large saucepan. Bring to a boil over medium-high heat; reduce heat to low. Cover and simmer about 5 minutes or until chicken is no longer pink.

Stir together cornstarch, soy sauce and sherry in small bowl until smooth. Add to chicken broth mixture. Cook and stir until mixture comes to a boil. Stir in green onions and egg. Cook about 1 minute, stirring in one direction, until egg is cooked. Ladle soup into bowls.

Makes 7 (1-cup) servings

HOT AND SOUR SOUP

TURKEY WONTON SOUP

3 ounces ground turkey sausage
2 green onions, sliced
½ teaspoon grated fresh ginger,
    divided
12 wonton skins
6 cups Chicken Broth (recipe
    follows) or canned chicken
    broth
2 medium carrots, peeled and
    thinly sliced
1 tablespoon lemon juice or dry
    sherry
    Sliced green onion tops for
    garnish

1. For wontons, cook sausage, 2 onions and ¼ teaspoon ginger in medium saucepan over medium heat until sausage is no longer pink, stirring to crumble meat. Drain on paper towels.

2. Stack wonton skins and cut in half horizontally to make rectangles. Place 2 rectangles at a time on waxed paper. Moisten edges of rectangles with water. Place heaping ½ teaspoonful of filling at 1 end of each rectangle. Fold wonton skin in half over filling, forming square. Pinch to seal; press edges with tines of fork. Repeat until all wontons are filled.

3. For soup, bring broth to a boil in saucepan over high heat. Stir in carrots, remaining ¼ teaspoon ginger and lemon juice. Add wontons; bring to a boil. Reduce heat to medium-low; simmer, uncovered, 5 minutes.

4. Spoon four wonton squares into each bowl using slotted spoon; add broth mixture. Garnish, if desired.   *Makes 6 servings*

CHICKEN BROTH

2 medium onions
1 (5-pound) capon,* cut into pieces
3 quarts cold water
2 medium carrots, halved
2 ribs celery including leaves, cut
    into halves
1 large clove garlic, crushed
6 sprigs fresh parsley
8 black peppercorns
1 bay leaf
½ teaspoon dried thyme leaves

*Capon provides a wonderfully rich flavor, but can be expensive. Chicken can be substituted for capon.

1. Trim tops and roots from onions, leaving most of the dried outer skin intact; cut into wedges.

2. Place onions, capon, water, carrots, celery, garlic, parsley, peppercorns, bay leaf and thyme into stockpot or 6-quart Dutch oven. Bring to a boil over high heat. Reduce heat to medium-low; simmer, uncovered, 3 to 4 hours, skimming foam that rises to the surface with large spoon.

3. Remove from heat; cool. Remove large bones. Strain broth through large sieve or colander lined with several layers of damp cheesecloth, removing all bones and vegetables; discard bones and vegetables.

4. Use immediately, or refrigerate in covered container up to 2 days, or freeze in storage containers several months.   *Makes about 2½ quarts*

TURKEY WONTON SOUP

CLEAR SOUP
WITH SHRIMP

8 medium fresh shrimp in shells
2 cups water
1¼ teaspoons salt, divided
4 cups fish stock
2 pods fresh okra, cut into
⅛-inch-thick slices
1 teaspoon reduced-sodium soy
sauce
1 (1-inch) square lemon peel, cut
into 16 strips

1. Peel each shrimp, leaving tail and portion of shell nearest tail attached. Devein shrimp.

2. Mix water and ¼ teaspoon salt in medium saucepan over medium-high heat; bring to a boil. Add shrimp; reduce heat to low. Cook about 3 minutes until shrimp are pink and opaque. Drain; set aside.

3. Combine fish stock and remaining 1 teaspoon salt in medium saucepan over medium-high heat; bring to a boil. Cook and stir until salt is dissolved. Stir in okra and soy sauce. Remove from heat.

4. Place 2 shrimp in each of 4 individual serving bowls. Pour 1 cup soup over shrimp in each bowl. Garnish with lemon peel.   *Makes 4 servings*

JAPANESE EGG
DROP SOUP

3 ounces boneless skinless chicken
breast, cut into 1½×½×½-inch
pieces
1 teaspoon sake
½ teaspoon plus pinch salt, divided
¾ cup water
1 (1-inch) piece carrot, cut into
⅛-inch-thick slices
4 cups fish stock
1 teaspoon reduced-sodium soy
sauce
2 eggs, lightly beaten

1. Combine chicken, sake and pinch of salt in small bowl; set aside. Place water and ¼ teaspoon salt in small saucepan. Bring to a boil over medium heat; add carrot slices. Cook 2 minutes; drain.

2. Place fish stock in 3-quart saucepan; bring to a boil over medium-high heat. Add remaining ¼ teaspoon salt, soy sauce and chicken. Reduce heat to medium; boil 2 minutes.

3. Slowly pour about ⅓ of eggs at a time into boiling soup, stirring constantly. Return soup to a boil after each addition. Remove from heat immediately after last egg "threads" form.

4. Place 2 carrot slices in each of 4 individual soup bowls. Ladle about 1 cup soup over carrots in each bowl.   *Makes 4 servings*

SHANGHAI MEATBALL SOUP

1 pound ground turkey
¾ cup QUAKER® Oats (quick or old
    fashioned, uncooked)
2 tablespoons lite soy sauce
1 tablespoon dry sherry (optional)
2 teaspoons sesame oil (optional)
1½ teaspoons minced fresh ginger
½ teaspoon black pepper
2 cans (14½ ounces each) reduced-
    salt chicken broth, divided
1 cup water
1½ cups halved pea pods *or*
    1 (6-ounce) package frozen pea
    pods, thawed, cut in half
1 cup thinly sliced carrot strips
1½ cups bean sprouts
¼ cup thinly sliced green onion

Spray rack of broiler pan with no-stick cooking spray or oil lightly. Combine first seven ingredients and ¼ cup chicken broth; mix well. Shape into 1-inch meatballs; place on prepared rack. Broil 6 to 8 inches from heat 7 to 10 minutes or until cooked through. In large saucepan or Dutch oven, combine meatballs with water and remaining chicken broth; bring to a boil over high heat. Add pea pods and carrot strips; cook 1 to 2 minutes or until vegetables are crisp-tender. Turn off heat; add bean sprouts and green onion. Serve immediately.

Makes about 6 (1-cup) servings

PIEROGY WONTON SOUP

1 tablespoon peanut or vegetable oil
2½ cups bok choy cabbage,* cut into ½-inch pieces
½ cup carrots, cut into matchsticks**
1 teaspoon minced garlic
½ teaspoon ground ginger
2 cans (about 15 ounces each) ready-to-serve chicken broth
1 teaspoon soy sauce
1 package (16.9 ounces) MRS. T'S® Frozen Potato And Cheddar Cheese or Potato And Onion Pierogies
¼ cup sliced radishes
Sesame seeds (optional)

If bok choy cabbage is not available, use fresh spinach, adding just before pierogies are cooked through.

**For carrot matchsticks, cut carrot into thin diagonal slices; stack 3 or 4 slices and cut into narrow sticks.*

In large saucepan, heat oil over medium-high heat. Add bok choy, carrots, garlic and ginger; cook and stir constantly until bok choy is barely tender, about 1 minute. Add broth and soy sauce; bring to a boil. Add pierogies and cook until heated through, about 5 to 7 minutes. Stir in radishes. Sprinkle with sesame seeds, if desired.   *Makes 6 cups*

Tip ■■■

Pierogi are Polish noodle dumplings filled with minced meat and/or vegetables. They are similar to wontons used in Chinese cuisine.

PIEROGY WONTON SOUP

TURKEY TERIYAKI UDON

Turkey Teriyaki with Grilled Mushrooms (recipe page 180)
12 ounces fresh udon or soba noodles
3 cups water
1 can (14 ounces) chicken broth
2 tablespoons sake or sherry wine
1 tablespoon minced fresh ginger
1 tablespoon soy sauce
2 teaspoons sugar
1½ cups chopped fresh or frozen spinach, thawed
1 cup fresh bean sprouts
Carrot flowers

Prepare Turkey Teriyaki with Grilled Mushrooms. Cook noodles according to package directions; drain and keep warm. Combine water, broth, sake, ginger, soy sauce and sugar in 5-quart Dutch oven. Bring to a boil over high heat. Reduce heat to medium-low and simmer 5 minutes. Stir in spinach and bean sprouts; heat through. Place noodles in 4 large soup bowls; spoon broth mixture over noodles. Slice turkey into bite-size pieces; arrange turkey, mushrooms and green onions on noodles. Garnish with carrot flowers. Serve immediately. *Makes 4 servings*

TURKEY TERIYAKI UDON

ASIAN PASTA & SHRIMP SOUP

1 package (3½ ounces) fresh
    shiitake mushrooms
2 teaspoons Oriental sesame oil
2 cans (14½ ounces each)
    vegetable broth
4 ounces angel-hair pasta, broken
    into 2-inch lengths (about
    1 cup)
½ pound medium shrimp, peeled
    and deveined
4 ounces snow peas, cut into thin
    strips
2 tablespoons *French's*® Napa
    Valley Style Dijon Mustard
1 tablespoon *Frank's*® *RedHot*®
    Original Cayenne Pepper Sauce
⅛ teaspoon ground ginger

1. Remove and discard stems from mushrooms. Cut mushrooms into thin strips. Heat oil in large saucepan over medium-high heat. Add mushrooms; stir-fry 3 minutes or just until tender.

2. Add broth and *½ cup water* to saucepan. Heat to boiling. Stir in pasta. Cook 2 minutes or just until tender.

3. Add remaining ingredients, stirring frequently. Heat to boiling. Reduce heat to medium-low. Cook 2 minutes or until shrimp turn pink and peas are tender.
                                               Makes 4 servings

Prep Time: 10 minutes
Cook Time: about 10 minutes

COUNTRY JAPANESE NOODLE SOUP

1 can (14½ ounces) DEL MONTE®
   Stewed Tomatoes — Original
   Recipe
1 can (14 ounces) low-salt chicken
   broth
3 ounces linguine
1 to 1½ teaspoons minced
   gingerroot *or* ¼ teaspoon
   ground ginger
2 teaspoons low-salt soy sauce
¼ pound sirloin steak, cut crosswise
   into thin strips
5 green onions, cut into thin 1-inch
   slivers
4 ounces firm tofu, cut into small
   cubes

1. Combine tomatoes, broth, pasta, ginger and soy sauce with 1¾ cups water in large saucepan; bring to boil.

2. Cook, uncovered, over medium-high heat 5 minutes.

3. Add meat, green onions and tofu; cook 4 minutes or until pasta is tender. Season to taste with pepper and additional soy sauce, if desired.

Makes 4 servings (1¼ cups each)

Prep Time: 10 minutes
Cook Time: 15 minutes

EGG DROP SOUP

2 cans (14 ounces each) reduced-
   sodium chicken broth
1 tablespoon reduced-sodium soy
   sauce
2 teaspoons cornstarch
½ cup cholesterol-free egg
   substitute
¼ cup thinly sliced green onions

1. Bring broth to a boil over high heat in large saucepan; reduce heat and simmer.

2. Blend soy sauce and cornstarch in cup until smooth; stir into broth. Cook and stir 2 minutes or until soup boils and thickens slightly.

3. Stirring constantly in one direction, slowly pour egg substitute in thin stream into soup.

4. Ladle into soup bowls. Sprinkle with onions.

Makes 4 appetizer servings (about 3½ cups)

HANOI BEEF AND RICE SOUP

1½ pounds ground beef chuck
2 tablespoons cold water
2 tablespoons soy sauce
2 teaspoons sugar
2 teaspoons cornstarch
2 teaspoons lime juice
½ teaspoon black pepper
2 cloves garlic, minced
2 teaspoons fennel seeds
1 teaspoon anise seeds
1 cinnamon stick (3 inches long)
2 bay leaves
6 whole cloves
1 tablespoon vegetable oil
1 cup uncooked long-grain rice
1 medium yellow onion, sliced and
    separated into rings
1 tablespoon minced fresh ginger
4 cans (about 14 ounces each) beef
    broth
2 cups water
½ pound fresh snow peas, trimmed
1 fresh red Thai chili or red
    jalapeño pepper,* cut into
    slivers, for garnish

*Thai chilies and jalapeño peppers can sting
and irritate the skin; wear rubber gloves when
handling chilies and do not touch eyes. Wash
hands after handling.

1. Combine beef, 2 tablespoons water, soy sauce, sugar, cornstarch, lime juice, black pepper and garlic in large bowl; mix well. Place meat mixture on cutting board; pat evenly into 1-inch-thick square. Cut meat into 36 squares; shape each square into a ball.

2. Bring 4 inches water to a boil in wok over high heat. Add meatballs and return water to a boil. Cook meatballs 3 to 4 minutes or until firm, stirring occasionally. Transfer meatballs to bowl with slotted spoon. Discard water.

3. Place fennel seeds, anise seeds, cinnamon, bay leaves and cloves on 12-inch double-thick square of dampened cheesecloth. Tie with string into spice bag; set aside.

4. Heat wok over medium heat 1 minute or until hot. Drizzle oil into wok and heat 30 seconds. Add rice; stir-fry 3 to 4 minutes or until lightly browned. Add onion and ginger. Stir-fry 1 minute. Add beef broth, 2 cups water and spice bag. Cover and bring to a boil. Reduce heat to low; simmer 25 minutes.

5. Remove spice bag and discard. Add meatballs and snow peas to soup. Cook and stir until heated through. Ladle soup into individual serving bowls. Garnish, if desired.   *Makes 6 main-dish servings*

HANOI BEEF AND RICE SOUP

CURRIED VEGETABLE-RICE SOUP

1 package (16 ounces) frozen
    vegetable medley, such as
    broccoli, cauliflower, sugar
    snap peas and red bell peppers
1 can (about 14 ounces) vegetable
    broth
¾ cup uncooked instant brown rice
2 teaspoons curry powder
½ teaspoon salt
½ teaspoon hot pepper sauce or to
    taste
1 can (14 ounces) unsweetened
    coconut milk
1 tablespoon fresh lime juice

1. Combine vegetables and broth in large saucepan. Cover; bring to a boil over high heat. Stir in rice, curry powder, salt and pepper sauce; reduce heat to medium-low. Cover and simmer 8 minutes or until rice is tender, stirring once.

2. Stir in coconut milk; cook 3 minutes or until heated through. Remove from heat. Stir in lime juice. Ladle into shallow bowls and serve immediately.
Makes 4 servings

Prep and Cook Time: 16 minutes

SPICY PEANUT SOUP

1 tablespoon vegetable oil
1 large onion, chopped
1 medium sweet potato, diced
2 cloves garlic, minced
8 cups chicken broth
1 teaspoon dried crushed thyme leaves
½ teaspoon ground cumin
1 cup MAHATMA® or CAROLINA® rice
1½ cups thick and chunky salsa
3 (16-ounce) cans garbanzo beans
    (chick-peas), drained and rinsed
1 cup diced unpeeled zucchini
⅔ cup creamy peanut butter

In a large saucepan, heat vegetable oil and sauté onions, sweet potato and garlic, stirring occasionally until onion is softened (about 5 minutes). Add chicken broth, thyme, cumin and rice. Bring to a boil, reduce heat to simmer. Simmer for 20 minutes. Add salsa, beans and zucchini; cook 10 minutes. Add peanut butter and stir until completely combined. Remove from heat.
Makes 8 servings

CURRIED VEGETABLE-RICE SOUP

Incredible Salads

CHINESE CABBAGE SALAD

6 tablespoons cider vinegar
3 tablespoons sugar
1 tablespoon dark sesame oil
1 teaspoon minced fresh ginger
1 large crisp red apple, diced
1 medium (1 to 1¼ pounds) head green cabbage *or* 1 bag (16 ounces) prepackaged shredded cabbage salad mix
⅓ cup golden raisins
2 green onions, thinly sliced
2 tablespoons chopped fresh cilantro
1 tablespoon toasted sesame seeds

1. Combine vinegar, sugar, oil and ginger in large bowl; stir until sugar dissolves. Stir in apple.

2. Add cabbage, raisins, onions, cilantro and sesame seeds; gently stir until well combined. *Makes 6 servings*

NOTE: Store cabbage tightly wrapped in a plastic bag in the refrigerator for up to two weeks. A one-pound cabbage will yield about 4 cups shredded cabbage.

CHINESE CABBAGE SALAD

ASIAN BROWN RICE AND PEANUT SALAD TOSS

1½ **cups water**
¾ **cup uncooked brown rice**
3 **ounces dry-roasted peanuts**
1 **(8-ounce) can sliced water chestnuts, drained**
3 **ounces frozen snow peas, thawed and patted dry**
½ **cup chopped red onion**
½ **cup chopped green bell pepper**
¼ **cup raisins or dried sweetened cranberries**
2 **tablespoons cider vinegar**
2 **tablespoons honey**
2 **tablespoons light soy sauce**
¼ **teaspoon dried red pepper flakes**

1. Bring water to a boil over high heat in medium saucepan. Stir in rice; return to a boil. Reduce heat; simmer, covered, 25 minutes or until rice is tender and liquid is absorbed. With fork, fluff rice and spread out on greased baking sheet. Cool to room temperature, about 30 to 40 minutes.

2. Meanwhile, place large skillet over medium-high heat. Add peanuts; toast, 3 to 4 minutes, stirring frequently, or until fragrant and beginning to lightly brown. Place in medium bowl. Add water chestnuts, snow peas, onion, bell pepper and raisins. Add cooled rice.

3. Combine vinegar, honey, soy sauce and pepper flakes in small bowl. Combine dressing with rice mixture and serve. *Makes 6 servings*

ASIAN BROWN RICE AND PEANUT SALAD TOSS

ORIENTAL CRAB & NOODLE SALAD

1 package (10 ounces) Chinese curly noodles or 10 ounces vermicelli
1 package (8 ounces) flaked imitation crabmeat
6 ounces (1½ cups) fresh snow peas or sugar snap peas
⅓ cup soy sauce
2 tablespoons dark sesame oil
2 tablespoons seasoned rice vinegar
1 teaspoon minced ginger
½ teaspoon minced garlic
¼ teaspoon red pepper flakes
1 red bell pepper, cut into strips
¼ cup thinly sliced green onions

1. Bring 3 quarts water to a boil in covered Dutch oven over high heat. Add noodles; return to a boil. Cook 2 minutes. Add crabmeat and peas; cook 1 minute or until noodles are al dente.

2. Meanwhile, to prepare dressing, combine soy sauce, sesame oil, vinegar, ginger, garlic and pepper flakes in large bowl; mix well.

3. Drain noodle mixture. Add noodle mixture and bell pepper to dressing; toss to coat. Arrange noodle mixture on salad plates; sprinkle with green onions.

Makes 4 servings

Prep and Cook Time: 20 minutes

CHINESE PORK SALAD

1 pound pork strips
½ cup Oriental stir-fry sauce
½ red onion, peeled and sliced
2 packages (10 ounces each) frozen snow peas, thawed and drained
1 can (8 ounces) mandarin oranges, drained
1 can (3 ounces) chow mein noodles

Marinate pork in stir-fry sauce. In large nonstick skillet, stir-fry pork and onion over medium-high heat 4 to 5 minutes. In large bowl, toss pork mixture together with remaining ingredients.

Makes 4 servings

Prep Time: 5 minutes
Cook Time: 5 minutes

Favorite recipe from **National Pork Board**

ORIENTAL CRAB & NOODLE SALAD

ORIENTAL SPA SALAD

1 can (20 ounces) DOLE® Pineapple
    Chunks
5 cups hot cooked rice
    Spa Dressing (recipe follows)
8 ounces cooked baby shrimp
2 cups bean sprouts
1½ cups DOLE® Broccoli cut into
    florettes
6 green onions, thinly sliced
1 large DOLE® Carrot, thinly sliced
    Salad greens

- Drain pineapple chunks; reserve ¼ cup juice for dressing. Prepare Spa Dressing. In a large bowl, combine hot rice and Spa Dressing. Cool. Add pineapple chunks, shrimp, bean sprouts, broccoli, onions and carrot. Toss. Chill 1 hour.

- Serve over salad greens. *Makes 8 servings*

SPA DRESSING

¼ cup sugar
¼ cup white vinegar
¼ cup reserved pineapple juice
1 tablespoon soy sauce
1 tablespoon sesame seeds, toasted

- Whisk together all ingredients in medium bowl until well blended.

ASIAN CABBAGE & CARROT SLAW

3 cups finely shredded Napa (Chinese) cabbage or green cabbage
1 cup finely shredded red cabbage
1 cup finely shredded carrots
1 can (8 ounces) sliced water chestnuts, rinsed and drained
¼ cup orange juice
2 tablespoons olive oil
2 tablespoons *Frank's® RedHot®* Original Cayenne Pepper Sauce
1 tablespoon soy sauce
2 teaspoons grated peeled fresh ginger
½ teaspoon sugar
½ teaspoon Oriental sesame oil

1. Combine Napa and red cabbage, carrots and water chestnuts in large bowl; set aside.

2. Whisk orange juice, olive oil, **Frank's RedHot** Sauce, soy sauce, ginger, sugar and sesame oil in small measuring cup. Pour over cabbage mixture; toss to coat evenly. Cover; refrigerate 1 hour.

Makes 6 servings (5 cups salad, about ½ cup dressing)

Prep Time: 30 minutes
Chill Time: 1 hour

JAPANESE PEAR SALAD

2 tablespoons rice vinegar, red wine vinegar or balsamic vinegar
2 tablespoons packed brown sugar
2 fresh USA Anjou or Bosc pears, cored and sliced
⅓ cup thinly sliced mushrooms
¼ cup each thinly sliced green bell pepper and radishes
4 Green Onion Brushes

Combine vinegar and sugar; gently toss pears in mixture. Allow to stand 30 minutes to 1 hour to blend flavors; stir occasionally. Drain pears and arrange with vegetables on individual trays or plates.   *Makes 4 servings*

GREEN ONION BRUSHES: Cut 3-inch pieces off root ends of 4 green onions. Cut three 1-inch lengthwise slashes through root end; rotate onion half-turn and make three more 1-inch lengthwise slashes. Place in iced water. Drain before using.

Favorite recipe from **Pear Bureau Northwest**

SESAME PORK SALAD

3 cups cooked rice
1½ cups slivered cooked pork
¼ pound fresh snow peas, trimmed
    and julienned
1 medium cucumber, peeled,
    seeded and julienned
1 medium red bell pepper,
    julienned
½ cup sliced green onions
2 tablespoons sesame seeds,
    toasted (optional)
¼ cup chicken broth
3 tablespoons rice or white wine
    vinegar
3 tablespoons soy sauce
1 tablespoon peanut oil
1 teaspoon sesame oil

Combine rice, pork, snow peas, cucumber, bell pepper, onions and sesame seeds in large bowl. Combine broth, vinegar, soy sauce and oils in small jar with lid; shake well. Pour over rice mixture; toss lightly. Serve at room temperature or slightly chilled. *Makes 6 servings*

Favorite recipe from **USA Rice Federation**

NOTE: Chicken can be substituted for pork if desired.

ORIENTAL SALAD SUPREME

¼ cup peanut or vegetable oil
¼ cup rice vinegar
2 tablespoons brown sugar
½ medium unpeeled cucumber,
    halved and sliced
6 cups torn romaine or leaf lettuce
1 cup chow mein noodles
¼ cup peanut halves or coarsely
    chopped cashews (optional)

1. Combine oil, vinegar and brown sugar in small bowl; whisk until sugar dissolves.* Toss with cucumbers. Marinate, covered, in refrigerator up to 4 hours.

2. Just before serving, toss dressing with remaining ingredients.

Makes 4 servings

*At this point, dressing may be tossed with remaining ingredients and served immediately.

SESAME PORK SALAD

TUNA CURRY PASTA SALAD

2 cups uncooked rotini pasta
½ cup plain nonfat yogurt
½ cup reduced-fat mayonnaise
2 tablespoons reduced-fat Italian salad dressing
1 tablespoon mild curry powder
2 teaspoons fresh lemon juice
1 can (8 ounces) sliced water chestnuts, drained
1 small carrot, shredded
⅓ cup raisins
1 can (6 ounces) water-packed solid albacore tuna, drained and flaked
4 cups mixed salad greens
1 medium tomato, cut into wedges
1 small cucumber, sliced

1. Cook rotini according to package directions; drain. Rinse with cold water; drain.

2. Combine yogurt, mayonnaise, salad dressing, curry powder and lemon juice in medium bowl. Add water chestnuts, carrot, raisins, rotini and tuna. Toss gently to coat evenly.

3. Divide mixed salad greens evenly among 4 serving plates. Top with tuna mixture, tomato wedges and cucumber slices. *Makes 4 servings*

Prep and Cook Time: 15 minutes

NOTE: Perfectly cooked pasta should be al dente—tender but still firm to the bite. Test pasta shortly before the cooking time recommended on the package to avoid overcooking.

TUNA CURRY PASTA SALAD

SHANGHAI SALAD

1 pound cooked shelled, deveined
 small shrimp
½ head bok choy or iceberg lettuce,
 finely shredded
½ pound bean sprouts
1 cup shredded carrot
3 ribs celery, thinly sliced
3 green onions, shredded
1 tablespoon finely slivered fresh
 ginger
½ cup vegetable oil
¼ cup lemon juice
2 tablespoons soy sauce
2 teaspoons honey
 Green onion brushes, for garnish

Combine shrimp, bok choy, bean sprouts, carrot, celery, onions and ginger in large bowl. Blend oil, lemon juice, soy sauce and honey in small bowl; pour over shrimp mixture. Toss to coat. Spoon shrimp mixture onto individual salad plates; garnish with onion brushes.

Makes 4 main-dish servings

Tip ...

To devein shrimp, cut a shallow slit along the back of the shrimp with a paring knife. Lift out the vein. (You may find this easier to do under cold running water.)

The veins of large and jumbo shrimp are gritty; they must always be removed. Medium and small shrimp are not gritty and do not need removed unless you wish a more elegant presentation.

SHANGHAI SALAD

THAI PEANUT SALAD

1 cup picante sauce
¼ cup chunky-style peanut butter
2 tablespoons honey
2 tablespoons orange juice
1 teaspoon soy sauce
½ teaspoon ground ginger
2 cups (12 ounces) chopped CURE 81® ham
1 (7-ounce) package spaghetti, cooked
¼ cup dry roasted unsalted peanuts
¼ cup red bell pepper, cut into julienne strips
2 tablespoons chopped cilantro

In small saucepan, combine picante sauce, peanut butter, honey, orange juice, soy sauce and ginger. Cook, stirring over low heat until mixture is smooth. Add ¼ cup sauce mixture to ham. Gently toss remaining sauce mixture with hot cooked pasta. Toss pasta mixture with ham mixture, peanuts and pepper strips. Cover and chill 1 to 2 hours. Before serving, sprinkle with cilantro.   *Makes 4 servings*

ORIENTAL GINGER DRESSING

½ cup pineapple juice
2 tablespoons cider vinegar
1 tablespoon sugar
1 tablespoon soy sauce
1 teaspoon grated fresh ginger
½ teaspoon sesame oil

Combine all ingredients in a jar. Cover and shake vigorously. (Or combine ingredients in food processor.) Chill or serve over green salad, chicken salad or pasta salad.   *Makes 4 servings*

Favorite recipe from **The Sugar Association, Inc.**

THAI PEANUT SALAD

MANDARIN STEAK SALAD

⅓ cup *French's®* **Bold n' Spicy Brown Mustard**
2 tablespoons teriyaki sauce
1 tablespoon sugar
½ teaspoon garlic powder
½ teaspoon ground ginger
1 can (11 ounces) mandarin oranges, *reserve ¼ cup liquid*
1 pound boneless sirloin steak (1 inch thick)
8 cups mixed salad greens, torn
2 green onions, thinly shredded
⅓ cup dry roasted peanuts, chopped

1. Combine mustard, teriyaki sauce, sugar, garlic powder and ginger in small bowl. Stir in reserved mandarin orange liquid. Pour *½ cup* dressing into serving bowl.

2. Brush remaining dressing on steak. Broil or grill steak 10 minutes or until desired doneness. Let stand 5 minutes.

3. Thinly slice steak. Serve over mixed greens. Top with oranges, green onions and peanuts. Drizzle with reserved dressing.   *Makes 4 servings*

Prep Time: 10 minutes
Cook Time: 10 minutes

THAI PORK SALAD

8 cups lightly packed shredded cabbage or packaged coleslaw mix
1 cup lightly packed cilantro leaves, coarsely chopped
30 large mint leaves, coarsely chopped
6 grilled pork loin chops *or* 6 grilled ½-inch-thick boneless pork chops
2 tablespoons vegetable oil
½ large red onion, cut into thin slivers
½ cup lightly salted roasted cashews or peanuts
½ teaspoon salt
¼ to ½ teaspoon cayenne pepper
⅓ cup lime juice
1 tablespoon sugar

Combine cabbage, cilantro and mint in large bowl; set aside. Cut pork chops into ¼-inch-thick strips. Heat oil in large skillet over medium-high heat. Add pork, onion, nuts, salt and cayenne pepper. Cook and stir 2 minutes; remove from heat. Stir in lime juice and sugar. Spoon pork mixture over cabbage; toss well to coat. Garnish with lime wedges.

Makes 5 main-dish servings or 8 to 10 side-dish servings

GINGERED PORK TENDERLOIN SALAD

3 pounds pork tenderloin, thinly sliced
¼ cup teriyaki sauce
3 tablespoons grated fresh ginger
3 tablespoons chopped cilantro
1 tablespoon cracked black pepper
1 tablespoon olive oil
12 artichoke hearts, quartered
2 tablespoons butter
Tangy Vinaigrette Dressing (recipe follows)
6 red potatoes, boiled, peeled and sliced
2 red onions, peeled and thinly sliced
Lettuce leaves

¾ cup rice vinegar
¼ cup chopped parsley
¼ cup chopped chives
2 tablespoons chopped gherkins
3 chopped anchovies
1 tablespoon capers
2 cloves garlic, minced
1 cup olive oil
2 teaspoons curry powder
Salt and pepper to taste

Marinate pork slices in teriyaki sauce, ginger, cilantro and pepper for 1 hour. Drain pork and stir-fry quickly in hot oil; set aside. Sauté artichoke pieces in butter until lightly browned. Prepare Tangy Vinaigrette Dressing. Toss pork, potatoes, artichokes and onions with dressing. Refrigerate. Arrange salad on lettuce-lined plates. Pass remaining dressing. *Makes 12 servings*

TANGY VINAIGRETTE DRESSING

Combine all ingredients in small jar with tight-fitting lid. Shake well.
Makes about 2 cups dressing

Prep Time: 20 minutes

*Favorite recipe from **National Pork Board***

SHRIMP AND PASTA TOSS

8 cups water
3 cups fresh broccoli florets
1 cup diagonally cut carrot slices
1 cup frozen snow peas, thawed
⅓ cup soy sauce
¼ cup orange juice
3 tablespoons sesame oil
2 teaspoons grated fresh ginger
2 cups medium pasta shells, cooked
    and drained
1 pound peeled and deveined
    medium shrimp, cooked
1 cup red bell pepper strips
2 green onions, chopped
1 to 2 teaspoons sesame seeds,
    toasted

Bring 8 cups water to a boil in large saucepan. Add broccoli, carrots and snow peas; cook 1 to 2 minutes or until crisp-tender. Immediately plunge vegetables into very cold water to stop cooking. Cover with ice water; let stand 5 minutes. Drain.

Combine soy sauce, orange juice, sesame oil and ginger in large bowl. Add cooked vegetables, pasta, shrimp and bell pepper. Toss lightly. Sprinkle with green onions and sesame seeds just before serving.

Makes 4 servings

Tip ■■■

    Low in fat and cholesterol, pasta is easy to prepare and goes with almost every meal. It is available in a multitude of shapes, sizes and colors.

SHRIMP AND PASTA TOSS

ORIENTAL STEAK SALAD

1 package (3 ounces) Oriental
    flavor instant ramen noodles,
    uncooked
4 cups water
1 bag (16 ounces) BIRDS EYE®
    frozen Farm Fresh Mixtures
    Cauliflower, Carrots & Snow
    Pea Pods
2 tablespoons vegetable oil
1 pound boneless beef top loin
    steak, cut into thin strips
⅓ cup Oriental sesame salad
    dressing
¼ cup chow mein noodles
    Lettuce leaves

- Reserve seasoning packet from noodles.

- In large saucepan, bring water to boil. Add ramen noodles and vegetables; return to boil and cook 5 minutes, stirring occasionally. Drain.

- Heat oil in large nonstick skillet over medium-high heat. Add beef; cook and stir about 8 minutes or until browned.

- Stir in reserved seasoning packet until beef is well coated.

- In large bowl, toss together beef, vegetables, ramen noodles and salad dressing. Sprinkle with chow mein noodles. Serve over lettuce.

Makes 4 servings

Prep Time: 10 minutes
Cook Time: 12 to 15 minutes

SERVING SUGGESTION: This salad also can be served chilled. Moisten with additional salad dressing, if necessary. Sprinkle with chow mein noodles and spoon over lettuce just before serving.

ORANGE-ONION SALAD

1. Combine vinegar, soy sauce and sesame oil in small bowl.

2. Place orange and onion slices in single layer in shallow baking dish; drizzle with soy sauce mixture. Cover and refrigerate at least 30 minutes or up to 8 hours.

3. Transfer orange and onion slices to lettuce-lined serving platter or individual lettuce-lined dishes; drizzle with juices from dish. Garnish with carrot curls.

Makes 4 servings

1 tablespoon rice vinegar
1 tablespoon soy sauce
2 teaspoons dark sesame oil
1 large navel orange, peeled and sliced
1 small red onion, thinly sliced
 Romaine lettuce or spinach leaves
 Carrot curls for garnish

ROASTED SHANGHAI PEPPER SALAD

1. Drain and rinse peppers; pat dry with paper towels. Cut peppers lengthwise into ½-inch strips; place in small bowl.

2. Combine soy sauce, vinegar, sesame oil, honey and garlic; mix well. Pour over peppers; cover and refrigerate at least 2 hours. Serve over lettuce leaves. Sprinkle with cilantro.

Makes 4 servings

NOTE: This salad will keep up to 1 week covered and refrigerated.

1 jar (14 to 15 ounces) roasted red or red and yellow peppers
1½ tablespoons soy sauce
1 tablespoon rice vinegar
1 tablespoon dark sesame oil
2 teaspoons honey
1 clove garlic, minced
 Romaine lettuce or spinach leaves
2 tablespoons coarsely chopped fresh cilantro

TOP TO BOTTOM: ORANGE-ONION SALAD AND
ROASTED SHANGHAI PEPPER SALAD

ORIENTAL SHRIMP AND PASTA SALAD

⅓ cup reduced-fat sour cream
¼ cup reduced-fat mayonnaise
1 tablespoon seasoned rice vinegar
1 teaspoon minced fresh garlic
¾ teaspoon minced fresh ginger
¼ teaspoon salt
¼ teaspoon white pepper
3 cups water
¼ pound fresh snow peas, trimmed
1 pound medium shrimp, peeled,
    deveined and cooked
2 cups mostaccioli, cooked and
    drained
½ cup red bell pepper strips
⅓ cup sliced green onions
6 cherry tomatoes, halved
  Salad greens (endive, leaf lettuce,
    etc.)

1. Combine sour cream, mayonnaise, vinegar, garlic, ginger, salt and white pepper in small bowl. Mix well and set aside.

2. Bring water to a boil in medium saucepan. Add snow peas. Cook 2 minutes or until slightly softened and bright green. Drain and rinse with cold water. Place in large bowl. Add shrimp, mostaccioli, bell pepper and green onions. Pour sour cream mixture over shrimp mixture. Toss well to blend. Cover and refrigerate 1 hour. Add tomatoes and toss gently.

3. Arrange salad greens on 4 individual serving plates; spoon shrimp salad over greens. Serve immediately. *Makes 4 servings*

SERVING SUGGESTION: Serve this salad on chilled plates with chilled forks.

ORIENTAL SHRIMP AND PASTA SALAD

SPICY ORIENTAL SHRIMP SALAD

1 head iceberg lettuce
½ cup fresh basil leaves
¼ cup rice wine vinegar
1 piece fresh ginger (2 inches), peeled
1 tablespoon reduced-sodium soy sauce
3 cloves garlic
2 teaspoons dark sesame oil
1 teaspoon red pepper flakes
28 large shrimp, peeled and deveined
1 to 2 limes, cut into wedges (optional)
Vinaigrette Dressing (recipe follows)

1. Core, rinse and thoroughly drain lettuce. Refrigerate in airtight container to crisp. Combine basil, vinegar, ginger, soy sauce, garlic, sesame oil and pepper flakes in blender or food processor fitted with metal blade. Blend to form rough paste, using on/off pulsing action, scraping sides as needed. Transfer paste to large mixing bowl. Add shrimp; stir until coated. Cover and refrigerate 2 hours or overnight.

2. Preheat broiler. Broil shrimp in shallow pan 2 minutes per side, turning once, just until opaque. Shred lettuce; arrange on four plates. Top with cooked shrimp. Garnish with lime, if desired. Serve with Vinaigrette Dressing.

Makes 4 servings

VINAIGRETTE DRESSING: Whisk 3 tablespoons red wine vinegar with 1½ tablespoons olive oil in small bowl until blended.

MARINATED CUCUMBERS

1 large cucumber (about
   12 ounces)
2 tablespoons rice vinegar
2 tablespoons peanut or vegetable
   oil
2 tablespoons soy sauce
1½ teaspoons sugar
1 clove garlic, minced
¼ teaspoon red pepper flakes

1. Score cucumber lengthwise with tines of fork. Cut in half lengthwise; scrape out and discard seeds. Cut crosswise into ⅛-inch slices; place in medium bowl.

2. Combine remaining ingredients in cup; pour over cucumber. Toss to coat. Cover and refrigerate at least 4 hours or up to 2 days.

Makes 4 to 6 servings

JADE SALAD WITH SESAME VINAIGRETTE

5 cups fresh spinach or romaine
   leaves, torn
1 (7-ounce) pouch of STARKIST®
   Premium Albacore or Chunk
   Light Tuna
1 cup frozen cooked bay shrimp,
   thawed
¾ cup shredded cucumber
½ cup shredded red radishes

Sesame Vinaigrette
3 tablespoons rice vinegar
2 tablespoons sesame oil
2 tablespoons vegetable oil
2 teaspoons soy sauce
2 teaspoons sesame seeds
1 teaspoon sugar
   Salt and pepper to taste

In a large salad bowl toss together spinach, tuna, shrimp, cucumber and radishes. For dressing, in a shaker jar combine vinaigrette ingredients. Cover and shake until well blended. Drizzle over salad, toss well.

Makes 4 servings

Prep Time: 15 minutes

SINGAPORE SPAM™ SALAD

Warm Sesame Dressing
1 cup sugar
⅓ cup rice vinegar
¼ cup CARAPELLI® Extra Virgin Olive Oil
2 tablespoons sesame oil
¼ teaspoon garlic salt

Salad
½ head iceberg lettuce, thinly sliced
½ head romaine lettuce, thinly sliced
1 (12-ounce) can SPAM® Classic, cubed
3 carrots, grated
1 cup chopped green onions
1 cup chopped celery
1 green bell pepper, chopped
1 cup thinly sliced radishes
1 (6½-ounce) package sliced almonds, toasted

In small saucepan over low heat, combine all dressing ingredients. Stir constantly until sugar dissolves. In large bowl, toss together all salad ingredients. Serve warm dressing with salad.   *Makes 8 servings*

Tip ∎∎∎

Radishes are root vegetables that were first cultivated thousands of years ago in China. They belong to the crucifer family, which also includes cabbage and broccoli. Radishes range from the common small red spheres to one- to two-pound Japanese daikon roots. All radishes have distinctive flavors ranging from peppery to pungent.

SINGAPORE SPAM™ SALAD

CHINESE CRAB & CUCUMBER SALAD

1 large cucumber, peeled
2 packages (6 ounces each) fresh
　　pasteurized or thawed frozen
　　crabmeat, flaked
½ red bell pepper, diced
½ cup mayonnaise
3 tablespoons soy sauce
1 tablespoon sesame oil
1 teaspoon ground ginger
½ pound bean sprouts
1 tablespoon sesame seeds, toasted

Cut cucumber in half lengthwise; scoop out seeds. Cut cucumber into 1-inch pieces. Combine cucumber, crabmeat and bell pepper in large bowl. Blend mayonnaise, soy sauce, sesame oil and ginger in small bowl. Pour over crabmeat mixture; toss to mix well. Refrigerate 1 hour to allow flavors to blend. To serve, arrange bean sprouts on individual serving plates. Spoon crabmeat mixture on top; sprinkle with sesame seeds. Garnish with fresh chives, if desired.　　*Makes 4 main-dish servings*

ASIAN SLAW

½ small head napa cabbage,
　　shredded (about 4 cups)
3 carrots, shredded
2 red or yellow bell peppers, cut
　　into very thin strips
¼ pound snow peas, trimmed and
　　cut into thin strips
⅓ cup peanut oil
¼ cup rice vinegar
3 tablespoons *French's*®
　　Worcestershire Sauce
1 tablespoon Oriental sesame oil
1 tablespoon honey
2 cloves garlic, minced

Place vegetables in large bowl. Whisk together peanut oil, vinegar, Worcestershire, sesame oil, honey and garlic in small bowl until well blended. Pour dressing over vegetables; toss well to coat evenly. Cover and refrigerate 1 hour before serving.　　*Makes 6 side-dish servings*

Prep Time: 20 minutes
Chill Time: 1 hour

CHINESE CRAB & CUCUMBER SALAD

Sizzling Side Dishes

BUTTERNUT SQUASH IN COCONUT MILK

⅓ cup sweetened flaked coconut
2 teaspoons vegetable oil
½ small onion, finely chopped
2 cloves garlic, minced
1 cup canned unsweetened
    coconut milk
¼ cup packed brown sugar
1 tablespoon fish sauce
⅛ to ¼ teaspoon red pepper flakes
1 butternut squash (about
    2 pounds), peeled and cut into
    large cubes
1 tablespoon chopped fresh
    cilantro
  Cilantro sprig and purple kale for
    garnish

1. Preheat oven to 350°F. Spread coconut in baking pan. Bake 6 minutes or until golden, stirring occasionally. Set aside to cool and crisp.

2. Heat oil in large saucepan over medium-high heat. Add onion and garlic; cook and stir 3 minutes or until tender. Add coconut milk, brown sugar, fish sauce and red pepper flakes; stir until sugar is dissolved.

3. Bring mixture to a boil; add squash. Reduce heat to medium; cover and simmer 30 minutes or until squash is tender. Transfer squash to serving bowl with slotted spoon.

4. Increase heat to high; boil remaining liquid until thick, stirring constantly. Pour liquid over squash in bowl. Sprinkle with toasted coconut and chopped cilantro. Garnish, if desired. *Makes 4 to 6 servings*

BUTTERNUT SQUASH IN COCONUT MILK

BRAISED ORIENTAL CABBAGE

½ small head green cabbage (about ½ pound)
1 small head bok choy (about ¾ pound)
½ cup fat-free reduced-sodium chicken broth
2 tablespoons rice wine vinegar
2 tablespoons reduced-sodium soy sauce
1 tablespoon brown sugar
¼ teaspoon red pepper flakes (optional)
1 tablespoon water
1 tablespoon cornstarch

1. Cut cabbage into 1-inch pieces. Cut woody stems from bok choy leaves; slice stems into ½-inch pieces. Cut tops of leaves into ½-inch slices; set aside.

2. Combine cabbage and bok choy stems in large nonstick skillet. Add broth, vinegar, soy sauce, brown sugar and red pepper flakes, if desired.

3. Bring to a boil over high heat. Reduce heat to medium. Cover and simmer 5 minutes or until vegetables are crisp-tender.

4. Blend water into cornstarch in small bowl until smooth. Stir into skillet. Cook and stir 1 minute or until sauce boils and thickens.

5. Stir in reserved bok choy leaves; cook 1 minute.

Makes 6 side-dish servings

STIR-FRIED SPINACH WITH GARLIC

2 teaspoons peanut or vegetable oil
1 large clove garlic, minced
6 cups packed fresh spinach leaves (about 8 ounces)
2 teaspoons soy sauce
1 teaspoon rice vinegar
¼ teaspoon sugar
1 teaspoon toasted sesame seeds*

To toast sesame seeds, spread seeds in small skillet. Shake skillet over medium heat 2 minutes or until seeds begin to pop and turn golden.

1. Heat wok or large skillet over medium-high heat. Add oil; heat until hot. Add garlic; cook 1 minute.

2. Add spinach, soy sauce, vinegar and sugar; stir-fry 1 to 2 minutes until spinach is wilted. Sprinkle with sesame seeds. *Makes 2 servings*

BRAISED ORIENTAL CABBAGE

STIR-FRIED BROCCOLI

1 pound broccoli
1 medium onion
2 ribs celery
4 ounces fresh bean sprouts
1 tablespoon cornstarch
1 tablespoon cold water
1 tablespoon oyster sauce
¼ teaspoon salt
¼ teaspoon sugar
1 tablespoon vegetable oil
2 cloves garlic, minced
¾ cup vegetable or chicken broth
¼ cup pimiento strips, drained

1. Cut woody stems from broccoli; discard. Peel stems and cut diagonally into slices. Cut tops into florets; rinse. Cut onion into wedges and celery diagonally into ¼-inch-thick slices. Rinse bean sprouts and drain, removing any green hulls. Set aside.

2. Combine cornstarch, water, oyster sauce, salt and sugar in small bowl; stir until smooth. Set aside.

3. Heat wok over high heat about 1 minute or until hot. Drizzle oil into wok and heat 30 seconds. Add broccoli stems, onion and celery; stir-fry 2 to 3 minutes or until vegetables are crisp-tender. Add broccoli florets and garlic; stir-fry 30 seconds. Add broth. Cover and cook about 3 minutes or until broccoli is crisp-tender.

4. Stir cornstarch mixture until smooth. Add to wok. Cook and stir until sauce boils and thickens.

5. Add bean sprouts and pimiento; stir-fry just until heated through. Transfer to serving dish.

Makes 6 servings

Tip ∎∎∎

For successful stir-frying, make sure the ingredients are cut into uniform sizes and shapes. This will ensure even cooking. Also keep the food in constant motion, tossing and stirring it with a flat metal or wooden spatula.

STIR-FRIED BROCCOLI

HONG KONG FRIED RICE CAKES

1 box (about 6 ounces) chicken-flavored rice mix
½ cup sliced green onions
2 eggs, beaten
2 tablespoons chopped fresh parsley
1 tablespoon hoisin sauce
1 tablespoon soy sauce
1 teaspoon minced fresh ginger
1 clove garlic, minced
2 to 3 tablespoons vegetable oil, divided

1. Prepare rice according to package directions, omitting butter. Cover and refrigerate one hour or until completely chilled. Add remaining ingredients, except oil, to rice; mix well. Form rice mixture into cakes, 3 inches in diameter.

2. Heat 1 tablespoon oil in large skillet over medium heat until hot. Cook 4 cakes at a time 3 to 4 minutes on each side or until golden brown. Add additional oil to skillet as needed. *Makes 4 to 6 servings*

HOT AND SOUR ZUCCHINI

2 teaspoons minced fresh ginger
1 clove garlic, minced
¼ teaspoon red pepper flakes or crushed Szechuan peppercorns
1 pound zucchini
2 teaspoons sugar
1 teaspoon cornstarch
2 tablespoons red wine vinegar
2 tablespoons soy sauce
1 tablespoon peanut or vegetable oil
1 teaspoon dark sesame oil

1. Combine ginger, garlic and red pepper in small bowl. Cut zucchini into ¼-inch slices. If zucchini is large, cut each slice in half. Toss zucchini with ginger mixture.

2. Combine sugar and cornstarch in small bowl. Stir in vinegar and soy sauce until smooth.

3. Heat large nonstick skillet over medium-high heat. Add peanut oil; heat until hot. Add zucchini mixture; stir-fry 4 to 5 minutes until zucchini is crisp-tender.

4. Stir vinegar mixture and add to skillet. Stir-fry 15 seconds or until sauce boils and thickens. Stir in sesame oil. *Makes 4 servings*

HONG KONG FRIED RICE CAKES

SESAME SNOW PEAS

½ **pound snow peas (Chinese pea pods)**
2 **teaspoons dark sesame oil**
2 **teaspoons vegetable oil**
2 **green onions, cut into ¼-inch slices**
½ **teaspoon grated fresh ginger** *or* ¼ **teaspoon ground ginger**
1 **medium carrot, cut into matchstick pieces**
1 **teaspoon soy sauce**
1 **tablespoon sesame seeds, toasted***

*To toast sesame seeds, heat small skillet over medium heat. Add sesame seeds; cook and stir about 5 minutes or until golden. Set aside.

1. To de-stem peas, pinch off stem end from each pod and pull strings down pod to remove, if present. (Young tender pods may have no strings.) Make a "V-shaped" cut at opposite end of pod.

2. To stir-fry, place wok or large skillet over high heat. Add sesame and vegetable oils, swirling to coat sides. Heat oils until hot, about 30 seconds. Add onions, ginger, peas and carrot; stir-fry 4 minutes or until peas are bright green and crisp-tender.

3. Stir in soy sauce. Transfer to warm serving dish; sprinkle with reserved sesame seeds. Serve immediately.   *Makes 4 side-dish servings*

ORIENTAL RICE PILAF

½ **cup chopped onion**
1 **clove garlic, minced**
1 **tablespoon sesame oil**
1¾ **cups beef broth**
1 **cup uncooked long grain white rice**
1 **tablespoon reduced-sodium soy sauce**
⅛ to ¼ **teaspoon red pepper flakes**
⅓ **cup thinly sliced green onions**
⅓ **cup diced red bell pepper**
2 **tablespoons sesame seeds, toasted**

Cook onion and garlic in oil in 2- to 3-quart saucepan over medium heat until onion is tender. Add broth, rice, soy sauce and pepper flakes. Bring to a boil; stir once or twice. Reduce heat; cover and simmer 15 minutes or until rice is tender and liquid is absorbed. Stir green onions, red bell pepper and sesame seeds into cooked rice; cover and let stand 5 minutes. Fluff with fork.   *Makes 6 servings*

Favorite recipe from **USA Rice Federation**

SESAME SNOW PEAS

SPICED MUSHROOM PILAU

5 whole cardamom pods
1 teaspoon cumin seeds
5 whole cloves
2 cinnamon sticks, broken, divided
1 tablespoon butter
1 tablespoon vegetable oil
1 onion, finely chopped
8 ounces button mushrooms, sliced ¼-inch thick
1 cup basmati rice*
1 bay leaf
½ teaspoon turmeric
¼ teaspoon salt
1 can (about 14 ounces) chicken broth plus enough water to make 2 cups
¼ cup cashews for garnish

Some packages of rice recommend washing rice before using. Consult package for specific directions.

1. Preheat oven to 250°F.

2. Remove seeds from cardamom pods; discard pods. Combine cardamom seeds, cumin, cloves and 1 broken cinnamon stick on pizza pan or pie plate. Bake 30 minutes, stirring every 10 minutes. Transfer warm spices to clean coffee or spice grinder and grind until fine powder or use mortar and pestle to pulverize. Set aside.

3. Heat butter and oil in large skillet over medium heat. Add onion; stir-fry 5 minutes or until onion is soft. Add mushrooms; stir-fry 5 minutes.

4. Stir in rice, bay leaf, turmeric, salt, ground roasted spices and remaining cinnamon stick. Stir-fry 2 minutes or until spices become fragrant.

5. Add chicken broth and water; bring to a boil over high heat. Reduce heat to low; cover and simmer 15 minutes or until rice is tender and all liquid is absorbed.

6. Remove and discard bay leaf and pieces of cinnamon stick; fluff rice with fork. Let stand, covered, 5 minutes. Transfer to serving dish; garnish with cashews.

Makes 4 to 6 servings

SPICED MUSHROOM PILAU

STIR-FRY VEGETABLES

¼ cup GRANDMA'S® Molasses
¼ cup chicken broth
2 tablespoons soy sauce
4 teaspoons cornstarch
1 tablespoon minced ginger
1 teaspoon minced garlic
⅛ teaspoon ground red pepper
1 tablespoon canola oil
2 pounds fresh vegetables, cut into bite-sized pieces (celery, zucchini, onion, peppers, Chinese cabbage and snow peas)

In large bowl, combine molasses, broth, soy sauce, cornstarch, ginger, garlic and red pepper. Set aside. Heat oil in wok or large heavy skillet. Add vegetables and stir-fry 2 minutes until crisp and tender. Mix in molasses mixture. Cook just until sauce thickens and vegetables are well coated.

Makes 4 to 6 servings

MA PO TOFU

1 package (about 12 ounces) firm tofu, drained
2 tablespoons soy sauce
2 teaspoons minced fresh ginger
1 cup chicken broth, divided
1 tablespoon cornstarch
1½ cups broccoli florets
1 teaspoon hot chili oil
2 teaspoons dark sesame oil
¼ cup coarsely chopped fresh cilantro or green onion tops

1. Press tofu lightly between paper towels; cut into ¾-inch squares or triangles. Place in shallow dish; sprinkle with soy sauce and ginger.

2. Blend ¼ cup broth into cornstarch in cup until smooth. Combine remaining ¾ cup broth, broccoli and chili oil in 10-inch skillet. Bring to a boil over high heat. Reduce heat to medium. Cover and cook 3 minutes or until broccoli is crisp-tender.

3. Stir broth mixture and add to skillet. Cook and stir 1 minute or until sauce boils and thickens. Stir in tofu mixture. Simmer, uncovered, until tofu is hot. Stir in sesame oil. Sprinkle with cilantro.

Makes 2 main-dish or 4 side-dish servings

STIR-FRY VEGETABLES

ASPARAGUS WITH SESAME-GINGER SAUCE

1 tablespoon SPLENDA® Granular
1 tablespoon water
1 tablespoon peanut oil
1 tablespoon rice vinegar
1 tablespoon soy sauce
1 tablespoon tahini* (puréed sesame seeds)
1 teaspoon chopped fresh ginger
½ teaspoon chopped garlic
Pinch crushed red pepper
48 medium asparagus spears, trimmed and peeled

Look for tahini in the ethnic foods section of your supermarket.

1. In a food processor, combine all ingredients except asparagus and mix until thoroughly blended. Set aside.

2. Fill large skillet half-full of water; cover and bring to a boil. Add asparagus and simmer just until crisp-tender, approximately 4 to 5 minutes. Drain well. (Do not rinse.)

3. Transfer to serving platter. Pour sauce over hot asparagus. Serve warm or at room temperature. *Makes 7 servings*

Prep Time: 10 minutes
Cook Time: 5 minutes

CASHEW GREEN BEANS

1 package (10 ounces) frozen julienne-cut green beans, thawed and drained
1 tablespoon peanut or vegetable oil
1 small onion, cut into thin wedges
2 cloves garlic, minced
2 tablespoons oyster sauce
1 tablespoon rice vinegar
1 tablespoon honey
¼ cup coarsely chopped cashews

1. Pat green beans dry with paper towels.

2. Heat wok or large skillet over medium-high heat. Add oil; heat until hot. Add onion and garlic; stir-fry 3 minutes.

3. Add beans; stir-fry 2 minutes. Add oyster sauce, vinegar and honey; stir-fry 1 minute or until heated through. Remove from heat; stir in cashews. *Makes 4 servings*

ASPARAGUS WITH SESAME-GINGER SAUCE

SWEET & HOT MARINATED MUSHROOMS

⅓ cup honey
¼ cup white wine vinegar
¼ cup dry white wine or vegetable broth
2 tablespoons vegetable oil
1 tablespoon soy sauce
1 tablespoon sesame oil
1 clove garlic, minced
1 small green onion, chopped
1 teaspoon grated fresh gingerroot
½ teaspoon grated orange peel
¼ teaspoon ground red pepper
1 pound fresh small button mushrooms
Parsley sprigs and orange wedges for garnish (optional)

Combine honey, vinegar, wine, vegetable oil, soy sauce, sesame oil, garlic, green onion, gingerroot, orange peel and red pepper in small saucepan. Cook and stir mixture over low heat until hot. Place mushrooms in heat-proof bowl; pour hot marinade over mushrooms. Cover and marinate 3 hours in refrigerator, stirring occasionally. Arrange mushrooms in serving dish; garnish with parsley sprigs and orange wedges, if desired.

Makes 4 to 6 servings

Favorite recipe from **National Honey Board**

GREEN RICE

2 cups chicken broth
1 cup uncooked rice
¼ cup chopped fresh parsley
¼ cup chopped green onions with tops
1 tablespoon butter or margarine

1. Combine broth and rice in medium saucepan. Bring to a boil; stir.

2. Reduce heat to low; cover. Simmer, without stirring, 15 minutes or until rice is tender and liquid is absorbed. (Do not remove lid during cooking.)

3. Remove saucepan from heat; stir in parsley, onions and butter. Cover; keep warm until ready to serve.

Makes 4 servings

SWEET & HOT MARINATED MUSHROOMS

SPINACH AND MUSHROOM STIR-FRY

2 tablespoons peanut oil
2 cloves garlic, minced
1 teaspoon minced fresh ginger
¼ to ½ teaspoon red pepper flakes
1 red bell pepper, cut into 1-inch triangles
2 ounces fresh shiitake or button mushrooms,* sliced
10 ounces fresh spinach, washed, stemmed and coarsely chopped
1 teaspoon fish sauce

Or, substitute ½-ounce dried Oriental mushrooms, soaked according to package directions.

Heat wok over high heat 1 minute or until hot. Drizzle oil into wok; heat 30 seconds. Add garlic, ginger and pepper flakes; stir-fry 30 seconds. Add bell pepper and mushrooms; stir-fry 2 minutes. Add spinach and fish sauce; stir-fry 1 to 2 minutes or until spinach is wilted.

Makes 4 servings

ASIAN SPAGHETTI

3 tablespoons CRISCO® Oil,* divided
8 ounces uncooked spaghetti
3 tablespoons sesame seeds
3 tablespoons soy sauce
1 scallion or green onion, trimmed and thinly sliced

Use your favorite Crisco Oil product.

1. Bring large pot of salted water to a boil on high heat. Add 2 tablespoons oil and spaghetti. Boil according to package directions until al dente. Drain.

2. Heat remaining 1 tablespoon oil in small skillet on medium heat. Add sesame seeds. Sauté 2 minutes, or until brown.

3. Toss spaghetti with soy sauce, sesame seeds and scallion. Serve immediately.

Makes 4 servings

Prep Time: 10 minutes
Total Time: 25 minutes

SPINACH AND MUSHROOM STIR-FRY

WILTED SPINACH MANDARIN

1 tablespoon oil
½ pound fresh spinach, washed and stemmed
1 cup bean sprouts
1 can (11 ounces) mandarin oranges, drained
2 tablespoons reduced-sodium soy sauce
2 tablespoons orange juice
Quartered orange slices for garnish

Heat oil in wok or large skillet over medium-high heat. Add spinach, bean sprouts and mandarin oranges to wok. Stir-fry 1 or 2 minutes just until spinach wilts. Transfer to serving dish. Heat soy sauce and orange juice in wok; pour over spinach and toss gently to coat. Garnish, if desired.

Makes 4 side-dish servings

INDONESIAN HONEY-BAKED BEANS

2 cans (15 ounces each) white beans, drained
2 apples, pared and diced
1 small onion, diced
⅔ cup honey
½ cup golden raisins
⅓ cup sweet pickle relish
1 tablespoon prepared mustard
1 teaspoon curry powder or to taste
Salt to taste

Combine all ingredients in 2½-quart casserole. Add enough water just to cover. Bake at 300°F about 1½ hours, adding more water if needed.

Makes 8 servings

Favorite recipe from **National Honey Board**

WILTED SPINACH MANDARIN

SESAME GREEN BEANS AND RED PEPPER

1 tablespoon sesame seeds
3 tablespoons *Frank's® RedHot®*
  Original Cayenne Pepper Sauce
1 tablespoon olive oil
1 tablespoon soy sauce
2 teaspoons grated peeled fresh
  ginger
¼ teaspoon Oriental sesame oil
1 clove garlic, minced
1 pound fresh green beans, washed,
  trimmed and cut in half
  crosswise
¼ teaspoon salt
½ red bell pepper, seeded and cut
  into very thin strips
  Lettuce (optional)

1. Heat large nonstick skillet over medium heat. Add sesame seeds. Cook 1 to 2 minutes or until golden; shaking skillet often. Transfer to small bowl. Whisk in *Frank's RedHot* Sauce, olive oil, soy sauce, ginger, sesame oil and garlic; set aside.

2. Bring 1 cup water to a boil in large saucepan over high heat. Place green beans and salt in steamer basket; set into saucepan. Do not let water touch beans. Cover; steam 5 to 6 minutes or until beans are crisp-tender. Rinse with cold water; drain well.

3. Combine beans and bell pepper in large bowl. Pour sesame dressing over vegetables; toss to coat evenly. Cover; refrigerate 1 hour. Toss just before serving. Serve on lettuce-lined plates, if desired.

Makes 6 servings

Tip ■■■

From Asian cuisine to breads and vegetables, toasted sesame seeds enhance the flavor of foods as well as add a little crunch. They are widely available packaged in supermarkets and are sold in bulk in specialty stores and ethnic markets.

SESAME GREEN BEANS AND RED PEPPER

MOO SHU VEGETABLES

½ package dried Chinese black
  mushrooms (6 or
  7 mushrooms)
2 tablespoons vegetable oil
2 cloves garlic, minced
2 cups shredded napa or green
  cabbage
1 red bell pepper, cut into short,
  thin strips
1 cup fresh bean sprouts or canned
  bean sprouts, rinsed and
  drained
2 large green onions, cut into
  short, thin strips
1 tablespoon teriyaki sauce
⅓ cup plum sauce
8 (6-inch) flour tortillas, warmed

1. Soak mushrooms in warm water 20 minutes. Drain; squeeze out excess water. Discard stems; slice caps.

2. Heat oil in wok or large nonstick skillet over medium heat. Add garlic; stir-fry 30 seconds.

3. Add cabbage, mushrooms and bell pepper; stir-fry 3 minutes. Add bean sprouts and green onions; stir-fry 2 minutes. Add teriyaki sauce; stir-fry 30 seconds or until mixture is hot.

4. Spread about 2 teaspoons plum sauce on each tortilla. Spoon heaping ¼ cup of vegetable mixture over sauce. Fold bottom of each tortilla up over filling, then fold sides over filling.   *Makes 8 servings*

NOT FRIED ASIAN RICE

2 teaspoons sesame oil
¾ cup chopped green onions
½ cup chopped red bell pepper
2 cloves garlic, minced
2 cups water
1 cup uncooked converted rice
2 egg whites
1 tablespoon light soy sauce
2 teaspoons sugar

Heat oil in nonstick skillet over medium-high heat until hot. Add onions, bell pepper and garlic; cook and stir 1 minute. Add water and bring to a boil. Reduce heat to low; stir in rice and egg whites. Simmer 20 minutes or until rice is tender, stirring frequently. Stir in soy sauce and sugar. Cook 3 to 5 minutes more until sugar caramelizes.   *Makes 6 servings*

Favorite recipe from **The Sugar Association, Inc.**

MOO SHU VEGETABLES

CARROTS CHINOISE

8 ounces medium carrots, peeled
2 teaspoons vegetable oil
¼ cup water
1 can (8 ounces) sliced water chestnuts, drained
1 package (6 ounces) frozen Chinese pea pods, partially thawed
1 teaspoon dark sesame oil
½ teaspoon salt
⅛ teaspoon black pepper

1. Cut carrots diagonally into thin slices.

2. Heat wok over medium-high heat 1 minute or until hot. Drizzle vegetable oil into wok and heat 30 seconds. Add carrots; stir-fry until lightly browned. Reduce heat to medium.

3. Add water; cover and cook about 4 minutes or until carrots are crisp-tender.

4. Add water chestnuts, pea pods, sesame oil, salt and black pepper; stir-fry until heated through. Transfer to serving dish.   *Makes 4 servings*

BROCCOLI & CAULIFLOWER STIR-FRY

2 dry-pack sun-dried tomatoes
1 tablespoon plus 1 teaspoon reduced-sodium soy sauce
1 tablespoon rice wine vinegar
1 teaspoon brown sugar
1 teaspoon dark sesame oil
⅛ teaspoon red pepper flakes
2¼ teaspoons vegetable oil
2 cups cauliflower florets
2 cups broccoli florets
1 clove garlic, finely chopped
⅓ cup thinly sliced red or green bell pepper

1. Place tomatoes in small bowl; cover with boiling water. Let stand 5 minutes. Drain; coarsely chop. Meanwhile, blend soy sauce, vinegar, sugar, sesame oil and red pepper in small bowl.

2. Heat vegetable oil in wok or large nonstick skillet over medium-high heat until hot. Add cauliflower, broccoli and garlic; stir-fry 4 minutes. Add tomatoes and bell pepper; stir-fry 1 minute or until vegetables are crisp-tender. Add soy sauce mixture; cook and stir until heated through. Serve immediately.   *Makes 2 servings*

CARROTS CHINOISE

BRAISED EGGPLANT IN GARLIC SAUCE

1 medium eggplant (1¼ pounds), peeled and cut into chunks
1 teaspoon salt
2 tablespoons light soy sauce
1 tablespoon rice vinegar or white vinegar
1 tablespoon rice wine or dry sherry
1 tablespoon dark sesame oil
2 teaspoons cornstarch
2 teaspoons sugar
2 tablespoons vegetable oil
2 cloves garlic, minced
¼ cup chicken broth
1 small red bell pepper, cut into strips
1 green onion with tops, cut into 1-inch lengths
Lemon balm for garnish

1. Place eggplant in large colander over bowl; sprinkle with salt. Let stand 30 minutes to extract moisture.

2. Combine soy sauce, vinegar, rice wine, sesame oil, cornstarch and sugar in cup; mix well. Set aside.

3. Rinse eggplant with cold water; pat dry with paper towels. Heat wok over high heat about 1 minute or until hot. Drizzle vegetable oil into wok; heat 15 seconds. Add eggplant and stir-fry about 5 minutes or until lightly browned. Add garlic; stir-fry 15 seconds.

4. Add chicken broth to wok; cover and reduce heat to medium. Cook eggplant 3 minutes.

5. Uncover wok. Increase heat to medium-high. Add bell pepper and onion; stir-fry 2 minutes. Stir cornstarch mixture; add to wok. Cook and stir until liquid boils and thickens. Transfer to warm serving dish. Garnish, if desired. Serve immediately.

Makes 6 servings

BRAISED EGGPLANT IN GARLIC SAUCE

FRIED RICE WITH HAM

2 tablespoons vegetable oil, divided
2 eggs, beaten
1 small onion, chopped
1 carrot, peeled and chopped
⅔ cup diced ham
½ cup frozen green peas
1 large clove garlic, minced
3 cups cold cooked rice
3 tablespoons reduced-sodium soy sauce
⅛ teaspoon black pepper

1. Heat 1 tablespoon oil in wok or large skillet over medium-high heat until hot. Add eggs; rotate wok to swirl eggs into thin layer. Cook eggs until set and slightly brown; break up with wooden spoon. Remove from wok to small bowl.

2. Heat remaining 1 tablespoon oil until hot. Add onion and carrot; stir-fry 2 minutes. Add ham, peas and garlic; stir-fry 1 minute.

3. Add rice; stir-fry 2 to 3 minutes or until rice is heated through. Stir in soy sauce and pepper until well blended. Stir in cooked eggs.

Makes 4 servings

Prep and Cook Time: 18 minutes

NOTE: Substitute leftover cooked vegetables for the carrots and peas in this recipe.

SESAME HONEY VEGETABLE CASSEROLE

1 package (16 ounces) frozen mixed vegetables such as baby carrots, broccoli, onions and red peppers, thawed and drained
3 tablespoons honey
1 tablespoon dark sesame oil
1 tablespoon reduced-sodium soy sauce
2 teaspoons sesame seeds

1. Heat oven to 350°F. Place mixed vegetables in shallow 1½-quart casserole dish or quiche dish.

2. Combine honey, oil, soy sauce and sesame seeds; mix well. Drizzle evenly over vegetables. Bake 20 to 25 minutes or until vegetables are hot, stirring after 15 minutes.

Makes 4 side-dish servings

FRIED RICE WITH HAM

HOT CHINESE POTATOES

3 tablespoons vegetable oil, divided
4 medium COLORADO Potatoes, halved lengthwise, thinly sliced
1 cup *each* thin diagonal carrot and celery slices
½ cup green bell pepper strips
½ cup sliced mushrooms
1 clove garlic, minced
½ cup water
2 tablespoons soy sauce
1½ teaspoons cornstarch
1 large tomato, cut into thin wedges
⅓ cup sliced green onions

Heat 1½ tablespoons oil in wok or large skillet. Add potatoes; cook and stir over medium-high heat about 10 minutes until barely tender. Remove and keep warm. Add remaining oil to wok. Add carrot, celery, pepper, mushrooms and garlic; cook and stir 3 to 4 minutes until crisp-tender.

Combine water, soy sauce and cornstarch in small bowl. Return potatoes to wok with cornstarch mixture. Cook and stir about 2 minutes, just until sauce thickens and mixture is heated through. Spoon onto platter; garnish with tomato and onions.

Makes 6 servings

*Favorite recipe from **Colorado Potato Administrative Committee***

SZECHUAN-GRILLED MUSHROOMS

1 pound large fresh mushrooms
2 tablespoons soy sauce
2 teaspoons peanut or vegetable oil
1 teaspoon dark sesame oil
1 clove garlic, minced
½ teaspoon crushed Szechuan peppercorns or red pepper flakes

1. Place mushrooms in large plastic bag. Add remaining ingredients to bag. Close bag securely; shake to coat mushrooms with marinade. Marinate at room temperature 15 minutes or cover and refrigerate up to 8 hours. (Mushrooms will absorb marinade.)

2. Thread mushrooms onto skewers. Grill or broil mushrooms 5 inches from heat 10 minutes or until lightly browned, turning once. Serve immediately.

Makes 4 servings

HOT CHINESE POTATOES

ZESTY MIXED VEGETABLES

8 ounces green beans
½ small head cauliflower
2 green onions with tops
1 or 2 jalapeño or Thai chili
    peppers*
2 tablespoons vegetable oil
2 cloves garlic, minced
8 ounces peeled fresh baby carrots
1 cup reduced-sodium chicken
    broth, divided
1 tablespoon cornstarch
1 teaspoon sugar
¼ teaspoon salt
2 tablespoons oyster sauce
    Red and yellow bell pepper strips
    for garnish

*Jalapeño and other chili peppers can sting
and irritate the skin; wear rubber gloves when
handling peppers and do not touch eyes. Wash
hands after handling.

• Trim ends from beans and discard. Cut beans diagonally into thirds or quarters. Cut cauliflower into florets. Cut onions into ½-inch pieces, keeping white part and green tops of onions separate. Cut jalapeño peppers lengthwise in half; remove stem and seeds. Cut jalapeño peppers crosswise into thin slices.

• Heat wok or large skillet over high heat about 1 minute or until hot. Drizzle oil into wok and heat 30 seconds. Add white part of onions, beans, cauliflower, jalapeño peppers and garlic; stir-fry until tender. Add carrots and ¾ cup broth. Cover; bring to a boil. Reduce heat to low; cook until carrots and beans are crisp-tender.

• Combine cornstarch, sugar and salt in cup; stir in remaining ¼ cup broth and oyster sauce until smooth. Stir into wok. Cook until sauce boils and thickens. Stir in green onion tops. Transfer to serving dish. Garnish, if desired.   *Makes 4 servings*

NOTE: Jalapeño peppers are small, dark green chilies, normally 2 to 3 inches long and ¾ inch wide with a slightly tapered end. Their flavor varies from hot to very hot. Use 1 or 2 in this dish depending on your preference.

ZESTY MIXED VEGETABLES

MARINATED VEGETABLES

¼ cup rice wine vinegar
3 tablespoons reduced-sodium soy
    sauce
2 tablespoons fresh lemon juice
1 tablespoon vegetable oil
1 clove garlic, minced
1 teaspoon minced fresh ginger
½ teaspoon sugar
2 cups broccoli florets
2 cups cauliflower florets
2 cups diagonally sliced carrots
    (½-inch pieces)
8 ounces whole fresh mushrooms
1 large red bell pepper, cut into
    1-inch pieces
Lettuce leaves

1. Combine vinegar, soy sauce, lemon juice, oil, garlic, ginger and sugar in large bowl. Set aside.

2. To blanch broccoli, cauliflower and carrots, cook 1 minute in enough salted boiling water to cover. Remove and plunge into cold water, then drain immediately. Toss with oil mixture while still warm. Cool to room temperature.

3. Add mushrooms and bell pepper to bowl; toss to coat. Cover and marinate in refrigerator at least 4 hours or up to 24 hours. Drain vegetables; reserve marinade.

4. Arrange vegetables on lettuce-lined platter. Serve chilled or at room temperature with toothpicks. If desired, serve remaining marinade in small cup for dipping.

Makes 12 servings

Tip ■■■

Food is blanched for one or more of the following reasons: to loosen and remove skin (tomatoes, peaches, almonds); to enhance color and reduce bitterness (raw vegetables for dips); and to extend storage life (raw vegetables to be frozen).

MARINATED VEGETABLES

GRILLED BOK CHOY PACKETS

12 fresh or dried shiitake
    mushrooms*
½ small onion, thinly sliced
1 head bok choy (1 pound),
    coarsely chopped
1 can (about 8¾ ounces) whole
    baby corn, rinsed and drained
1 large red bell pepper, cut into
    strips
2 tablespoons water
2 tablespoons sweet cooking rice
    wine
2 tablespoons reduced-sodium soy
    sauce
1½ teaspoons dark sesame oil
1 teaspoon minced fresh ginger
½ teaspoon salt

*For dried mushrooms, place in small bowl; cover
with warm water and soak 30 minutes to soften.
Drain and squeeze dry.*

1. Remove and discard mushroom stems; set aside. (Mushroom caps can be thinly sliced, if desired.)

2. Spray 6 (16-inch-long) sheets of foil with nonstick cooking spray. In center of each sheet, layer onion slices, bok choy, corn, bell pepper and mushrooms.

3. Combine water, rice wine, soy sauce, oil, ginger and salt in small bowl. Drizzle over vegetables in each packet.

4. Seal packets by bringing two long sides of foil together over vegetables; fold down in series of locked folds, allowing for heat circulation and expansion. Fold short ends up and over again. Press folds firmly to seal packets. Turn packets over several times to coat vegetables completely.

5. Grill packets on covered grill over medium to low coals about 10 minutes, turning every 2 to 3 minutes. (Vegetables will continue to cook once removed from heat.) To serve, carefully open one end of each packet and slide vegetables onto plates. *Makes 6 servings*

SERVING SUGGESTION: Grilled bok choy goes great with grilled shrimp.

GRILLED BOK CHOY PACKET

BUDDHA'S DELIGHT

1 package (1 ounce) dried black
    Chinese mushrooms
1 package (about 12 ounces) firm
    tofu, drained
1 tablespoon peanut or vegetable
    oil
2 cups diagonally cut 1-inch
    asparagus pieces *or* 1 package
    (10 ounces) frozen cut
    asparagus, thawed and drained
1 medium onion, cut into thin
    wedges
2 cloves garlic, minced
½ cup chicken broth
3 tablespoons hoisin sauce
¼ cup coarsely chopped fresh
    cilantro or thinly sliced green
    onions

1. Place mushrooms in small bowl; cover with warm water. Soak 20 minutes to soften. Drain, squeezing out excess water over fine strainer into measuring cup; reserve. Discard mushroom stems; slice caps.

2. Press tofu lightly between paper towels; cut into ¾-inch squares or triangles.

3. Heat wok or large skillet over medium-high heat. Add oil; heat until hot. Add asparagus, onion wedges and garlic; stir-fry 4 minutes for fresh or 3 minutes for frozen asparagus.

4. Add mushrooms, ¼ cup reserved mushroom liquid,* broth and hoisin sauce. Reduce heat to medium-low. Simmer, uncovered, until asparagus is crisp-tender, 2 to 3 minutes for fresh or 1 minute for frozen asparagus.

5. Stir in tofu; heat through, stirring occasionally. Ladle into shallow bowls. Sprinkle with cilantro. *Makes 2 main-dish or 4 side-dish servings*

Remaining mushroom liquid may be covered and refrigerated up to 3 days or frozen up to 3 months. It may be used in soups and stews.

BUDDHA'S DELIGHT

Vegetarian Delights

SPICY FRIED RICE WITH TOFU

4 ounces firm tofu, drained
2 eggs
4½ teaspoons vegetable oil, divided
1 tablespoon minced garlic
1 tablespoon minced fresh ginger
½ teaspoon red pepper flakes
2 cups thinly sliced Chinese cabbage
1 cup chopped carrots
1 cup frozen green peas, thawed
3 cups cooked white rice
¼ cup canned chicken broth
¼ cup reduced-sodium soy sauce
3 tablespoons dry sherry
2 teaspoons balsamic vinegar

1. Cut tofu into ½-inch cubes; set aside.

2. Beat eggs in small bowl with wire whisk. Heat 1½ teaspoons oil in wok or large skillet over medium-high heat. Add beaten eggs; cook and stir 2 to 3 minutes until soft curds form.

3. Remove eggs from wok. Cut eggs into small pieces with spoon; set aside.

4. Heat remaining 3 teaspoons oil in wok over high heat. Add garlic, ginger and red pepper flakes; cook about 30 seconds or until fragrant. Add cabbage, carrots and peas; cook about 5 to 10 minutes until carrots are crisp-tender.

5. Stir in rice, tofu, chicken broth, soy sauce, sherry and vinegar; cook and stir 3 minutes. Stir in eggs just before serving. Garnish as desired.

Makes 4 servings

SPICY FRIED RICE WITH TOFU

SPINACH AND TOMATO TOFU TOSS

Nonstick cooking spray
¾ cup chopped onion
1 teaspoon chopped garlic
1 package (10 ounces) extra-firm tofu, drained and cut into ½-inch cubes
2 teaspoons soy sauce
¼ teaspoon black pepper
¼ pound washed spinach leaves, divided
4 whole wheat pitas, cut in half
2 large ripe tomatoes, chopped
¾ cup chopped red bell pepper

1. Spray large nonstick skillet with cooking spray; heat over medium heat until hot. Add onion and garlic. Cook and stir 2 minutes or until onion is crisp-tender.

2. Add tofu, soy sauce and black pepper to skillet; toss until well combined. Cook over medium heat 3 to 4 minutes or until heated through. Remove from heat and cool slightly.

3. Set aside 8 whole spinach leaves; tear remaining leaves into bite-size pieces. Line pita halves with whole spinach leaves. Add tomatoes, torn spinach and bell peppers to tofu mixture; toss to combine. Fill pita halves with tofu mixture. Serve immediately.

Makes 4 servings

Tip ...

Pitas, also known as pocket bread, are round, flat Middle Eastern bread made from white or whole wheat flour. It is usually about 6 to 7 inches in diameter. The bread splits horizontally to form a pocket, which can be filled with a variety of ingredients to make a sandwich. Pita bread may also be cut into wedges, toasted and used as dippers for Middle Eastern dishes like hummus.

SPINACH AND TOMATO TOFU TOSS

STEWED MUSHROOMS ON ASPARAGUS WITH VEGETARIAN OYSTER SAUCE

7 ounces asparagus, trimmed
Salt
Vegetable oil
2 slices ginger
4 ounces fresh black mushrooms
4 ounces baby corn
3 tablespoons LEE KUM KEE®
   Vegetarian Oyster Flavored
   Sauce
¼ teaspoon sugar
1 teaspoon cornstarch mixed with
   1 tablespoon water
¼ teaspoon LEE KUM KEE® Sesame
   Oil

1. Cook asparagus in boiling water with salt and vegetable oil 3 minutes. Remove and arrange on plate.

2. Heat 2 tablespoons vegetable oil in wok. Sauté ginger until fragrant. Add mushrooms and baby corn. Stir-fry 1 minute.

3. Combine Vegetarian Oyster Flavored Sauce, ⅔ cup water and sugar in small bowl; add to wok. Simmer 5 minutes. Add cornstarch mixture; simmer until thickened. Place mixture over asparagus and sprinkle with Sesame Oil.

Makes 4 to 6 servings

Black mushrooms, also called black trumpet mushrooms, can be found in specialty produce markets from midsummer through midfall. These trumpet-shaped mushrooms have thin, brittle flesh and stand 2 to 5 inches tall. They range in color from grayish brown to almost black.

TOFU SATAY WITH PEANUT SAUCE

Satay

    1 package (15 ounces) extra firm tofu, drained and pressed*
    ⅓ cup water
    ⅓ cup soy sauce
    1 teaspoon prepared crushed garlic
    1 teaspoon prepared crushed ginger
    1 tablespoon sesame oil
   24 small to medium white button mushrooms, trimmed
    1 large red bell pepper, cored, seeded and cut into 12 pieces
    8 (8-inch) wooden skewers

Peanut Sauce

    1 can (14 ounces) reduced-fat coconut milk
    ½ cup smooth natural peanut butter
    2 tablespoons packed brown sugar
    1 tablespoon rice vinegar
    1 to 2 teaspoons red Thai curry paste

*Remove tofu from water pack and place on paper towels in a colander in the sink. Place a small flat plate on top of tofu and weight with a 28-ounce can of beans or tomatoes. Let drain 30 minutes.

1. Cut tofu into 24 cubes.

2. Combine water, soy sauce, garlic, ginger and sesame oil. Add tofu cubes, mushrooms and bell pepper in large, resealable plastic food storage bag. Turn bag gently to coat. Marinate 30 minutes, turning occasionally.

3. Preheat oven to 400°F.

4. Drain tofu mixture; discard marinade. Thread skewers as follows: tofu, red pepper, tofu, mushroom, tofu.

5. Spray sides and bottom of 13×9-inch glass baking pan with nonstick cooking spray. Place skewers in baking pan. Bake 25 minutes or until tofu cubes are lightly browned and vegetables are cooked but not mushy.

6. Meanwhile, combine all peanut sauce ingredients in small saucepan over medium heat, whisking to blend. Stir until sauce comes to a boil. Immediately reduce heat to low; cook about 20 minutes over very low heat, stirring often, until creamy and thick. Serve sauce over satay.

VEGETABLE PILAF WITH SPICED BEAN SAUCE

2 cups basmati rice or brown rice
½ pound broccoli
   Spiced Bean Sauce (recipe
     follows)
1 tablespoon vegetable oil
2 carrots, chopped
½ teaspoon ground cinnamon
   Peanuts

1. Cook rice according to package directions.

2. Meanwhile, to prepare broccoli, trim leaves from stalks. Trim ends of stalks. Cut broccoli into florets. Peel stalks; cut into 1-inch pieces.

3. Steam broccoli until tender.

4. Prepare Spiced Bean Sauce.

5. Heat oil in large skillet over medium heat until hot. Add carrots; cook and stir 5 minutes or until tender. Stir in broccoli and cinnamon. Cook until broccoli is heated through. Stir carrot mixture into rice.

6. Serve Spiced Bean Sauce over rice. Sprinkle with peanuts.

Makes 6 servings

SPICED BEAN SAUCE

1 serrano chili
1 tablespoon vegetable oil
½ cup chopped leek
½ teaspoon ground ginger
¼ teaspoon ground turmeric
1 bay leaf
1 can (15 ounces) red kidney
    beans, drained
1⅓ cups vegetable broth
   Salt and black pepper

1. Mince chili.* Heat oil in small skillet over medium heat until hot. Add leek, chili, ginger, turmeric and bay leaf; cook and stir 3 to 5 minutes or until leek is tender.

2. Add beans and broth; bring to a boil over high heat. Reduce heat to low. Simmer, uncovered, 5 minutes. Remove bay leaf; discard. Process bean mixture in food processor until coarsely chopped. Return to skillet; cook over low heat 2 to 3 minutes or until heated through. Season to taste with salt and pepper.

Makes about 2 cups sauce

*Chilies can sting and irritate the skin; wear rubber gloves when handling and do not touch eyes. Wash hands after handling.

VEGETABLE PILAF WITH SPICED BEAN SAUCE

ROASTED VEGETABLES WITH NOODLES

5 tablespoons soy sauce, divided
3 tablespoons peanut or vegetable oil
2 tablespoons rice vinegar
2 cloves garlic, minced
½ pound large fresh mushrooms
4 ounces shallots
1 medium zucchini, cut in half lengthwise then crosswise into 1-inch pieces
1 medium yellow crookneck squash, cut in half lengthwise then crosswise into 1-inch pieces
1 red bell pepper, cut into 1-inch pieces
1 yellow bell pepper, cut into 1-inch pieces
2 small Asian eggplants, cut into ½-inch slices *or* 2 cups cubed eggplant
8 ounces Chinese egg noodles or vermicelli, cooked, drained and kept warm
1 tablespoon dark sesame oil

1. Preheat oven to 425°F. Combine 2 tablespoons soy sauce, peanut oil, vinegar and garlic in small bowl; mix well.

2. Combine vegetables in shallow roasting pan (do not line pan with foil). Toss with soy sauce mixture to coat well.

3. Roast vegetables 20 minutes or until browned and tender, stirring well after 10 minutes.

4. Place noodles in large bowl. Toss hot noodles with remaining 3 tablespoons soy sauce and sesame oil.

5. Toss roasted vegetables with noodle mixture; serve warm or at room temperature.

Makes 6 servings

ROASTED VEGETABLES WITH NOODLES

BRAISED VEGETARIAN E-FU NOODLES

7 ounces uncooked E-Fu noodles
4 ounces sliced straw mushrooms
2 ounces sliced button mushrooms
5 Chinese mushrooms, soaked and
    shredded
2 ounces shredded carrot
1 tablespoon vegetable oil
½ cup water
5 tablespoons LEE KUM KEE®
    Vegetarian Oyster Flavored
    Sauce
2 ounces snow peas, shredded
1 teaspoon LEE KUM KEE® Sesame
    Oil

1. Blanch noodles in boiling water until soft; drain.

2. In wok, sauté mushrooms and carrot in vegetable oil until fragrant.

3. Add noodles, water, Vegetarian Oyster Flavored Sauce and snow peas to wok; stir-fry until liquid evaporates. Sprinkle with Sesame Oil.

Makes 4 to 6 servings

Tip ■■■

E-fu noodles are a type of Chinese egg noodles made with wheat flour and deep-fried. They are long and flat, and pale yellow in color. They should be cooked briefly in boiling water before using.

CELLENTANI WITH ASIAN DRESSING

1 package (16 ounces) uncooked
   BARILLA® cellentani
1 medium cucumber
1 cup shredded red cabbage
1 cup shredded Savoy or green
   cabbage
1 cup shredded carrots
3 green onions, sliced
2 tablespoons chopped cilantro

Dressing
½ cup rice vinegar
¼ cup soy sauce
¼ cup creamy peanut butter
2 teaspoons minced garlic
1 teaspoon ground ginger
   Sesame seeds and chopped,
     toasted peanuts, for garnish

Prepare cellentani according to package directions; drain. Peel cucumber and cut into ¼-inch-thick circles; slice circles in half. Combine cooked cellentani with cucumber, cabbage, carrots, green onions and cilantro in large bowl; mix well.

Combine vinegar, soy sauce, peanut butter, garlic and ginger in small saucepan; cook and stir over medium-low heat 4 minutes or until peanut butter melts and ingredients are thoroughly mixed. Add dressing to cellentani mixture; toss well. Garnish with sesame seeds and chopped, toasted peanuts, if desired.

Makes 4 to 6 servings

CHUNKY GARDEN STEW

Spicy Hot Sauce (recipe follows)
1 tablespoon olive or canola oil
3 medium Colorado Sangre red potatoes, cut into chunks
1 large carrot, sliced diagonally
1 medium onion, quartered
1 large yellow squash or zucchini, sliced
1 Japanese eggplant *or* ½ regular eggplant, cut into cubes
2 stalks celery, sliced
1 small red or green bell pepper, cut into chunks
1 teaspoon *each* ground cinnamon, coriander and turmeric
½ teaspoon *each* ground cumin, ground cardamom and salt
2 cans (14½ ounces each) vegetable broth
1 can (15 ounces) chick-peas, drained
⅔ cup raisins
6 cups hot cooked rice

⅓ cup coarsely chopped fresh cilantro
¼ cup water
1 tablespoon olive or canola oil
2 cloves garlic
½ teaspoon *each* salt and turmeric
¼ to ½ teaspoon ground red pepper
¼ teaspoon *each* sugar, ground cumin, ground cardamom and ground coriander

Prepare Spicy Hot Sauce; set aside. Heat oil in Dutch oven over medium-high heat. Add potatoes and carrot; cook and stir 5 minutes. Add onion, squash, eggplant, celery, bell pepper, spices and salt; cook and stir 3 to 5 minutes. Add broth, chick-peas and raisins; bring to a simmer. Simmer, covered, about 15 minutes or until potatoes are tender. Serve vegetable stew over rice. Serve with Spicy Hot Sauce.   *Makes 5 to 6 servings*

SPICY HOT SAUCE

Combine cilantro, water, olive oil, garlic, salt, turmeric, ground red pepper, sugar, ground cumin, ground cardamom and ground coriander in blender; process until smooth. Adjust flavors to taste.

Makes about ½ cup sauce

*Favorite recipe from **Colorado Potato Administrative Committee***

CHUNKY GARDEN STEW

CAVATELLI AND VEGETABLE STIR-FRY

¾ cup uncooked cavatelli or elbow
   macaroni
   Nonstick cooking spray
6 ounces fresh snow peas, cut
   lengthwise into halves
½ cup thinly sliced carrot
1 teaspoon minced fresh ginger
½ cup chopped yellow or green bell
   pepper
½ cup chopped onion
¼ cup chopped fresh parsley
1 tablespoon chopped fresh
   oregano *or* 1 teaspoon dried
   oregano leaves, crushed
1 tablespoon reduced-fat margarine
2 tablespoons water
1 tablespoon reduced-sodium soy
   sauce

1. Prepare cavatelli according to package directions, omitting salt; drain and set aside.

2. Coat wok or large skillet with cooking spray. Add snow peas, carrot and ginger; stir-fry 2 minutes over medium-high heat. Add bell pepper, onion, parsley, oregano and margarine. Stir-fry 2 to 3 minutes or until vegetables are crisp-tender. Stir in water and soy sauce. Stir in pasta; heat through.
Makes 4 servings

CAVATELLI AND VEGETABLE STIR-FRY

STUFFED HAIRY GOURD VEGETARIAN STYLE

15 ounces hairy gourd
2 tablespoons vegetable oil
2 ounces diced carrot
5 Chinese dried mushrooms, rehydrated and diced
2 ounces diced baby corn
2 ounces diced celery
2 ounces diced dried bean curd
1 ounce dried black fungus, soaked
4 tablespoons LEE KUM KEE® Vegetarian Oyster Flavored Sauce
½ teaspoon sugar
1 teaspoon cornstarch mixed with 1 tablespoon water

1. Peel hairy gourd and cut into halves; scrape away pith. Cook in boiling water 3 minutes. Rinse and drain.

2. Heat oil in wok. Add carrot, mushrooms, baby corn, celery, bean curd and black fungus; stir-fry until fragrant. Combine 1 cup water, Vegetarian Oyster Flavored Sauce and sugar in small bowl; add to wok with hairy gourd. Stir until mixture comes to a boil. Reduce heat and simmer 5 minutes or until hairy gourd softens.

3. Remove hairy gourd and arrange on plate. Add cornstarch mixture to wok; cook until thickened. Divide mixture over hairy gourd halves and serve.
Makes 4 to 6 servings

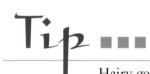

Hairy gourds are cylinder shaped and about 2 to 3 inches in diameter. Other names include Mao Qwa, fuzzy gourd, or "Little Winter Melon". Their skin is hairy and green, while their flesh is white, firm and mildly flavored. Cucumbers can be substituted for hairy gourd.

VEGETARIAN BROWN RICE SALAD

1 bag SUCCESS® Brown Rice
1 medium cucumber, chopped
¾ cup sliced green onions
¾ cup chopped celery
½ cup sliced radishes
½ cup chopped red bell pepper
¼ cup snow pea pods, trimmed and blanched
2 tablespoons chopped fresh parsley
2 tablespoons rice vinegar
1 teaspoon lemon juice
1 teaspoon reduced-sodium soy sauce
1 teaspoon black pepper
2 tablespoons safflower oil

Prepare rice according to package directions. Cool.

Place rice in large bowl. Add cucumber, green onions, celery, radishes, red pepper, pea pods and parsley; mix lightly.

Blend together vinegar, lemon juice, soy sauce and black pepper in small bowl. Gradually whisk in oil until well blended. Pour over rice mixture; toss lightly to coat. Refrigerate at least 2 hours. *Makes 10 servings*

TOFU STIR-FRY

1 pound firm tofu cakes, rinsed and drained
4 tablespoons cornstarch, divided
½ teaspoon salt
1 can (14½ ounces) vegetable broth
1 tablespoon soy sauce
1 tablespoon dry sherry
1 teaspoon dark sesame oil
¼ cup vegetable oil
8 ounces broccoli, cut into florets
8 ounces fresh mushrooms, sliced
1 cup drained canned baby corn, cut in half
Chow mein noodles

Dry tofu on paper towels. Cut tofu into 1-inch cubes. Place 2 tablespoons cornstarch on waxed paper. Coat tofu with cornstarch. Set aside.

Combine remaining 2 tablespoons cornstarch and salt in small bowl. Stir in broth, soy sauce, sherry and sesame oil until smooth; set aside.

Heat wok over medium-high heat 1 minute or until hot. Drizzle vegetable oil into wok and heat 30 seconds. Ease tofu into hot oil; stir-fry about 10 minutes or until golden brown on all sides. Place tofu in large bowl. Reduce heat to medium.

Add broccoli, mushrooms and corn to wok; stir-fry until mushrooms are tender. Cover and cook 3 minutes or until broccoli is crisp-tender. Stir broth mixture until smooth and add to wok. Cook, uncovered, until sauce boils and thickens. Return tofu to wok; stir gently to mix. Serve over noodles.

Makes 4 servings

TOFU STIR-FRY

THAI PASTA SALAD WITH PEANUT SAUCE

¼ cup evaporated skimmed milk
1 tablespoon plus 1½ teaspoons creamy peanut butter
1 tablespoon plus 1½ teaspoons finely chopped red onion
1 teaspoon lemon juice
¾ teaspoon brown sugar
½ teaspoon reduced-sodium soy sauce
⅛ teaspoon red pepper flakes
½ teaspoon finely chopped fresh ginger
1 cup hot cooked whole wheat spaghetti
2 teaspoons finely chopped green onion

1. Combine milk, peanut butter, red onion, lemon juice, sugar, soy sauce and red pepper flakes in medium saucepan. Bring to a boil over high heat, stirring constantly. Boil 2 minutes, stirring constantly. Reduce heat to medium-low. Add ginger; blend well. Add spaghetti; toss to coat.

2. Top servings evenly with green onion. *Makes 2 servings*

Whole wheat pasta should be used within a month after buying for guaranteed freshness.

VEGETABLES WITH SPICY HONEY PEANUT SAUCE

½ cup honey
¼ cup peanut butter
2 tablespoons soy sauce
1 tablespoon chopped fresh
   cilantro
⅛ teaspoon crushed red pepper
   flakes
4 cups broccoli florets
4 cups sliced carrots
4 cups snow peas
6 cups cooked white rice

Combine honey, peanut butter, soy sauce, cilantro and red pepper in small bowl; mix well and set aside. Steam vegetables until crisp-tender; drain well. Toss steamed vegetables with peanut sauce in large bowl. Serve immediately over rice. *Makes 6 servings*

Favorite recipe from **National Honey Board**

ASIAN CHILI PEPPER LINGUINE

1 (12-ounce) package PASTA
   LABELLA™ Chili Pepper
   Linguine
¼ cup vegetable oil
1 small carrot, julienned
1 small yellow squash, julienned
1 medium Spanish onion, chopped
2 cloves garlic, crushed
2 tablespoons toasted sesame seeds
2 tablespoons soy sauce

Cook pasta according to package directions. In large skillet, heat oil. Add carrot, squash, onion and garlic; sauté 4 minutes. Add sesame seeds and soy sauce; simmer 2 minutes. Season with salt and pepper to taste. Serve over hot chili pepper linguine. *Makes 3 dinner servings*

VEGETABLE LO MEIN

8 ounces uncooked vermicelli or
    thin spaghetti, cooked and
    drained
¾ teaspoon dark sesame oil
½ teaspoon vegetable oil
3 cloves garlic, minced
1 teaspoon grated fresh ginger
2 cups sliced bok choy
½ cup sliced green onions
2 cups shredded carrots
6 ounces firm tofu, drained and
    cubed
¼ cup plus 2 tablespoons rice wine
    vinegar
¼ cup water
¼ cup plum preserves
1 teaspoon reduced-sodium soy
    sauce
½ teaspoon red pepper flakes

Toss vermicelli with sesame oil in large bowl until well coated; set aside. Heat vegetable oil in large nonstick skillet or wok over medium heat. Stir in garlic and ginger; stir-fry 10 seconds. Add bok choy and onions; stir-fry 3 to 4 minutes or until crisp-tender. Add carrots and tofu; stir-fry 2 to 3 minutes or until carrots are crisp-tender.

Combine vinegar, water, preserves, soy sauce and red pepper flakes in small saucepan. Heat over medium heat until preserves are melted, stirring constantly. Combine noodles, vegetable mixture and sauce in large bowl; mix well.

Makes 6 servings

Tip ∎∎∎

Plum preserves are a sweet mixture of plums and sugar, cooked together to make a spread. Similar to jam, preserves are distinguished by having chunky bits of fruit left intact in the mixture.

VEGETABLE LO MEIN

WHOLE WHEAT PASTA WITH CUCUMBER AND SPICY PEANUT SAUCE

1 cup hot water
¾ cup creamy peanut butter
3 tablespoons soy sauce
3 tablespoons lemon juice
2 garlic cloves, minced
1 teaspoon dried hot red pepper flakes
1 teaspoon sugar
20 ounces whole wheat pasta
2 cucumbers, peeled, seeded and cut diagonally into ⅛-inch slices
1 cup thinly sliced scallions
1 cup red peppers, thinly sliced and 1 inch in length
Salt and pepper to taste

In blender, combine hot water, peanut butter, soy sauce, lemon juice, garlic, red pepper flakes and sugar until smooth. In pot of boiling salted water, boil pasta until just tender; transfer to colander and rinse briefly under cold water. Drain pasta well. In large bowl, toss noodles with peanut sauce, cucumbers, scallions and red peppers. Add salt and pepper to taste. Serve immediately at room temperature. *Makes 8 servings*

Favorite recipe from **Peanut Advisory Board**

Tip ■■■

Cucumbers found in supermarket produce sections are often waxed to preserve the vegetable's moisture content. Wash cucumbers thoroughly in cold water in order to remove this waxy protective covering. Refrigerate whole cucumbers up to one week in a plastic bag. To seed cucumbers, cut in half lengthwise and scrape out seeds with a small spoon.

VEGETARIAN STIR-FRY

2 tablespoons vegetable oil
5 ounces sliced carrots
3 ounces sliced onion
3 ounces baby corn
5 tablespoons LEE KUM KEE®
   Vegetarian Stir-Fry Sauce,
   divided
6 ounces snow peas
3 ounces sliced mushrooms
2 tablespoons pine nuts

Heat skillet over medium heat. Add oil. Sauté carrots, onion and baby corn in 2 tablespoons Vegetarian Stir-Fry Sauce until tender. Add snow peas, mushrooms and remaining 3 tablespoons sauce. Stir-fry until heated through. Sprinkle with pine nuts and serve. *Makes 4 servings*

THAILAND PEANUT PESTO

1 cup unsalted roasted peanuts
½ cup soy sauce
½ cup sesame oil
1 teaspoon TABASCO® brand
   Pepper Sauce
¼ cup honey
⅓ cup water
3 cloves garlic, minced
12 ounces bow tie pasta, cooked
   according to package
   directions, drained
   Chopped green onions for
   garnish

Place peanuts in food processor; process until finely ground. With motor running, add soy sauce, sesame oil, TABASCO® Sauce, honey, water and garlic one at a time, through feed tube. Process until a thick, smooth paste has formed. Transfer mixture to bowl; refrigerate, covered, until ready to use. Toss with bow tie pasta and garnish with chopped green onions.

Makes 4 servings

VEGETABLE STIR-FRY IN SPICY BLACK BEAN SAUCE

1 teaspoon vegetable oil
1 medium onion, chopped
1 medium-size green bell pepper,
    cut into strips
3 carrots, cut into julienne strips
    (matchstick size)
3 cups shredded cabbage (green,
    red or napa)
1 cup tofu, crumbled
4 cups cooked rice, kept warm
    Fresh chives and radishes
    (optional)

Black Bean Sauce
1 cup GUILTLESS GOURMET®
    Spicy Black Bean Dip
2 teaspoons water
¼ cup low-sodium soy sauce
¼ cup cooking sherry
1 tablespoon minced peeled fresh
    ginger
1 clove garlic, minced

Heat oil in wok or large skillet over medium-high heat until hot. Add onion, pepper, carrots, cabbage and tofu; stir-fry until crisp-tender.

To prepare Black Bean Sauce, combine bean dip and water in small bowl; mix well. Stir in remaining Black Bean Sauce ingredients; pour over stir-fried vegetables. Stir-fry over high heat 2 minutes more. Reduce heat to low; cook 2 to 4 minutes more or until heated through, stirring often. Serve over hot rice. Garnish with chives and radishes, if desired.

Makes 6 servings

Tip ■■■

The wok, the primary cooking vessel in Asia, was developed centuries ago as a result of fuel shortages. Its rounded shape and long sloping side provide an extended cooking surface, which may be heated to very high temperatures with little fuel. The wok is commonly associated with the technique of stir-frying, but it can be used to braise, deep-fry, roast, simmer, smoke and steam.

VEGETABLE STIR-FRY IN SPICY BLACK BEAN SAUCE

STIR-FRY VEGETABLES

1 tablespoon peanut oil
¾ cup *each* (or combination of any): snow peas; broccoli, cut into 1-inch pieces; carrots, cut into 1-inch strips; green onions, cut into 1-inch pieces; celery, cut into 1-inch pieces; mushrooms, sliced (drained if canned); bamboo shoots, sliced (drained if canned); and water chestnuts, sliced (drained if canned)
¼ cup dry-roasted Texas peanuts
¼ cup molasses
¼ cup soy sauce
1½ tablespoons cornstarch
1 large clove garlic, minced
⅛ teaspoon ground ginger
Dash ground red pepper
¼ cup sherry
2 cups uncooked rice, cooked and kept hot

Heat oil in medium skillet or wok. Add vegetables. Cook until onions begin to turn translucent, about 3 to 5 minutes. Add peanuts, molasses, soy sauce, cornstarch, garlic, ginger and pepper; cook, stirring, until thickened. Cover; cook over low heat 5 to 10 minutes, stirring occasionally. Add sherry; heat through. Serve over rice.

Makes 8 servings

Favorite recipe from **Texas Peanut Producers Board**

VEGETARIAN
FRIED RICE

4 dried mushrooms
4 cups cooked long-grain rice
3 eggs
¾ teaspoon salt, divided
2 tablespoons plus 1½ teaspoons vegetable oil, divided
3 green onions with tops, thinly sliced
1 teaspoon minced fresh ginger
1 clove garlic, minced
4 ounces extra firm tofu, cut into ¼-inch cubes and deep-fried
1 tablespoon soy sauce
¼ teaspoon sugar
1 cup bean sprouts, coarsely chopped
½ cup thawed frozen peas

1. Place mushrooms in small bowl; cover with hot water. Let stand 30 minutes; drain, reserving liquid. Squeeze out excess water. Remove stems; discard. Chop caps.

2. Rub rice with wet hands so all the grains are separated.

3. Beat eggs with ¼ teaspoon salt in medium bowl. Heat 1½ teaspoons oil in wok or large skillet over medium heat. Add eggs; cook and stir until soft curds form.

4. Remove wok from heat; cut eggs into small pieces with spoon. Remove from wok; set aside.

5. Heat remaining 2 tablespoons oil in wok over high heat. Add onions, ginger and garlic; stir-fry 10 seconds. Add mushrooms, ¼ cup reserved mushroom liquid, tofu, soy sauce and sugar. Cook until most of the liquid evaporates, about 4 minutes. Add bean sprouts and peas; cook 30 seconds.

6. Stir in rice and remaining ½ teaspoon salt; heat thoroughly. Stir in eggs just before serving.
Makes 4 servings

ORANGE-GINGER TOFU & NOODLES

⅔ cup orange juice
3 tablespoons reduced-sodium soy sauce
½ to 1 teaspoon minced ginger
1 clove garlic, minced
¼ teaspoon red pepper flakes
5 ounces extra-firm tofu, well drained and cut into ½-inch cubes
1½ teaspoons cornstarch
1 teaspoon canola or peanut oil
2 cups fresh cut-up vegetables, such as broccoli, carrots, onion and snow peas
1½ cups hot cooked vermicelli

1. Combine orange juice, soy sauce, ginger, garlic and red pepper in resealable plastic food storage bag; add tofu. Marinate 20 to 30 minutes. Drain tofu, reserving marinade. Stir marinade into cornstarch until smooth.

2. Heat oil in large nonstick skillet or wok over medium-high heat. Add vegetables; stir-fry 2 to 3 minutes or until vegetables are crisp-tender. Add tofu; stir-fry 1 minute. Stir reserved marinade mixture; add to skillet. Bring to a boil; boil 1 minute. Serve over vermicelli.   *Makes 2 servings*

ORANGE-GINGER TOFU & NOODLES

CHINESE SWEET AND SOUR VEGETABLES

3 cups broccoli florets
2 medium carrots, diagonally sliced
1 large red bell pepper, cut into
    short, thin strips
¼ cup water
2 teaspoons cornstarch
1 teaspoon sugar
⅓ cup unsweetened pineapple juice
1 tablespoon soy sauce
1 tablespoon rice vinegar
½ teaspoon dark sesame oil
¼ cup diagonally sliced green
    onions or chopped fresh
    cilantro (optional)

1. Combine broccoli, carrots and red pepper in large skillet with tight-fitting lid. Add water; bring to a boil over high heat. Reduce heat to medium. Cover and steam 4 minutes or until vegetables are crisp-tender.

2. Meanwhile, combine cornstarch and sugar in small bowl. Blend in pineapple juice, soy sauce and vinegar until smooth.

3. Transfer vegetables to colander; drain. Stir pineapple mixture and add to skillet. Cook and stir 2 minutes or until sauce boils and thickens.

4. Return vegetables to skillet; toss with sauce. Stir in sesame oil. Garnish with onions.

Makes 4 servings

HOT SESAME NOODLES

1 package (16 ounces) uncooked linguini
1 teaspoon Oriental sesame oil
3 tablespoons olive oil
3 tablespoons sesame seeds
2 cloves garlic, minced
⅔ cup chunky peanut butter
1 cup chicken broth
⅓ cup reduced-sodium soy sauce
3 to 4 tablespoons *Frank's® RedHot®* Original Cayenne Pepper Sauce
1½ teaspoons sugar
1 large green onion, sliced

1. Cook linguini according to package directions. Rinse under cold water; drain well. Toss linguini with sesame oil in large bowl.

2. Heat olive oil in large nonstick skillet over medium heat. Add sesame seeds and garlic; cook and stir constantly 1 minute or until seeds are golden. Add peanut butter; stir until well blended. Stir in broth, soy sauce, *Frank's RedHot* Sauce and sugar. Bring just to a boil.

3. Pour sauce over linguini; toss to coat evenly. Sprinkle with green onions. Serve immediately. *Makes 4 servings (2 cups sauce)*

Prep Time: 20 minutes
Cook Time: 15 minutes

NOTE: Sesame noodles may be served cold, if desired. Chill linguini and sauce separately. Toss just before serving.

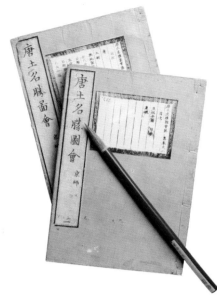

SWEET AND SPICY CHICKEN STIR-FRY

1½ cups uncooked long-grain white rice
1 can (8 ounces) **DEL MONTE®** Pineapple Chunks In Its Own Juice
4 boneless, skinless chicken breast halves, cut into bite-size pieces
2 tablespoons vegetable oil
1 large green bell pepper, cut into strips
¾ cup sweet and sour sauce
⅛ to ½ teaspoon red pepper flakes

1. Cook rice according to package directions.

2. Drain pineapple, reserving ⅓ cup juice.

3. Stir-fry chicken in hot oil in large skillet over medium-high heat until no longer pink in center. Add green pepper and reserved pineapple juice; stir-fry 2 minutes or until tender-crisp.

4. Add sweet and sour sauce, red pepper flakes and pineapple; stir-fry 3 minutes or until heated through.

5. Spoon rice onto serving plate; top with chicken mixture. Garnish, if desired.

Makes 4 servings

Prep Time: 5 minutes
Cook Time: 20 minutes

SWEET AND SPICY CHICKEN STIR-FRY

ASIAN CHICKEN AND NOODLES

1 package (3 ounces) chicken flavor instant ramen noodles
1 bag (16 ounces) BIRDS EYE® frozen Farm Fresh Mixtures Broccoli, Carrots and Water Chestnuts*
1 tablespoon vegetable oil
1 pound boneless skinless chicken breasts, cut into thin strips
¼ cup stir-fry sauce

*Or, substitute 1 bag (16 ounces) Birds Eye® frozen Broccoli Cuts.

- Reserve seasoning packet from noodles.

- Bring 2 cups water to a boil in large saucepan. Add noodles and vegetables. Cook 3 minutes, stirring occasionally; drain.

- Meanwhile, heat oil in large nonstick skillet over medium-high heat. Add chicken; cook and stir until browned, about 8 minutes.

- Stir in noodles, vegetables, stir-fry sauce and reserved seasoning packet; heat through. *Makes about 4 servings*

Prep Time: 5 minutes
Cook Time: 20 minutes

CHICKEN AND WALNUT FRIED RICE

4½ teaspoons vegetable oil, divided
2 eggs, beaten
½ cup chopped walnuts
¾ pound boneless, skinless chicken breast, cut into strips
½ teaspoon ground white pepper
1 cup thinly sliced fresh mushrooms
½ cup thinly sliced carrots
½ cup thinly sliced green onions
1½ teaspoons grated fresh ginger
3 cups cooked brown rice, chilled
2 tablespoons soy sauce

Heat 1½ teaspoons oil in large skillet or wok over medium heat until hot. Add eggs and cook, without stirring, until set. Invert skillet over baking sheet to remove cooked eggs; cut into strips. Set aside. Heat remaining 3 teaspoons oil in skillet over medium-high heat until hot. Add walnuts; stir-fry until lightly browned. Sprinkle chicken with pepper. Add chicken, mushrooms, carrots, onions and ginger to skillet; stir-fry about 3 to 4 minutes or until carrots are tender. Stir in rice and egg strips; sprinkle with soy sauce. Toss lightly; heat thoroughly. Serve immediately.

Makes 4 servings

*Favorite recipe from **USA Rice Federation***

ASIAN CHICKEN AND NOODLES

TURKEY TERIYAKI WITH GRILLED MUSHROOMS

1¼ **pounds turkey breast slices, tenderloins or medallions**
¼ **cup sake or sherry wine**
¼ **cup soy sauce**
3 **tablespoons granulated sugar, brown sugar or honey**
1 **piece (1-inch cube) fresh ginger, minced**
3 **cloves garlic, minced**
1 **tablespoon vegetable oil**
½ **pound mushrooms**
4 **green onions, cut into 2-inch pieces**

Cut turkey slices into long 2-inch-wide strips.* Combine sake, soy sauce, sugar, ginger, garlic and oil in 2-quart glass dish. Add turkey; turn to coat. Cover and refrigerate 15 minutes or overnight. Remove turkey from marinade; discard marinade. Thread turkey onto metal or wooden skewers, alternating with mushrooms and green onions. (Soak wooden skewers in hot water 30 minutes to prevent burning.) Grill on covered grill over medium-hot KINGSFORD® Briquets about 3 minutes per side until turkey is cooked through. *Makes 4 servings*

*Do not cut tenderloins or medallions.

OLYMPIC SEOUL CHICKEN

8 **chicken thighs, skinned**
¼ **cup white vinegar**
3 **tablespoons soy sauce**
2 **tablespoons honey**
¼ **teaspoon ground ginger**
2 **tablespoons peanut oil**
10 **cloves garlic, coarsely chopped**
½ **to 1 teaspoon crushed red pepper**
2 **ounces Chinese rice stick noodles, cooked *or* 2 cups hot cooked rice**
Snow peas, steamed
Diagonally sliced yellow squash, steamed

Combine vinegar, soy sauce, honey and ginger in small bowl; set aside. Heat oil in large skillet over medium-high heat. Add chicken; cook about 10 minutes or until evenly browned on all sides. Add garlic and red pepper; cook, stirring frequently, 2 to 3 minutes. Drain off excess fat. Add vinegar mixture. Cover; reduce heat and simmer about 15 minutes or until juices run clear. Uncover; cook about 2 minutes or until sauce has reduced and thickened. Serve with rice stick noodles, peas and squash. Garnish as desired. *Makes 4 servings*

*Favorite recipe from **Delmarva Poultry Industry, Inc.***

TURKEY TERIYAKI WITH GRILLED MUSHROOMS

KUNG PAO CHICKEN

1 pound boneless, skinless chicken breasts, cut into 1-inch pieces
1 tablespoon cornstarch
2 teaspoons CRISCO® Oil*
3 tablespoons chopped green onions with tops
2 cloves garlic, minced
¼ to 1½ teaspoons crushed red pepper
¼ to ½ teaspoon ground ginger
¼ cup rice vinegar
¼ cup soy sauce
1 tablespoon sugar
⅓ cup unsalted dry roasted peanuts
4 cups hot cooked rice

*Use your favorite Crisco Oil product.

1. Combine chicken and cornstarch in small bowl; toss. Heat oil in large skillet or wok on medium-high heat. Add chicken. Stir-fry 5 to 7 minutes or until no longer pink in center. Remove from skillet. Add onions, garlic, red pepper and ginger to skillet. Stir-fry 15 seconds. Remove from heat.

2. Combine vinegar, soy sauce and sugar in small bowl. Stir well. Add to skillet. Return chicken to skillet. Stir until coated. Stir in nuts. Heat thoroughly, stirring occasionally. Serve over hot rice.   *Makes 4 servings*

ORIENTAL CHICKEN & RICE

1 (6.9-ounce) package RICE-A-RONI® Chicken Flavor
2 tablespoons margarine or butter
1 pound boneless, skinless chicken breasts, cut into thin strips
¼ cup teriyaki sauce
½ teaspoon ground ginger
1 (16-ounce) package frozen Oriental-style mixed vegetables

1. In large skillet over medium heat, sauté rice-vermicelli mix with margarine until vermicelli is golden brown. Slowly stir in 2 cups water, chicken, teriyaki sauce, ginger and Special Seasonings; bring to a boil. Reduce heat to low. Cover; simmer 10 minutes.

2. Stir in vegetables. Cover; simmer 5 to 10 minutes or until rice is tender and chicken is no longer pink inside. Let stand 3 minutes.

Makes 4 servings

Prep Time: 5 minutes
Cook Time: 25 minutes

KUNG PAO CHICKEN

SWIMMING RAMA

1¾ to 2 pounds fresh spinach, washed and stemmed *or* 2 packages (10 ounces each) fresh spinach
3 boneless skinless chicken breasts (about 1¼ pounds), sliced crosswise into ½-inch-wide strips
Peanut Sauce (recipe page 185)
1 fresh red chili pepper, seeded and finely chopped* *or* ¼ cup diced red bell pepper
Marigold petals for garnish

Chili peppers can sting and irritate the skin; wear rubber gloves when handling peppers and do not touch eyes. Wash hands after handling.

1. Set steamer basket in Dutch oven or large skillet; add water to within ¼ inch of bottom of basket.

2. Bring water to a boil over high heat. Layer about ¼ of spinach in basket; cover and steam 15 seconds. Quickly turn leaves over with tongs. Cover and steam 15 seconds or until leaves are bright green and barely wilted.

3. Transfer spinach to colander. Repeat with remaining spinach. Lay spinach on serving platter or individual plates.

4. Bring 6 cups water to a boil in large saucepan over high heat. Add chicken to boiling water; remove saucepan from heat. Let stand, covered, 5 minutes or until chicken is no longer pink in center.

5. Prepare Peanut Sauce.

6. Drain chicken; stir into hot Peanut Sauce and pour mixture over spinach. Sprinkle with reserved chili pepper. Garnish, if desired.

Makes 4 servings

PEANUT SAUCE

2 teaspoons vegetable oil
½ cup finely chopped onion
3 cloves garlic, minced
½ cup chunky or creamy peanut
    butter
3 tablespoons packed brown sugar
2 tablespoons fish sauce
1 teaspoon paprika
¼ teaspoon ground red pepper
1 cup unsweetened coconut milk
    or 1 cup milk plus 1 teaspoon
    coconut extract
1 tablespoon water
1 tablespoon cornstarch
2 tablespoons lime juice

1. Heat oil in medium saucepan over medium-high heat. Add onion and garlic; cook and stir 2 to 3 minutes or until tender.

2. Reduce heat to medium. Add peanut butter, brown sugar, fish sauce, paprika and red pepper; stir until smooth. Slowly stir in coconut milk until well blended. (At this point, sauce may be cooled, covered and refrigerated up to 2 days in advance.)

3. Stir sauce constantly over medium heat until bubbling gently. Reduce heat to medium-low. Combine water and cornstarch in small cup; stir into sauce. Cook and stir 1 to 2 minutes or until sauce is thickened. Stir in lime juice.

Makes about 2 cups sauce

TANDOORI-SPICED GAME HENS

4 cups (32 ounces) plain nonfat yogurt
1 tablespoon curry powder
1 tablespoon sweet paprika
1 teaspoon bottled puréed ginger
1 teaspoon bottled puréed garlic
4 fresh Cornish game hens, all visible fat removed

1. Mix yogurt with curry powder, paprika, ginger and garlic in large bowl.

2. Cut game hens in half by cutting through breast bone. Remove triangular breast bone; discard. Rinse hens.

3. Place hens in resealable plastic food storage bags. Pour yogurt mixture into each bag; seal bags. Marinate in refrigerate 2 to 3 hours or overnight, turning bags once or twice.

4. Preheat oven to 500°F. Remove game hens from bags; discard marinade. Lay hens, skin side down on cutting board; brush off excess marinade. Place hens on racks lightly sprayed with nonstick cooking spray. Place racks in shallow baking pans. Bake about 30 to 35 minutes or until no longer pink in center and juices run clear. Garnish with fresh celery leaves, if desired. *Makes 8 servings*

NOTE: To keep the hens moist, cook them with the skin on.

TANDOORI-SPICED GAME HEN

CHICKEN RIBBONS SATAY

½ **cup creamy peanut butter**
½ **cup water**
¼ **cup soy sauce**
 4 **cloves garlic, sliced**
 3 **tablespoons lemon juice**
 2 **tablespoons packed brown sugar**
¾ **teaspoon ground ginger**
½ **teaspoon crushed red pepper
   flakes**
 4 **boneless skinless chicken breast
   halves**
   Sliced green onion tops

Combine peanut butter, water, soy sauce, garlic, lemon juice, brown sugar, ginger and red pepper flakes in a small saucepan. Cook over medium heat 1 minute or until smooth; cool. Remove garlic from sauce; discard. Reserve half of sauce for dipping. Cut chicken lengthwise into 1-inch-wide strips. Thread onto 8 metal or bamboo skewers. (Soak bamboo skewers in water at least 20 minutes to keep them from burning.)

Oil hot grid to help prevent sticking. Grill chicken, on a covered grill, over medium-hot KINGSFORD® Briquets, 6 to 8 minutes until chicken is no longer pink in center, turning once. Baste with sauce once or twice during cooking. Serve with reserved sauce garnished with sliced green onion.

Makes 4 servings

PEANUT CHICKEN

 4 **boneless, skinless chicken breast
   halves**
 2 **tablespoons vegetable oil**
 1 **can (14½ ounces) DEL MONTE®
   Diced Tomatoes with Garlic &
   Onion**
 2 **cloves garlic, minced,** *or*
   ¼ **teaspoon garlic powder**
¼ **teaspoon ground ginger** *or*
   1 **teaspoon grated gingerroot**
⅛ **to** ¼ **teaspoon crushed red
   pepper flakes**
 3 **tablespoons chunky peanut butter**

1. Cook chicken in hot oil in large skillet over medium-high heat about 4 minutes on each side or until chicken is no longer pink in center. Remove chicken from skillet.

2. Add tomatoes, garlic, ginger and red pepper flakes to skillet; cook 2 minutes. Stir in peanut butter.

3. Return chicken to skillet; heat through. Garnish with chopped cilantro and peanuts, if desired.

Makes 4 servings

Prep Time: 4 minutes
Cook Time: 12 minutes

CHICKEN RIBBONS SATAY

ASIAN TURKEY BURGERS

1 pound ground turkey
1⅓ cups *French's*® French Fried
    Onions, divided
1 egg
½ cup finely chopped water chestnuts
¼ cup dry bread crumbs
3 tablespoons Oriental stir-fry sauce
    or teriyaki baste & glaze sauce
1 tablespoon *Frank's*® *RedHot*®
    Original Cayenne Pepper Sauce
2 teaspoons grated fresh ginger *or*
    ½ teaspoon ground ginger
4 sandwich buns
    Shredded lettuce

Combine turkey, *1 cup* French Fried Onions, egg, water chestnuts, bread crumbs, stir-fry sauce, *Frank's RedHot* Sauce and ginger in large bowl. Shape into 4 patties.

Broil patties 6 inches from heat, or grill over medium coals, 10 minutes or until no longer pink in center, turning once. Serve on buns. Top with remaining ⅓ *cup* onions and lettuce. *Makes 4 servings*

Prep Time: 15 minutes
Cook Time: 10 minutes

PINEAPPLE-HOISIN HENS

2 cloves garlic
1 can (8 ounces) crushed pineapple
    in juice, undrained
2 tablespoons rice vinegar
2 tablespoons soy sauce
2 tablespoons hoisin sauce
2 teaspoons minced fresh ginger
1 teaspoon Chinese five-spice
    powder
2 large Cornish hens (about
    1½ pounds each), split in half

1. Mince garlic in blender or food processor. Add pineapple with juice; process until fairly smooth. Add remaining ingredients except hens; process 5 seconds.

2. Place hens in large resealable plastic food storage bag; pour pineapple mixture over hens. Seal bag; turn to coat. Marinate in refrigerator at least 2 hours or up to 24 hours, turning bag once.

3. Preheat oven to 375°F. Drain hens; reserve marinade. Place hens, skin side up, on rack in shallow, foil-lined roasting pan. Roast 35 minutes.

4. Brush hens lightly with some of the reserved marinade; discard remaining marinade. Roast 10 minutes or until hens are browned and juices run clear (180°F). *Makes 4 servings*

ASIAN TURKEY BURGER

MU SHU TURKEY

1 can (16 ounces) plums, drained, rinsed and pitted
½ cup orange juice
¼ cup finely chopped onion
1 tablespoon minced fresh ginger
¼ teaspoon ground cinnamon
1 pound boneless turkey breast, cut into thin strips
6 (7-inch) flour tortillas
3 cups coleslaw mix

Slow Cooker Directions

1. Place plums in blender or food processor. Cover and blend until almost smooth. Combine plums, orange juice, onion, ginger and cinnamon in slow cooker; mix well. Place turkey over plum mixture. Cover; cook on LOW 3 to 4 hours.

2. Remove turkey from slow cooker and divide evenly among tortillas. Spoon about 2 tablespoons plum sauce over turkey in each tortilla; top with about ½ cup coleslaw mix. Fold bottom edge of tortilla over filling; fold in sides. Roll up to completely enclose filling. Repeat with remaining tortillas. Use remaining plum sauce for dipping. *Makes 6 servings*

ORIENTAL CHICKEN WITH ALMONDS

4 tablespoons I CAN'T BELIEVE IT'S NOT BUTTER!® Spread, divided
3 tablespoons orange juice
1 tablespoon soy sauce
1 tablespoon firmly packed brown sugar
4 boneless, skinless chicken breast halves (about 1¼ pounds)
¼ teaspoon salt
¼ teaspoon ground black pepper
¼ cup chicken broth
¼ cup sliced almonds, toasted

In small bowl, combine 2 tablespoons I Can't Believe It's Not Butter! Spread, orange juice, soy sauce and brown sugar; set aside.

Season chicken with salt and pepper. In 12-inch skillet, melt remaining 2 tablespoons I Can't Believe It's Not Butter! Spread over medium-high heat and lightly brown chicken. Add broth. Reduce heat to low and simmer covered 20 minutes or until chicken is thoroughly cooked. Remove chicken to serving platter and keep warm.

In same skillet, add soy sauce mixture. Bring to a boil over high heat and boil 1 minute. To serve, pour sauce over chicken and sprinkle with almonds. Serve, if desired, with hot cooked rice. *Makes 4 servings*

MU SHU TURKEY

GRILLED CHICKEN WITH ASIAN PESTO

4 boneless skinless chicken breast
  halves *or* 8 boneless skinless
  thighs *or* combination of both
Olive or vegetable oil
Salt and black pepper
Asian Pesto (recipe follows)
Lime wedges

Place chicken between two pieces of waxed paper; pound to ⅜-inch thickness. Brush chicken with oil; season to taste with salt and pepper. Spread about ½ tablespoon Asian Pesto on both sides of each breast or thigh.

Oil hot grid to help prevent sticking. Grill chicken, on an uncovered grill, over medium KINGSFORD® Briquets, 6 to 8 minutes until chicken is no longer pink in center, turning once. Serve with additional Asian Pesto and lime wedges.   *Makes 4 servings*

ASIAN PESTO

1 cup packed fresh basil leaves
1 cup packed fresh cilantro
1 cup packed fresh mint leaves
¼ cup olive or vegetable oil
2 cloves garlic, chopped
2½ to 3½ tablespoons lime juice
1 tablespoon sugar
1 teaspoon salt
1 teaspoon black pepper

Combine all ingredients in a blender or food processor; process until smooth.   *Makes about ¾ cup pesto*

NOTE: The Asian Pesto recipe makes enough for 6 servings. Leftovers can be saved and used as a spread for sandwiches.

MALAY SPICED CHICKEN

1 pound boneless skinless chicken breasts
2 medium onions
4 cloves garlic
1 small piece fresh ginger (¾ inch long), peeled
1 teaspoon ground cumin
1 teaspoon ground nutmeg
1 teaspoon turmeric
½ teaspoon ground cinnamon
¼ teaspoon ground red pepper
¼ teaspoon ground cloves
3 tablespoons vegetable oil
Grated peel of ½ lemon
⅔ cup water
2 tablespoons distilled white vinegar
1 tablespoon sugar
½ teaspoon salt
Hot cooked rice

Rinse chicken; pat dry with paper towels. Cut chicken crosswise into ½-inch-wide strips. Chop onions, garlic and ginger. Combine cumin, nutmeg, turmeric, cinnamon, red pepper and cloves in cup. Set aside.

Heat wok over medium heat until warm. Add spice mixture; cook and stir until lightly toasted and fragrant. Return spice mixture to bowl. Increase heat to high.

Drizzle oil into wok and heat 30 seconds. Add onions, garlic, ginger and lemon peel; stir-fry about 5 minutes or until lightly browned. Add chicken and spice mixture; stir-fry until chicken is no longer pink in center and is coated with spice mixture. Stir in water, vinegar, sugar and salt. Bring to a boil. Stir until half the liquid evaporates and mixture thickens. Spoon chicken mixture over rice. *Makes 4 servings*

GOLDEN CHICKEN STIR-FRY

½ **pound chicken tenders, cut into thin strips**
½ **cup stir-fry sauce, divided**
3 **tablespoons vegetable oil, divided**
1 **medium onion, thinly sliced**
1 **clove garlic, minced**
2 **carrots, cut diagonally into thin slices**
1 **rib celery, cut diagonally into thin slices**
1 **tablespoon sesame seeds, toasted**
½ **teaspoon five-spice powder**
¼ **teaspoon dark sesame oil**
2 **cups hot cooked white rice**

Toss chicken with 2 tablespoons stir-fry sauce in small bowl. Heat 1 tablespoon vegetable oil in hot wok or large skillet over medium-high heat. Add chicken and stir-fry 2 minutes; remove and set aside. Heat remaining 2 tablespoons vegetable oil in same pan. Add onion; stir-fry 2 minutes. Add garlic, carrots and celery; stir-fry 2 minutes longer. Add remaining stir-fry sauce, chicken, sesame seeds and five-spice powder to pan. Cook and stir until chicken and vegetables are coated with sauce. Remove from heat; stir in sesame oil. Serve with rice.

Makes 4 servings

PINEAPPLE TERIYAKI CHICKEN

½ **small red onion, halved and thinly sliced**
1 **medium green bell pepper, cut into 1-inch pieces**
6 **boneless, skinless chicken breasts (about 1½ pounds)**
1 **bottle (12 ounces) LAWRY'S® Teriyaki Marinade with Pineapple Juice, divided**
1 **can (20 ounces) pineapple rings, drained**

Preheat oven to 375°F. Spray 13×9×2-inch glass baking dish with nonstick cooking spray; add onion and bell pepper. Arrange chicken over vegetables; pour ⅔ cup Teriyaki Marinade over chicken, top with pineapple slices. Drizzle remaining Marinade over top. Bake until meat is no longer pink and juices run clear when cut (170°F), about 40 to 45 minutes. Spoon pan juices over chicken and vegetables once during baking and again just before serving.

Makes 6 servings

Prep Time: 10 minutes
Cook Time: 40 to 45 minutes

GOLDEN CHICKEN STIR-FRY

SAUCY-SPICY TURKEY MEATBALLS

1 pound ground turkey
⅓ cup dry bread crumbs
1 egg
1 clove garlic, minced
2 tablespoons light soy sauce, divided
1 teaspoon grated fresh ginger
¾ to 1 teaspoon red pepper flakes, divided
1 tablespoon vegetable oil
1 can (20 ounces) pineapple chunks, undrained
2 tablespoons lemon juice or orange juice
2 tablespoons honey
1 tablespoon cornstarch
1 large red bell pepper, seeded and cut into 1-inch triangles
Hot cooked rice

1. Combine turkey, bread crumbs, egg, garlic, 1 tablespoon soy sauce, ginger and ½ teaspoon red pepper flakes in large bowl. Shape turkey mixture into 1-inch meatballs.

2. Heat oil in wok or large skillet over medium-high heat. Add meatballs and cook 4 to 5 minutes or until no longer pink in centers, turning to brown all sides. Remove from wok; set aside.

3. Drain pineapple, reserving juice. Add enough water to juice to make 1 cup liquid. Whisk together pineapple juice mixture, lemon juice, honey, cornstarch, remaining 1 tablespoon soy sauce and ¼ teaspoon red pepper flakes. Pour into wok. Cook and stir over medium-high heat until sauce thickens.

4. Add meatballs, pineapple and bell pepper to sauce. Cook and stir until hot. Adjust seasoning with remaining ¼ teaspoon hot pepper flakes, if desired. Serve over rice. *Makes 4 to 5 servings*

To quickly shape uniform meatballs, place meat mixture on cutting board; pat evenly into large square, one inch thick. With sharp knife, cut meat into 1-inch squares; shape each square into a ball.

SAUCY-SPICY TURKEY MEATBALLS

INDIAN-SPICED CHICKEN WITH WILD RICE

½ teaspoon salt
½ teaspoon ground cumin
½ teaspoon black pepper
¼ teaspoon ground cinnamon
¼ teaspoon ground turmeric
4 boneless skinless chicken breasts
(about 1 pound)
2 tablespoons olive oil
2 carrots, sliced
1 red bell pepper, chopped
1 rib celery, chopped
2 cloves garlic, minced
1 package (6 ounces) long grain
and wild rice mix
2 cups reduced-sodium chicken
broth
1 cup raisins
¼ cup sliced almonds

Combine salt, cumin, black pepper, cinnamon and turmeric in small bowl. Rub spice mixture on both sides of chicken. Place chicken on plate; cover and refrigerate 30 minutes.

Preheat oven to 350°F. Spray 13×9-inch baking dish with nonstick cooking spray.

Heat oil in large skillet over medium-high heat until hot. Add chicken; cook 2 minutes per side or until browned. Remove chicken; set aside.

Place carrots, bell pepper, celery and garlic in same skillet. Cook and stir 2 minutes. Add rice; cook 5 minutes, stirring frequently. Add seasoning packet from rice mix and broth; bring to a boil over high heat. Remove from heat; stir in raisins. Pour into prepared dish. Place chicken on rice mixture; sprinkle with almonds.

Cover tightly with foil and bake 35 minutes or until chicken is no longer pink in center and rice is tender. *Makes 4 servings*

INDIAN-SPICED CHICKEN WITH WILD RICE

EASY ORIENTAL CHICKEN SANDWICHES

¼ **cup peanut butter**
2 **tablespoons honey**
2 **tablespoons light soy sauce**
½ **teaspoon garlic powder**
½ **teaspoon ground ginger**
4 **boneless skinless chicken breasts**
  (about 1¼ pounds)
4 **onion or Kaiser rolls, split**
  Lettuce leaves
1 **cup sliced cucumbers**
1 **cup bean sprouts**
¼ **cup sliced green onions**

1. Preheat oven to 400°F. Combine peanut butter, honey, soy sauce, garlic powder and ginger in large bowl; stir until well blended. Reserve ¼ cup peanut butter mixture.

2. Place chicken on foil-lined baking pan. Spread remaining peanut butter mixture over chicken. Bake 20 minutes or until chicken is no longer pink in center.

3. Fill rolls with lettuce, cucumbers, bean sprouts and chicken; sprinkle with green onions. Serve with reserved peanut butter mixture.

Makes 4 servings

ANGEL HAIR NOODLES WITH PEANUT SAUCE

¼ **cup Texas peanuts, puréed**
2 **tablespoons low-fat chicken broth**
  or water
1 **tablespoon soy sauce**
1 **tablespoon rice vinegar**
10 **ounces dried bean thread noodles**
1½ **teaspoons vegetable oil**
1 **pound chicken breast, boned,**
  skinned and thinly sliced
½ **cucumber, peeled, seeded and**
  cut into matchstick pieces
2 **medium carrots, shredded**
  Additional Texas peanuts for garnish

To make sauce, combine peanut purée, chicken broth, soy sauce and vinegar in small bowl; set aside.

Bring 4 cups water to a boil in medium saucepan. Add noodles, stirring to separate strands. Cook, stirring, 30 seconds or until noodles are slightly soft. Drain in colander and rinse under cold running water. Drain well; cut noodles in half and set aside.

Heat wok or wide skillet over high heat. Add oil, swirling to coat sides. Add chicken and stir-fry 1 minute or until opaque. Add cucumber, carrots and peanut sauce; cook, stirring to mix well. Remove from heat. Add noodles and toss until evenly coated. Sprinkle with additional peanuts, if desired.

Makes 6 servings

Favorite recipe from **Texas Peanut Producers Board**

EASY ORIENTAL CHICKEN SANDWICH

CHICKEN AND CURRIED FRUIT

6 skinless chicken breasts
    (2¼ pounds)
1 cup mixed diced dried fruit
½ cup chopped onion (about
    1 small)
¼ cup chopped chutney
3 cloves garlic, minced
1 to 1½ teaspoons curry powder
1 teaspoon ground cumin
¼ teaspoon ground red pepper
¼ teaspoon ground allspice
2½ cups fat-free reduced-sodium
    chicken broth
½ cup dry sherry or apple juice
3 cups hot cooked rice or couscous

1. Preheat oven to 350°F. Arrange chicken, breast side up, in single layer in 13×9-inch baking pan. Place dried fruit around chicken. Combine onion, chutney, garlic, curry powder, cumin, red pepper and allspice in medium bowl; stir in chicken broth and sherry. Pour mixture over chicken and fruit.

2. Cover; bake 30 minutes. Uncover; bake about 15 minutes or until chicken is no longer pink in center and juices run clear.

3. Remove chicken from pan; arrange over rice on serving platter. Process half the fruit and half the liquid mixture from pan in food processor or blender until smooth; spoon over chicken. Discard remaining liquid mixture. Arrange remaining fruit over chicken. *Makes 6 servings*

CHICKEN AND CURRIED FRUIT

TURKEY YAKITORI

½ teaspoon low-sodium chicken bouillon granules
2 tablespoons boiling water
2 tablespoons reduced-sodium soy sauce
2 tablespoons dry sherry
1 teaspoon ground ginger
1 garlic clove, minced
2 pounds turkey breast cutlets, cut into 1-inch-wide strips
8 metal skewers (9 inches long)
½ pound fresh whole mushrooms
½ large red bell pepper, cut into 1-inch cubes
½ large green bell pepper, cut into 1-inch cubes

1. Dissolve bouillon in boiling water in small bowl.

2. Combine bouillon mixture, soy sauce, sherry, ginger, garlic and turkey in large resealable plastic bag. Seal bag and turn mixture to coat. Refrigerate 4 hours or overnight. Drain marinade and discard.*

3. Weave turkey strips around mushrooms and pepper cubes on skewers.

4. Remove grill rack from charcoal grill and lightly coat with cooking spray; set aside. Preheat charcoal grill for direct-heat cooking. Grill turkey skewers 4 to 5 minutes or until turkey is no longer pink.

Makes 4 servings

*If desired, prepare another recipe of marinade by combining first six ingredients to use for brushing on grilled skewers or as dipping sauce. DO NOT use any original marinade as dipping sauce when serving.

*Favorite recipe from **National Turkey Federation***

INDONESIAN GRILLED TURKEY WITH SATAY SAUCE

2 disposable aluminum foil pans (9 inches each)
1 whole turkey breast (about 5 pounds)
2 tablespoons *French's®* Worcestershire Sauce
2 tablespoons olive oil
2 teaspoons seasoned salt
½ teaspoon ground black pepper
Satay Sauce (recipe follows)

To prepare grill, place doubled foil pans in center of grill under grilling rack. Arrange hot coals or lava rocks around foil pan. Fill pan with cold water. Place turkey on greased grid. Combine Worcestershire, oil and seasonings in small bowl; brush generously on turkey.

Grill, on covered grill, over medium-low to medium coals 1½ hours or until meat thermometer inserted into turkey reaches 170°F. Slice turkey. Serve with Satay Sauce.   *Makes 8 servings*

SATAY SAUCE

½ cup chunky-style peanut butter
⅓ cup *French's®* Worcestershire Sauce
¼ cup loosely packed fresh cilantro leaves
2 tablespoons *Frank's® RedHot®* Original Cayenne Pepper Sauce
2 tablespoons sugar
2 tablespoons water
1 tablespoon chopped peeled fresh ginger
2 cloves garlic, chopped

Place peanut butter, Worcestershire, cilantro, *Frank's RedHot* Sauce, sugar, water, ginger and garlic in food processor or blender. Cover and process until smooth.   *Makes 1⅓ cups sauce*

Prep Time: 20 minutes
Cook Time: 1 hour 30 minutes

ORANGE-GINGER BROILED CORNISH HENS

2 large Cornish hens, split (about 1½ pounds each)
2 teaspoons peanut or vegetable oil, divided
¼ cup orange marmalade
1 tablespoon minced fresh ginger

1. Place hens, skin side up, on rack of foil-lined broiler pan. Brush with 1 teaspoon oil.

2. Broil 6 to 7 inches from heat 10 minutes. Turn hens skin side down; brush with remaining 1 teaspoon oil. Broil 10 minutes.

3. Combine marmalade and ginger in cup; brush half of mixture over hens. Broil 5 minutes.

4. Turn hens skin side up; brush with remaining marmalade mixture. Broil 5 minutes or until juices run clear (180°F) and hens are browned and glazed.

Makes 4 servings

TERIYAKI CHICKEN MEDLEY

2 cups cooked white rice (about ¾ cup uncooked)
2 cups (10 ounces) cooked chicken, cut into strips
1⅓ cups *French's*® French Fried Onions, divided
1 package (12 ounces) frozen bell pepper strips, thawed and drained*
1 jar (12 ounces) chicken gravy
3 tablespoons teriyaki sauce

**Or, substitute 2 cups sliced bell peppers for frozen pepper strips.*

Preheat oven to 400°F. Grease 2-quart oblong baking dish. Press rice into bottom of prepared dish.

Combine chicken, ⅔ *cup* French Fried Onions, bell pepper strips, gravy and teriyaki sauce in large bowl; mix well. Pour mixture over rice layer. Cover; bake 30 minutes or until heated through. Top with remaining ⅔ *cup* onions. Bake 1 minute or until onions are golden.

Makes 4 to 6 servings

Prep Time: 10 minutes
Cook Time: 31 minutes

ORANGE-GINGER BROILED CORNISH HEN

TWICE-FRIED CHICKEN THIGHS WITH PLUM SAUCE

1 tablespoon ivory-colored sesame
seeds (optional)
½ cup Plum Sauce (recipe follows)
1 cup peanut oil
1 to 1¼ pounds boneless skinless
chicken thighs, cut into strips
4 medium carrots, cut into julienne
strips
4 green onions, sliced
½ teaspoon salt
½ teaspoon red pepper flakes
Hot cooked rice

1. Heat wok over medium-high heat until hot. Add sesame seeds; cook and stir 45 seconds or until golden. Remove to small bowl, reserve.

2. Prepare Plum Sauce.

3. Heat oil in wok over high heat until oil registers 375°F on deep-fry thermometer. Drop chicken into oil; fry 1 minute. Remove with slotted spoon; drain on paper towels. Drain oil from wok, reserving 2 tablespoons.

4. Add 1 tablespoon reserved oil to wok. Heat over high heat. Add carrots; stir-fry 5 minutes until crisp-tender. Remove from wok; set aside.

5. Add remaining 1 tablespoon oil to wok. Add chicken and onions; stir-fry 1 minute. Stir in Plum Sauce, carrots, salt and red pepper. Cook and stir 2 minutes. Serve over rice; top with sesame seeds, if desired.

Makes 4 servings

PLUM SAUCE

1 cup plum preserves
½ cup prepared chutney, chopped
2 tablespoons brown sugar
2 tablespoons lemon juice
2 cloves garlic, minced
2 teaspoons soy sauce
2 teaspoons minced fresh ginger

Combine plum preserves, chutney, brown sugar, lemon juice, garlic, soy sauce and ginger in small saucepan. Cook and stir over medium heat until preserves melt.

Makes 1 cup sauce

TWICE-FRIED CHICKEN THIGHS WITH PLUM SAUCE

CHICKEN WITH LYCHEES

3 whole boneless skinless chicken breasts
¼ cup plus 1 teaspoon cornstarch, divided
½ cup water, divided
½ cup tomato sauce
1 teaspoon sugar
1 teaspoon instant chicken bouillon granules
3 tablespoons vegetable oil
6 green onions with tops, cut into 1-inch pieces
1 red bell pepper, cut into 1-inch pieces
1 can (11 ounces) whole peeled lychees, drained
Vermicelli (recipe follows, optional)

1. Cut chicken breasts in half; cut each half into 6 pieces.

2. Place ¼ cup cornstarch in large resealable plastic food storage bag; add chicken pieces. Seal bag; shake until chicken is well coated; set aside.

3. Combine remaining 1 teaspoon cornstarch and ¼ cup water in small cup; mix well. Set aside.

4. Combine remaining ¼ cup water, tomato sauce, sugar and bouillon granules in small bowl; mix well. Set aside.

5. Heat oil in wok or large skillet over high heat. Add chicken; stir-fry until lightly browned, 5 to 8 minutes. Add onions and bell pepper; stir-fry 1 minute.

6. Pour tomato sauce mixture over chicken mixture. Stir in lychees. Reduce heat to low; cover. Simmer until chicken is tender and no longer pink in center, about 5 minutes.

7. Stir cornstarch mixture; add to wok. Cook and stir until sauce boils and thickens. Serve over hot Vermicelli. *Makes 4 servings*

VERMICELLI

8 ounces Chinese rice vermicelli or bean threads
Vegetable oil for frying

1. Cut bundle of vermicelli in half. Gently pull each half apart into small bunches.

2. Heat oil in wok or large skillet over medium-high heat to 375°F. Using slotted spoon or tongs, lower small bunch of vermicelli into hot oil. Cook until vermicelli rises to top, 3 to 5 seconds; remove immediately. Drain vermicelli. Repeat with remaining bunches. *Makes about 4 servings*

CHICKEN WITH LYCHEES

CHICKEN AND ASPARAGUS STIR-FRY

1 cup uncooked rice
2 tablespoons vegetable oil
1 pound boneless skinless chicken breasts, cut into ½-inch-wide strips
2 medium red bell peppers, cut into thin strips
½ pound fresh asparagus,* cut diagonally into 1-inch pieces
½ cup stir-fry sauce

*For stir-frying, select thin stalks of asparagus and cut them on the diagonal—they will cook more quickly.

1. Cook rice according to package directions. Keep hot.

2. Heat oil in wok or large skillet over medium-high heat until hot. Stir-fry chicken 3 to 4 minutes or until chicken is no longer pink in center.

3. Stir in bell peppers and asparagus; reduce heat to medium. Cover and cook 2 minutes or until vegetables are crisp-tender, stirring once or twice.

4. Stir in sauce. Serve immediately with rice.   *Makes 4 servings*

Prep and Cook Time: 18 minutes

Bell peppers are available in yellow, red, orange, purple and black. Cooks are using them to add an attractive splash of color to many dishes. Apart from their visual appeal, they each have their own distinctively pleasant taste.

CHICKEN AND ASPARAGUS STIR-FRY

SOY HONEY CHICKEN

½ cup honey
½ cup soy sauce
¼ cup dry sherry or water
1 teaspoon grated fresh gingerroot*
2 medium cloves garlic, crushed
1 broiler-fryer chicken, cut into
    serving pieces (2½ to
    3 pounds)

*Substitute 2 teaspoons ground ginger for fresh gingerroot, if desired.

Combine honey, soy sauce, sherry, gingerroot and garlic in small bowl. Place chicken in plastic food storage bag or large glass baking dish. Pour honey marinade over chicken, turning chicken to coat. Close bag or cover dish with plastic wrap. Marinate in refrigerator at least 6 hours, turning two or three times.

Remove chicken from marinade; reserve marinade. Arrange chicken on rack over roasting pan. Cover chicken with foil. Bake at 350°F 30 minutes. Bring reserved marinade to a boil in small saucepan over medium heat; boil 3 minutes and set aside.

Uncover chicken; brush with marinade. Bake, uncovered, 30 to 45 minutes longer or until juices run clear and chicken is no longer pink, brushing occasionally with marinade.

Makes 4 servings

Favorite recipe from **National Honey Board**

SOY HONEY CHICKEN

GINGER-MINT STIR-FRY CHICKEN

6 to 8 dried shiitake mushrooms
  (½ ounce)
  Fried Onions (recipe page 220)
2 tablespoons packed brown sugar
2 tablespoons fish sauce
2 tablespoons rice vinegar
4 to 6 teaspoons vegetable oil,
  divided
1½ pounds boneless skinless chicken
  breasts or thighs, cut into
  ½-inch strips
1 or 2 jalapeño peppers,* seeded
  and chopped
2 tablespoons finely chopped fresh
  ginger
3 cloves garlic, minced
1 large carrot**
1 can (5½ ounces) whole baby
  corn, drained
4 green onions, cut into 1-inch
  pieces
¼ cup slivered fresh mint leaves
  Red onion flower and mint leaves
  for garnish

*Jalapeños can sting and irritate the skin; wear rubber gloves when handling peppers and do not touch eyes. Wash hands after handling.

**To make scalloped edges, use citrus stripper to cut groove into carrot, from stem to tip. Continue to cut grooves around carrot about ¼ inch apart. Cut carrot into thin slices.

1. Place mushrooms in bowl; cover with hot water. Let stand 30 minutes or until caps are soft. Drain mushrooms; squeeze out excess water. Remove and discard stems. Slice caps into thin strips.

2. Prepare Fried Onions; set aside.

3. Combine brown sugar, fish sauce and vinegar in small bowl; stir until sugar is dissolved.

4. Heat wok or large skillet over high heat. Add 2 teaspoons oil and swirl to coat surface. Add ⅓ of chicken; stir-fry 3 minutes, stirring occasionally, until chicken is no longer pink in center. Transfer to bowl. Repeat with remaining chicken, adding 1 teaspoon oil with each batch to prevent sticking if necessary.

5. Add remaining 2 teaspoons oil to wok. Add jalapeño peppers, ginger and garlic; stir-fry 1 to 2 minutes or until fragrant but not browned.

6. Add fish sauce mixture to wok; boil until reduced by half. Return chicken to wok. Add mushrooms, carrots, baby corn and green onions; stir-fry 2 to 3 minutes or until heated through. Stir in mint. Transfer to serving platter and arrange Fried Onions around dish. Serve with rice and garnish, if desired.

Makes 4 to 6 servings

continued on page 220

GINGER-MINT STIR-FRY CHICKEN

Ginger-Mint Stir-Fry Chicken, *continued*

FRIED ONIONS

1 medium onion
¼ cup all-purpose flour
Peanut oil for frying

1. Trim ends from onion. Remove and discard peel. Slice onion into very thin rings; separate rings.

2. Place rings in resealable plastic food storage bag with flour. Seal bag and shake to coat onion evenly with flour. Remove onion rings from bag; shake off excess flour.

3. Heat 1 to 2 inches oil in Dutch oven or wok until oil registers 300°F to 325°F on deep-fry thermometer. Divide onions into 5 or 6 batches. Lower 1 batch into oil with slotted spoon. (Onion rings should be in single layer and overlap as little as possible).

4. Cook onion rings 6 to 8 minutes or until golden, turning once. Remove with slotted spoon to paper towels. Repeat with remaining onion rings, reheating oil between batches.

5. Let onion rings cool completely; store in airtight container at room temperature up to 1 day. (If onions soften overnight, arrange in single layer on baking sheets. Bake in preheated 375°F oven 5 to 10 minutes or until crisp, watching carefully to prevent burning.)

SWEET 'N' SOUR TURKEY MEATBALL STEW

2 pounds ground turkey
¾ cup dry bread crumbs
½ cup chopped onion
⅓ cup chopped water chestnuts
4 tablespoons reduced-sodium soy
    sauce, divided
1 clove garlic, minced
1 egg
½ teaspoon salt
½ teaspoon ground ginger
¼ teaspoon black pepper
2 tablespoons vegetable oil
2 cups water
¼ cup sugar
¼ cup apple cider vinegar
1 can (20 ounces) pineapple
    chunks in juice, drained and
    juice reserved
1 medium green bell pepper, cut
    into ½-inch pieces
1 medium red bell pepper, cut into
    ½-inch pieces
  Peel from 1 lemon, coarsely
    chopped
2 tablespoons cornstarch
  Hot cooked rice (optional)

Combine turkey, bread crumbs, onion, water chestnuts, 1 tablespoon soy sauce, garlic, egg, salt, ginger and black pepper in large bowl; mix well. Shape into meatballs.

Heat oil in 5-quart Dutch oven over medium heat. Brown meatballs in hot oil. Remove with slotted spoon. Discard fat. Combine water, sugar, vinegar and reserved pineapple juice in Dutch oven. Return meatballs to Dutch oven.

Bring to a boil over high heat. Reduce heat to low. Cover and simmer 20 to 25 minutes. Stir in pineapple, bell peppers and lemon peel. Simmer, uncovered, 5 minutes.

Blend remaining 3 tablespoons soy sauce into cornstarch in small bowl until smooth. Bring meatballs to a boil over medium-high heat; stir in cornstarch mixture. Cook 5 minutes or until mixture thickens, stirring constantly. Serve over rice, if desired. *Makes 6 servings*

HONEY-ORANGE TURKEY

1 pound boneless skinless turkey
   cutlets
½ teaspoon salt
¼ teaspoon black pepper
2 tablespoons cornstarch, divided
½ cup orange juice
2 tablespoons honey
1 tablespoon soy sauce
½ teaspoon ground ginger
2 tablespoons vegetable oil
1 tablespoon butter
   Hot cooked rice

Rinse turkey; pat dry with paper towels. Cut each cutlet into quarters. Place turkey on waxed paper; sprinkle with salt and pepper. Dust with 1 tablespoon cornstarch. Combine juice, honey, soy sauce and ginger in cup; stir until well blended. Set aside.

Heat wok or large skillet over high heat about 1 minute. Drizzle oil into wok. Add butter; swirl to coat bottom. Add turkey; stir-fry until browned on all sides. Remove to large plate. Reduce heat to medium.

Add remaining 1 tablespoon cornstarch to wok. Stir in juice mixture; bring to a boil. Boil 1 minute; pour over turkey. Serve with rice.

Makes 4 servings

STIR-FRIED BARBECUE CHICKEN WITH CASHEW NUTS

2 tablespoons LEE KUM KEE® Char
   Siu Sauce
1 tablespoon water
9 ounces boneless chicken, cut into
   cubes
2 tablespoons vegetable oil
½ onion, chopped
½ green bell pepper, chopped
½ red bell pepper, chopped
2 ounces cocktail cashew nuts

1. Combine Char Siu Sauce and water in large bowl; add chicken. Marinate chicken 15 minutes.

2. Heat oil in wok; sauté onion and peppers until fragrant. Add chicken and stir-fry until no longer pink.

3. Stir in nuts and serve.

Makes 4 servings

HONEY-ORANGE TURKEY

ORIENTAL STIR-FRY

1 bag SUCCESS® Rice
  Spicy Oriental Sauce (recipe
    follows)
¼ cup safflower oil, divided
¾ pound skinless, boneless turkey,
    cut into strips
½ teaspoon minced fresh ginger
1 clove garlic, minced
1 cup broccoli florets
1 medium onion, cut into wedges
1 yellow bell pepper, seeded and
    cut into strips
2 medium tomatoes, each cut into
    6 wedges

2 tablespoons cornstarch
½ cup water
2 tablespoons reduced-sodium soy
    sauce
1 tablespoon sherry
1 tablespoon Worcestershire sauce
1 teaspoon curry powder

Prepare rice according to package directions.

Prepare Spicy Oriental Sauce; set aside.

Heat 2 tablespoons oil in large skillet or wok. Add turkey, ginger and garlic; stir-fry until turkey is no longer pink in center. Remove turkey from skillet; set aside.

Heat remaining 2 tablespoons oil in same skillet. Add broccoli, onion and bell pepper; stir-fry 1 minute. Return turkey to skillet with tomatoes. Stir sauce. Add to skillet; cook and stir until sauce is thickened. Serve over hot rice. Garnish, if desired.

Makes 4 servings

SPICY ORIENTAL SAUCE

Combine cornstarch, water, soy sauce, sherry, Worcestershire sauce and curry powder in small bowl; mix well.

ORIENTAL STIR-FRY

PEANUT CHICKEN STIR-FRY

1 package (6.1 ounces)
  RICE-A-RONI® With ⅓ Less
  Salt Fried Rice
½ cup reduced-sodium or regular
  chicken broth
2 tablespoons creamy peanut
  butter
1 tablespoon reduced-sodium or
  regular soy sauce
1 tablespoon vegetable oil
¾ pound skinless, boneless chicken
  breasts, cut into ½-inch pieces
2 cloves garlic, minced
2 cups frozen mixed carrots,
  broccoli and red pepper
  vegetable medley, thawed,
  drained
2 tablespoons chopped peanuts
  (optional)

1. Prepare Rice-A-Roni® mix as package directs.

2. While Rice-A-Roni® is simmering, combine chicken broth, peanut butter and soy sauce; mix with fork. Set aside.

3. In second large skillet or wok, heat oil over medium-high heat. Stir-fry chicken and garlic 2 minutes.

4. Add vegetables and broth mixture; stir-fry 5 to 7 minutes or until sauce has thickened. Serve over rice. Sprinkle with peanuts, if desired.

Makes 4 servings

Tip ▪▪▪

Thoroughly wash cutting surfaces, utensils and your hands with hot soapy water after coming into contact with uncooked chicken. This eliminates the risk of contaminating other foods with salmonella bacteria that is often present in raw chicken. Salmonella is killed during cooking when allowed to reach a temperature of 165°F or higher.

PEANUT CHICKEN STIR-FRY

CHICKEN & VEGETABLES WITH MUSTARD SAUCE

1 pound boneless skinless chicken
    breasts
1 tablespoon sugar
2 teaspoons cornstarch
2 teaspoons dry mustard
3 tablespoons reduced-sodium soy
    sauce
2 tablespoons water
2 tablespoons rice vinegar
2 tablespoons vegetable oil, divided
2 cloves garlic, minced
1 small red bell pepper, cut into
    thin slices
½ cup thinly sliced celery
1 small onion, cut into thin wedges
    Chinese egg noodles
    Fresh chives and yellow bell
      pepper rose for garnish

1. Cut chicken into 1-inch pieces; set aside.

2. Combine sugar, cornstarch and mustard in small bowl. Stir soy sauce, water and vinegar into cornstarch mixture until smooth; set aside.

3. Heat wok over medium heat 2 minutes or until hot. Drizzle 1 tablespoon oil into wok and heat 30 seconds. Add chicken and garlic; stir-fry 5 to 6 minutes or until chicken is no longer pink in center. Transfer chicken to large bowl.

4. Drizzle remaining oil into wok and heat 30 seconds. Add red pepper, celery and onion; stir-fry 3 minutes or until vegetables are crisp-tender.

5. Stir soy sauce mixture; add to wok. Stir-fry 30 seconds or until sauce boils and thickens.

6. Return chicken and any accumulated juices to wok; cook until heated through. Serve with noodles. Garnish with fresh chives and yellow bell pepper rose, if desired.

Makes 4 servings

CHICKEN & VEGETABLES WITH MUSTARD SAUCE

LEMON-GINGER CHICKEN WITH PUFFED RICE NOODLES

Vegetable oil for frying
4 ounces rice noodles, broken in half
3 boneless skinless chicken breasts, cut into 2½×1-inch strips
1 stalk lemongrass, cut into 1-inch pieces*
3 cloves garlic, minced
1 teaspoon finely chopped fresh ginger
¼ teaspoon ground red pepper
¼ teaspoon black pepper
¼ cup water
1 tablespoon cornstarch
2 tablespoons peanut oil
6 ounces fresh snow peas, ends trimmed
1 can (8¾ ounces) baby corn, drained, rinsed and cut lengthwise into halves
¼ cup chopped fresh cilantro
2 tablespoons packed brown sugar
2 tablespoons fish sauce
1 tablespoon light soy sauce

Or, substitute 1½ teaspoons grated lemon peel.

1. Heat 3 inches vegetable oil in wok or Dutch oven until oil registers 375°F on deep-fry thermometer. Fry noodles in small batches 20 seconds or until puffy, holding down noodles in oil with slotted spoon to fry evenly. Drain on paper towels; set aside.

2. Combine chicken, lemongrass, garlic, ginger, red pepper and black pepper in medium bowl; toss to coat. Combine water and cornstarch in small bowl; set aside.

3. Heat wok over high heat 1 minute or until hot. Drizzle peanut oil into wok and heat 30 seconds. Add chicken mixture; stir-fry 3 minutes or until no longer pink.

4. Add snow peas and baby corn; stir-fry 1 to 2 minutes. Stir cornstarch mixture; add to wok. Cook 1 minute or until thickened.

5. Add cilantro, brown sugar, fish sauce and soy sauce; cook until heated through. Discard lemongrass. Serve over rice noodles.

Makes 4 servings

LEMON-GINGER CHICKEN WITH PUFFED RICE NOODLES

Perfect Pork

FRIED NOODLE AND PORK STIR-FRY

Noodle Bundles (recipe follows)
¹/₂ **cup stir-fry sauce**
¹/₄ **cup red wine**
 1 **teaspoon hot sauce**
¹/₂ **teaspoon cornstarch**
 2 **tablespoons peanut oil, divided**
³/₄ **pound boneless pork tenderloin,
      cut into thin pieces**
 1 **carrot, thinly sliced**
 1 **medium onion, chopped**
 2 **ribs celery, thinly sliced**
 1 **medium red bell pepper, cut into
      thin strips**

Prepare Noodle Bundles; set aside and keep warm.

Stir together stir-fry sauce, red wine, hot sauce and cornstarch in small bowl; set aside.

Heat 1 tablespoon oil in wok or large skillet over high heat. Add pork. Stir-fry 3 minutes; remove. Add remaining tablespoon of oil to wok. Add carrot to wok; stir-fry 1 minute. Add remaining ingredients; stir-fry 3 minutes or until vegetables are tender. Return pork to wok; add sauce mixture. Cook and stir until mixture boils and sauce is slightly thickened. Serve over noodle bundles. *Makes 4 to 6 servings*

NOODLE BUNDLES: Cook 8 ounces pasta according to package directions; rinse and drain. Arrange pasta into 4 to 6 bundles. Heat 1 tablespoon peanut oil in large nonstick skillet over medium-high heat. Add 2 or 3 bundles to skillet; cook 5 minutes or until bottom of bundles are golden. Repeat with remaining bundles, adding more oil to pan as needed.

FRIED NOODLE AND PORK STIR-FRY

EXOTIC PORK & VEGETABLES

¼ cup water
2 teaspoons cornstarch
4 tablespoons peanut oil, divided
6 whole dried hot red chili peppers
4 cloves garlic, sliced
1 pork tenderloin (about ¾ pound), thinly sliced
1 large carrot, peeled*
2 ounces fresh oyster, shiitake or button mushrooms,** cut into halves
1 baby eggplant, thinly sliced
5 ounces fresh snow peas, ends trimmed
3 tablespoons packed brown sugar
2 tablespoons fish sauce
1 tablespoon dark sesame oil
Hot cooked rice

*To make scalloped edges on carrot, use citrus stripper or grapefruit spoon to cut groove into carrot, cutting lengthwise from stem end to tip. Continue to cut grooves around carrot about ¼ inch apart. Cut carrot crosswise into ¼-inch-thick slices.

**Or, substitute ½ ounce dried Oriental mushrooms, soaked according to package directions.

1. Combine water and cornstarch in cup; set aside.

2. Heat wok or large skillet over high heat 1 minute or until hot. Drizzle 2 tablespoons peanut oil into wok and heat 30 seconds. Add peppers and garlic; stir-fry about 1 minute. Add pork; stir-fry 3 to 4 minutes or until no longer pink. Remove pork mixture to bowl and set aside.

3. Add remaining 2 tablespoons peanut oil to wok. Add carrot, mushrooms and eggplant; stir-fry 2 minutes. Add snow peas and pork mixture; stir-fry 1 minute.

4. Stir cornstarch mixture; add to wok. Cook 1 minute or until thickened. Stir in brown sugar, fish sauce and sesame oil; cook until heated through. Serve over rice.   *Makes 4 servings*

EXOTIC PORK & VEGETABLES

ASIAN POCKETS

1 pound **BOB EVANS®** Original
    Recipe Roll Sausage
¼ cup chopped green onions
2 teaspoons minced fresh ginger
¾ teaspoon garlic powder
1 tablespoon vegetable oil
1 large green bell pepper, sliced
    lengthwise
1 large red bell pepper, sliced
    lengthwise
6 small white pita bread pockets
12 tablespoons apple butter, divided

Combine sausage, green onions, ginger and garlic powder in medium bowl; mix well. Shape mixture into 6 patties. Cook patties in medium skillet over medium heat until browned and cooked through. Set aside and keep warm. Add oil and bell peppers to same skillet; cook and stir 1 to 2 minutes over medium heat just until peppers are slightly tender.

Open each pita bread pocket; fill with sausage patty, 2 tablespoons pepper mixture and 2 tablespoons apple butter. Serve warm. Refrigerate leftovers.

Makes 6 servings

PINEAPPLE PORK STIR-FRY

1 can (20 ounces) **DOLE®** Pineapple
    Chunks
½ pound lean pork loin
2 cloves garlic, pressed
1 yellow onion, cut into wedges
2 tablespoons minced gingerroot
    or 1 teaspoon ground ginger
1 tablespoon vegetable oil
2 tablespoons soy sauce
2 teaspoons cornstarch
1 bunch **DOLE®** Broccoli, cut into
    florets
½ cup chopped walnuts, toasted

- Drain pineapple chunks, reserving ½ cup juice.

- Cut pork into strips.

- In skillet or wok, stir-fry pork with garlic, onion and ginger in hot oil until pork is just pink.

- Mix reserved juice, soy sauce and cornstarch. Stir into pork mixture. Top with pineapple chunks, broccoli and nuts. Cover, cook 3 to 5 minutes longer until vegetables are tender-crisp. Stir before serving.

Makes 4 servings

ASIAN POCKET

STIR-FRIED PORK WITH ORANGES AND SNOW PEAS

1 cup uncooked rice
1 tablespoon vegetable oil
1 pound lean boneless pork, cut into ¼-inch-wide strips
½ pound snow peas, trimmed
½ cup bottled stir-fry sauce
2 tablespoons frozen orange juice concentrate, thawed
1 can (11 ounces) mandarin orange sections, drained

1. Cook rice according to package directions.

2. Heat oil in wok or large skillet over high heat until hot. Stir-fry pork 3 minutes or until brown.

3. Add snow peas; stir-fry 2 to 3 minutes or until crisp-tender. Add stir-fry sauce and juice concentrate; stir until well blended. Gently stir in orange sections. Serve with rice. *Makes 4 servings*

Prep and Cook Time: 20 minutes

Tip ■■■

Frozen orange juice concentrate can be scooped and measured when frozen. There's no need to thaw the entire can. A small amount, such as the 2 tablespoons here, will thaw in the time it takes to prepare steps 1 and 2.

STIR-FRIED PORK WITH ORANGES AND SNOW PEAS

SZECHUAN PORK

2 tablespoons soy sauce, divided
1 tablespoon cornstarch
1 pound boneless pork loin, thinly
    sliced into bite-size pieces
1 tablespoon dry sherry
½ to 1 teaspoon crushed red pepper
2 tablespoons FLEISCHMANN'S®
    Original Margarine
1 large red bell pepper, diced
⅓ cup sliced green onions
1 teaspoon grated gingerroot
    Hot cooked rice

1. Blend 1 tablespoon soy sauce and cornstarch in medium bowl; add pork, tossing to coat well. Blend remaining soy sauce and sherry in small bowl; set aside.

2. Cook and stir crushed red pepper in margarine in large skillet over medium heat until pepper turns black. Add pork mixture; cook and stir for 5 to 7 minutes or until pork is no longer pink. Remove pork from skillet; set aside.

3. Add red pepper, green onions and ginger to same skillet; cook and stir for 2 minutes or until tender-crisp. Return pork to skillet with sherry mixture; cook 2 to 3 minutes more, stirring constantly until pork is cooked. Serve over rice. *Makes 4 servings*

Prep Time: 20 minutes
Cook Time: 25 minutes
Total Time: 45 minutes

SZECHUAN PORK

MANDARIN PORK STIR-FRY

1½ cups DOLE® Pineapple Orange or
    Pineapple Juice, divided
    Vegetable cooking spray
12 ounces lean pork tenderloin,
    chicken breast or turkey
    tenderloin, cut into thin strips
1 tablespoon finely chopped fresh
    ginger *or* ½ teaspoon ground
    ginger
2 cups DOLE® Shredded Carrots
½ cup chopped DOLE® Pitted
    Prunes or Chopped Dates
4 green onions, cut into 1-inch
    pieces
2 tablespoons low-sodium soy
    sauce
1 teaspoon cornstarch

• Heat 2 tablespoons juice over medium-high heat in large nonstick skillet sprayed with vegetable cooking spray until juice bubbles.

• Add pork and ginger; cook and stir 3 minutes or until pork is no longer pink. Remove pork from skillet.

• Heat 3 more tablespoons juice in skillet; add carrots, prunes and green onions. Cook and stir 3 minutes.

• Stir soy sauce and cornstarch into remaining juice; add to carrot mixture. Stir in pork; cover and cook 2 minutes until heated through.

Makes 4 servings

Prep Time: 15 minutes
Cook Time: 15 minutes

MANDARIN PORK STIR-FRY

BARBECUED RIBS WITH ORIENTAL PLUM SAUCE

 3 pounds pork spareribs
½ cup water
   Oriental Plum Sauce (recipe
   follows)

Arrange ribs in single layer in 13×9-inch microwave-safe dish. Pour water over ribs. Cover loosely with plastic wrap. Microwave on MEDIUM-HIGH (70% power) 20 minutes, rearranging ribs once.

Place ribs on grid. Grill over medium coals 20 minutes or until barely pink near bone, basting with Oriental Plum Sauce during last 10 minutes of cooking. Serve with remaining sauce.   *Makes 4 servings*

ORIENTAL PLUM SAUCE

1 jar (10 ounces) plum jam
2 tablespoons *Frank's® RedHot®*
   Original Cayenne Pepper Sauce
2 tablespoons prepared seafood
   cocktail sauce or chili sauce
1 teaspoon grated peeled fresh
   ginger

Combine ingredients in small saucepan. Cook over medium heat 3 minutes or until hot and bubbly, stirring occasionally. Cool completely.
Makes about 1½ cups sauce

Prep Time: 20 minutes
Cook Time: 40 minutes

CHINESE PORK ROLL-UPS

¾ **pound boneless stir-fry-cut pork**
¼ **cup soy sauce**
2 **tablespoons cornstarch**
¼ **teaspoon freshly ground black**
   pepper
1 **package (½ ounce) dried shiitake**
   mushrooms (or other dried
   Asian mushrooms such as tree
   ear or cloud ear)
2 **tablespoons CRISCO® Oil***
½ **cup thinly sliced green onions,**
   white and 4-inches of green
   part
1 **tablespoon jarred minced garlic**
   or 2 **large cloves garlic, peeled**
   and minced
1 **cup shredded cabbage**
4 **eggs, lightly beaten**

For Serving
⅓ **cup plum sauce**
8 **(6-inch) flour tortillas**

*Use your favorite Crisco Oil product.

1. Combine pork, soy sauce, cornstarch and pepper in mixing bowl. Marinate 15 minutes. Pour very hot tap water over dried mushrooms while pork marinates. Keep mushrooms submerged with the back of a spoon. Soak 10 minutes. Drain. Squeeze out extra moisture. Discard stems. Slice caps thinly. Set aside.

2. Heat oil in large skillet or wok on medium-high heat. Add onions and garlic. Stir-fry 30 seconds. Add pork and cabbage. Stir-fry 4 minutes, or until pork has lost all its pink color and cabbage is wilted. Add mushrooms and eggs to pan. Stir. Cook 1 minute. Scrape to dislodge cooked eggs. Cook additional 1 to 2 minutes, or until eggs are set.

3. To serve: Spread plum sauce on surface of each tortilla, and place some of pork mixture in center. Tuck one edge over filling, and roll tightly but firmly to enclose filling. Serve immediately.

Makes 4 servings

Prep Time: 20 minutes
Total Time: 45 minutes

NOTE: Most supermarkets now carry pork already cut for stir-frying. If not available, use boneless pork loin. Cut into ¼-inch slices and then into ½-inch strips. The recipe can also be done with boneless, skinless chicken breasts, cut into thin slivers.

SERVING SUGGESTION: If you want the roll-ups to be crisp, wrap them as directed, spray with Crisco® No-Stick Cooking Spray and bake them at 375°F for 10 minutes.

SESAME PORK WITH BROCCOLI

1 can (14½ ounces) chicken broth
2 tablespoons cornstarch
1 tablespoon soy sauce
4 green onions with tops, finely diced
1 pound pork tenderloin, trimmed
1 tablespoon vegetable oil
1 clove garlic, minced
1½ pounds fresh broccoli, cut into bite-size pieces (about 7 cups)
2 tablespoons sliced pimiento, drained
   Hot cooked rice (optional)
2 tablespoons sesame seed, lightly toasted

Combine chicken broth, cornstarch and soy sauce in small bowl; blend well. Stir in green onions; set aside. Cut pork tenderloin lengthwise into quarters; cut each quarter into bite-size pieces. Heat oil in wok or heavy skillet over medium-high heat. Add pork and garlic; stir-fry 3 to 4 minutes or until pork is tender. Remove pork; keep warm. Stir broth mixture; add to wok with broccoli. Cover and simmer over low heat 8 minutes. Add cooked pork and pimiento to wok; cook just until mixture is hot, stirring frequently. Serve over rice, if desired. Sprinkle with sesame seed. Garnish as desired.

Makes 6 servings

*Favorite recipe from **National Pork Board***

Tip ▪▪▪

Sesame seeds are the seeds of a leafy green plant that is native to East Africa and Indonesia. These tiny round seeds are usually ivory colored, but brown, red and black are also available. Because of their high oil content, they easily turn rancid and are best stored in the refrigerator where they will keep up to six months or they may be frozen up to a year.

SESAME PORK WITH BROCCOLI

STIR-FRIED PORK WITH GREEN BEANS AND BABY CORN

¾ **pound pork tenderloin**
1 **tablespoon plus 1 teaspoon**
   cornstarch, divided
2 **tablespoons soy sauce**
1 **tablespoon rice wine or dry**
   sherry
1 **teaspoon sugar**
½ **teaspoon dark sesame oil**
⅓ **cup plus 2 tablespoons water,**
   divided
2 **tablespoons peanut oil, divided**
1 **pound fresh green beans,**
   trimmed and cut into 1½-inch
   pieces
2 **cloves garlic, minced**
1 **teaspoon finely chopped ginger**
1 **tablespoon black bean sauce**
1 **can (14 ounces) precut baby**
   corn, drained and rinsed *or*
   1 can (15 ounces) whole baby
   corn, drained, rinsed and cut
   into 1-inch lengths.

1. Slice pork across grain into thin slices; cut slices into ¾-inch strips.

2. Combine 1 teaspoon cornstarch, soy sauce, rice wine, sugar and sesame oil in medium bowl; mix well. Add pork; toss to coat. Set aside to marinate 20 to 30 minutes. Combine remaining 3 teaspoons cornstarch and ⅓ cup water in small cup; set aside.

3. Heat 1 tablespoon peanut oil in wok or large skillet over high heat. Add beans; stir-fry about 4 minutes. Add remaining 2 tablespoons water; reduce heat to medium-low. Cover and simmer 10 to 12 minutes or until crisp-tender. Remove from wok; set aside.

4. Heat remaining 1 tablespoon peanut oil in wok over high heat. Add garlic, ginger and pork; stir-fry about 3 minutes or until meat is no longer pink in center. Add black bean sauce; stir-fry 1 minute.

5. Return beans to wok. Stir cornstarch mixture; add to wok. Bring to a boil; cook until sauce thickens. Stir in baby corn; heat through.

Makes 4 servings

STIR-FRIED PORK WITH GREEN BEANS AND BABY CORN

SPAM™ HOT & SPICY STIR-FRY

⅓ cup reduced-sodium teriyaki
    sauce
⅓ cup water
2 to 3 teaspoons HOUSE OF
    TSANG® MONGOLIAN FIRE®
    Oil
½ teaspoon ground ginger
1 (12-ounce) can SPAM® Lite,
    cubed
1 cup broccoli florets
1 cup chopped onion
1 cup pea pods
1 red bell pepper, cut into strips
1 tablespoon plus 1½ teaspoons
    vegetable oil
1 (14-ounce) can whole baby corn,
    drained and cut in half
1 (7-ounce) jar mushrooms,
    drained
6 cups hot cooked white rice

In small bowl, combine teriyaki sauce, water, Chinese hot oil and ginger; set aside. In wok or large skillet, stir-fry SPAM®, broccoli, onion, pea pods and bell pepper in vegetable oil 2 minutes. Add teriyaki sauce mixture; cook until bubbly. Add baby corn and mushrooms; heat thoroughly. Serve over rice.

Makes 6 servings

Tip •••

Rice has a reputation for being difficult to cook. Since rice can be cooked by several methods, the choice is dependent upon the result you desire. The two most common cooking methods for polished white rice are the boiling method and the pilaf method. To prepare brown, converted, flavored or quick-cooking rices, follow the package directions.

SPAM™ HOT & SPICY STIR-FRY

GINGER PEANUT PORK TENDERLOIN

3 tablespoons soy sauce
1 tablespoon honey
1 tablespoon sesame oil
1 tablespoon creamy peanut butter
1 tablespoon minced fresh ginger
2 teaspoons TABASCO® brand
    Pepper Sauce
1 large clove garlic, minced
1 teaspoon curry powder
½ teaspoon salt
1½ pounds pork tenderloins

Combine all ingredients except pork in medium bowl. Set aside 2 tablespoons mixture. Add pork tenderloins to bowl; cover and marinate at least 2 hours or overnight, turning occasionally.

Preheat grill to medium, placing rack 5 to 6 inches above coals. Place tenderloins on rack; grill 20 to 25 minutes or until no longer pink in center, turning occasionally and brushing frequently with marinade during first 10 minutes of grilling. Let stand 10 minutes before slicing. Brush reserved 2 tablespoons soy sauce mixture over cooked meat.

Makes 6 servings

GRILLED ASIAN PORK

6 tablespoons CRISCO® Oil*
⅓ cup dark brown sugar
3 tablespoons soy sauce
3 teaspoons jarred minced garlic *or*
    1 large clove fresh garlic,
    peeled and minced
1½ to 4½ teaspoons curry powder
¾ teaspoon ground ginger
1½ pounds pork loin, trimmed of all
    fat and sliced ¼-inch thick
12 bamboo** or metal skewers

*Use your favorite Crisco Oil product.

**If using wooden skewers, soak in water 20 minutes before using.

1. Combine oil, sugar, soy sauce, garlic, curry and ginger in resealable plastic food storage bag or mixing bowl. Add sliced pork. Close bag; refrigerate for 45 minutes.

2. While meat is marinating, prepare grill or heat broiler. Thread meat onto skewers. Discard marinade. Grill skewers 3 minutes. Turn gently with tongs. Grill other side 3 minutes or until pork is brown on outside and no longer pink in center. Serve immediately.

Makes 4 servings

Prep Time: 15 minutes
Total Time: 1 hour 10 minutes

NOTE: Boneless skinless chicken breasts or lean steak such as flank steak can be marinated and grilled in the same manner. For beef, cook to desired degree of doneness. For chicken, grill until chicken is no longer pink in center.

GINGER PEANUT PORK TENDERLOIN

GARLIC-PEPPER SKEWERED PORK

1 boneless pork loin roast (about 2½ pounds)
6 to 15 cloves garlic, minced
⅓ cup lime juice
3 tablespoons firmly packed brown sugar
3 tablespoons soy sauce
2 tablespoons vegetable oil
2 teaspoons black pepper
¼ teaspoon cayenne pepper
8 green onions, cut into 2-inch pieces (optional)

Cut pork crosswise into six ½-inch-thick chops, reserving remaining roast. (Each chop may separate into 2 pieces.) Set chops aside in 13×9×2-inch glass dish. Cut remaining pork roast lengthwise into 2 pieces. Cut each piece into ⅛-inch-thick strips; place in dish with chops. To prepare marinade, combine all remaining ingredients except green onions in small bowl. Pour marinade over pork chops and slices; cover and refrigerate at least 1 hour or overnight. Thread pork slices ribbon style onto metal skewers, alternating pork with green onions. Grill skewered pork slices and chops over medium-hot KINGSFORD® Briquets about 3 minutes per side until no longer pink in center. (Chops may require 1 to 2 minutes longer.) *Do not overcook.* Serve skewered pork immediately. Cover and refrigerate chops for Thai Pork Salad (page 84).

Makes 4 to 6 servings (plus 6 chops for Thai Pork Salad)

GARLIC-PEPPER SKEWERED PORK

MOO SHU PORK

1 cup DOLE® Pineapple Juice
1 tablespoon low-sodium soy sauce
2 teaspoons sesame seed oil
2 teaspoons cornstarch
8 ounces pork tenderloin, cut into thin strips
1½ cups Oriental-style mixed vegetables
¼ cup hoisin sauce (optional)
8 (8-inch) flour tortillas, warmed
2 green onions, cut into thin strips

- **Stir** juice, soy sauce, sesame seed oil and cornstarch in shallow, nonmetallic dish until blended; remove ½ cup mixture for sauce.

- **Add** pork to remaining juice mixture in shallow dish. Cover and marinate 15 minutes in refrigerator. Drain pork; discard marinade.

- **Cook** and stir pork in large, nonstick skillet over medium-high heat 2 minutes or until pork is lightly browned. Add vegetables; cook and stir 3 to 4 minutes or until vegetables are tender-crisp. Stir in reserved ½ cup juice mixture; cook 1 minute or until sauce thickens.

- **Spread** hoisin sauce onto center of each tortilla, if desired; top with moo shu pork. Sprinkle with green onions. Fold opposite sides of tortilla over filling; fold remaining sides of tortilla over filling. Garnish with slivered green onions, kumquats and fresh herbs, if desired.

Makes 4 servings

Prep Time: 10 minutes
Marinate Time: 15 minutes
Cook Time: 10 minutes

MOO SHU PORK

SPICY MUSTARD STIR-FRY

4 tablespoons soy sauce, divided
1 tablespoon cornstarch
5 teaspoons vegetable oil, divided
1 teaspoon hot pepper sauce, divided
1 large pork tenderloin (about ¾ pound), cut into ¼-inch slices
3 tablespoons PLOCHMAN'S® Stone Ground Mustard
6 tablespoons water, divided
3 tablespoons Chinese rice wine or sherry, divided
4 cups cauliflower florets
1½ cups diagonally-cut carrot slices
1 tablespoon minced fresh ginger
2 cloves garlic, minced
4 green onions, cut into ¼-inch pieces
Hot cooked rice

1. In small bowl, combine 2 tablespoons soy sauce, cornstarch, 1 teaspoon oil and ½ teaspoon pepper sauce. Add pork, stirring to coat. Let stand at room temperature 15 minutes.

2. In another small bowl, combine mustard, remaining 2 tablespoons soy sauce, 2 tablespoons water, 1 tablespoon rice wine and remaining ½ teaspoon pepper sauce.

3. In large skillet or wok, heat 2 teaspoons oil over medium-high heat. Add cauliflower, carrots, ginger and garlic. Stir-fry 1 minute. Add remaining 2 tablespoons rice wine, then remaining 4 tablespoons water. Cover; cook 3 to 4 minutes or until vegetables are crisp-tender. Remove from skillet; wipe skillet clean.

4. Add remaining 2 teaspoons oil to skillet; heat over high heat. Stir pork mixture to separate slices; add to skillet. Stir-fry until almost done; add green onions. Continue cooking until pork is no longer pink.

5. Return vegetables to skillet; stir in mustard mixture. Heat 1 minute. Serve over rice.   *Makes 4 servings*

Prep and Cook Time: 40 minutes

VARIATION: Substitute 1 bag (16 ounces) frozen broccoli, cauliflower and carrot blend for fresh cauliflower and carrots.

EGG FOO YUNG

8 ounces fully cooked smoked ham
    steak, cut ½ inch thick
1 can (8 ounces) whole water
    chestnuts, drained
1 green onion with tops
1 tablespoon cornstarch
¼ teaspoon ground ginger
¼ teaspoon sugar
1 cup reduced-sodium chicken
    broth
1 teaspoon soy sauce
6 tablespoons vegetable oil, divided
1 rib celery, sliced
4 large eggs, beaten

Cut ham into ¼-inch strips; cut strips crosswise into ¼-inch pieces. Coarsely chop water chestnuts and onion. Set aside.

Combine cornstarch, ginger and sugar in small bowl. Stir broth and soy sauce into cornstarch mixture until smooth. Set aside.

Heat wok over medium-high heat 1 minute or until hot. Drizzle 1 tablespoon oil into wok and heat 30 seconds. Add ham, celery, water chestnuts and onion; stir-fry about 2 minutes or until ham is lightly browned. Remove ham mixture to medium bowl. Stir eggs into ham mixture until well mixed.

Heat wok over medium-high heat 1 minute or until hot. Drizzle 1 tablespoon oil into wok and heat 30 seconds. Ladle about ¼ cup egg mixture into wok and fry until underside is set and lightly browned. Turn over and fry other side just until set. Move to one side of wok. Repeat with remaining egg mixture, adding more oil as needed.

Transfer egg foo yung to serving plate and keep warm. Stir broth mixture until smooth and pour into wok. Cook and stir until sauce boils and thickens. Spoon sauce over egg foo yung. *Makes 4 servings*

STIR-FRIED SAUSAGE AND VEGETABLES

2 teaspoons vegetable oil
2 cups broccoli florets
1 cup red bell pepper strips
1 cup sliced carrots
1 to 2 cloves garlic, minced
1 pound cooked turkey sausage
1 can (8 ounces) sliced water
    chestnuts, drained
½ cup teriyaki sauce
    Hot cooked rice

Heat oil in wok or large skillet over medium-high heat. Add broccoli, pepper and carrots; stir-fry 2 to 3 minutes. Add garlic; stir-fry 1 to 2 minutes. Add sausage, water chestnuts and teriyaki sauce. Increase heat to high; cook until sausage is heated through. Serve over rice.

Makes 4 to 6 servings

SWEET AND SOUR HAM

1 tablespoon butter or margarine
1½ pounds HILLSHIRE FARM® Ham,
    cut into ½-inch cubes
3 tomatoes, cut into sixths
1 green bell pepper, cut into
    chunks
1 onion, chopped
½ cup apricot preserves
1 tablespoon cornstarch
1 tablespoon vinegar
1 tablespoon soy sauce
½ teaspoon ground ginger
2 cups drained pineapple chunks
    Hot cooked rice

Melt butter in large skillet over medium-high heat. Sauté Ham, tomatoes, bell pepper and onion 5 minutes.

Combine preserves, cornstarch, vinegar, soy sauce and ginger in small bowl. Pour preserves mixture into skillet; stir to mix thoroughly. Cook over low heat until sauce thickens. Mix in pineapple; cook until pineapple is heated through. Serve over rice. *Makes 6 servings*

HINT: Be prepared for unexpected company—keep plenty of Hillshire Farm products in your freezer.

STIR-FRIED SAUSAGE AND VEGETABLES

SZECHUAN PORK & VEGETABLES

**4 butterflied pork loin chops,
½ inch thick (1 to 1¼ pounds)**
**¼ cup plus 1 tablespoon stir-fry
sauce, divided**
**¾ teaspoon bottled minced ginger
or ½ teaspoon ground ginger**
**1 package (16 ounces) frozen
Asian-style vegetables, thawed**
**1 can (5 ounces) crisp chow mein
noodles**
2 tablespoons chopped green onion

1. Heat large, deep nonstick skillet over medium heat until hot. Add pork. Spoon 1 tablespoon stir-fry sauce over pork; sprinkle with ginger. Cook 3 minutes. Turn pork; cook 3 minutes. Transfer chops to plate; set aside.

2. Add vegetables and remaining ¼ cup stir-fry sauce to skillet. Cook over medium-low heat 3 minutes; add pork. Cook 3 minutes or until pork is barely pink in center, stirring vegetables and turning chops once.

3. While pork is cooking, arrange chow mein noodles around edges of 4 serving plates. Transfer chops to plates. Top noodles with vegetable mixture. Sprinkle with green onion. *Makes 4 servings*

Prep and Cook Time: 12 minutes

Tip ■■■

Succulent pork chops make a great summertime meal. Place two 5- to 6-ounce pork chops in a microwavable glass dish and cover with plastic wrap. Heat at MEDIUM (50% power) about 3 minutes, turning chops over halfway through cooking time. Proceed with your favorite grilling recipe, reducing the grilling time to 5 to 10 minutes, or until no longer pink in center.

SZECHUAN PORK & VEGETABLES

VEGETABLE PORK STIR-FRY

¾ **pound pork tenderloin**
1 **tablespoon vegetable oil**
1½ **cups (about 6 ounces) sliced fresh mushrooms**
1 **large green pepper, cut into strips**
1 **zucchini, thinly sliced**
2 **ribs celery, cut into diagonal slices**
1 **cup thinly sliced carrots**
1 **clove garlic, minced**
1 **cup chicken broth**
2 **tablespoons reduced-sodium soy sauce**
1½ **tablespoons cornstarch**
3 **cups hot cooked rice**

Slice pork across the grain into ⅛-inch strips. Brown pork strips in oil in large skillet over medium-high heat. Push meat to side of skillet. Add mushrooms, pepper, zucchini, celery, carrots and garlic; stir-fry about 3 minutes. Combine broth, soy sauce and cornstarch. Add to skillet and cook, stirring, until thickened; cook 1 minute longer. Serve over rice.

Makes 6 servings

Favorite recipe from **USA Rice Federation**

ASIAN PORK & VEGETABLES

4 **cups cut-up fresh broccoli**
1 **pound boneless loin pork chops, cut into thin strips**
1 **teaspoon *each* minced garlic and ginger**
1 **onion, sliced**
4 **tablespoons *Frank's® RedHot® Original Cayenne Pepper Sauce,* divided**
½ **cup chicken broth or water**
2 **teaspoons cornstarch**
1 **teaspoon soy sauce**

1. Microwave broccoli with ¼ *cup water* on HIGH 3 to 5 minutes or until crisp-tender; drain. Toss pork with garlic and ginger.

2. Heat *1 tablespoon oil* in large nonstick skillet until hot. Add onion, broccoli and *1 tablespoon **Frank's RedHot*** Sauce. Stir-fry 2 minutes. Remove from skillet.

3. Heat *1 tablespoon oil* in same skillet; stir-fry pork 3 minutes or until browned. Combine remaining *3 tablespoons **Frank's RedHot*** Sauce, broth, cornstarch and soy sauce. Add to skillet with vegetables. Cook, stirring, until sauce is thickened. Serve with hot cooked rice or ramen noodles, if desired.

Makes 4 servings

Prep Time: 15 minutes
Cook Time: 10 minutes

VEGETABLE PORK STIR-FRY

HOT 'N SPICY PORK

Sauce

- ¼ cup water
- 3 tablespoons LA CHOY® Soy Sauce
- 2 tablespoons dry sherry
- 1 tablespoon cornstarch
- 1 teaspoon sugar
- ½ teaspoon crushed red pepper
- ¼ teaspoon sesame oil

Pork and Vegetables

- 1 tablespoon LA CHOY® Soy Sauce
- 1 tablespoon cornstarch
- 1 pound lean boneless pork, cut into thin 2-inch strips
- 4 tablespoons WESSON® Oil, divided
- 1½ tablespoons minced fresh garlic
- 1 tablespoon minced gingerroot
- 1 green bell pepper, cut into ½-inch pieces
- ½ cup diagonally sliced celery
- 1 can (8 ounces) LA CHOY® Sliced Water Chestnuts, drained
- 1 can (8 ounces) LA CHOY® Bamboo Shoots, drained
- ¼ cup sliced green onions
- 1 can (5 ounces) LA CHOY® Chow Mein Noodles

In small bowl, combine sauce ingredients; set aside. In medium bowl, combine soy sauce and cornstarch; mix well. Add pork; toss gently to coat. In large nonstick skillet or wok, heat 3 tablespoons Wesson Oil. Add half of pork mixture; stir-fry until pork is no longer pink in center. Remove pork from skillet; drain. Set aside. Repeat with remaining pork mixture. Heat remaining 1 tablespoon oil in same skillet. Add garlic and ginger; cook and stir 30 seconds. Add green pepper and celery; stir-fry 1 to 2 minutes or until crisp-tender. Stir sauce; add to skillet with water chestnuts and bamboo shoots. Cook, stirring constantly, until sauce is thick and bubbly. Return pork to skillet with green onions; heat thoroughly, stirring occasionally. Serve over noodles.

Makes 4 to 6 servings

Cornstarch is used as a thickener. It has about twice the thickening ability of flour. Unlike flour, cornstarch becomes clear when cooked. For this reason, it is often preferred for Asian stir-fry sauces. In order to avoid lumps, it should be mixed with a cold liquid until smooth before cooking or adding it to a hot liquid. (This mixture is sometimes called a "slurry".) If overcooked or stirred too long, sauces made with cornstarch will become thin.

HOT 'N SPICY PORK

PORK WITH THREE ONIONS

⅓ **cup teriyaki sauce**
2 **cloves garlic, minced**
1 **pound pork tenderloin**
2 **tablespoons peanut or vegetable oil, divided**
1 **small red onion, cut into thin wedges**
1 **small yellow onion, cut into thin wedges**
1 **teaspoon sugar**
1 **teaspoon cornstarch**
2 **green onions, cut into 1-inch pieces**
  Fried bean threads* (optional)

*To fry bean threads, follow package directions.

1. Combine teriyaki sauce and garlic in shallow bowl. Cut pork across the grain into ¼-inch slices; cut each slice in half. Toss pork with teriyaki mixture. Marinate at room temperature 10 minutes.

2. Heat large skillet over medium-high heat. Add 1 tablespoon oil; heat until hot. Drain pork; reserve marinade. Stir-fry pork 3 minutes or until no longer pink. Remove and reserve.

3. Heat remaining 1 tablespoon oil in skillet; add red and yellow onions. Reduce heat to medium. Cook 4 to 5 minutes until softened, stirring occasionally. Sprinkle with sugar; cook 1 minute more.

4. Blend reserved marinade into cornstarch in cup until smooth. Stir into skillet. Stir-fry 1 minute or until sauce boils and thickens.

5. Return pork along with any accumulated juices to skillet; heat through. Stir in green onions. Serve over bean threads, if desired.

Makes 4 servings

PORK WITH THREE ONIONS

PORK AND RED CHILI STIR-FRY

1 pound lean boneless pork loin,
  cut into thin slices
1 teaspoon vegetable oil
2 cloves garlic, minced
¾ pound fresh green beans, cut into
  2-inch lengths *or* 1 (10-ounce)
  package frozen cut green
  beans, thawed
2 teaspoons sugar
2 teaspoons soy sauce
2 small red chili peppers, thinly
  sliced *or* ½ teaspoon red
  pepper flakes
1 teaspoon shredded fresh ginger
  or ½ teaspoon ground ginger
1 teaspoon sesame oil
1 teaspoon rice vinegar

Heat vegetable oil in nonstick skillet. Add pork and garlic; cook and stir until lightly browned. Add green beans; stir-fry until beans and pork are tender, about 5 minutes. Push meat and beans to one side of skillet. Add sugar, soy sauce, chili peppers and ginger; stir to dissolve sugar. Add sesame oil and vinegar. Stir to coat meat and beans. Serve immediately with cooked rice or shredded lettuce.

Makes 4 servings

Prep Time: 15 minutes

Favorite recipe from **National Pork Board**

Mincing refers to the technique of chopping food into very tiny, irregular pieces. Minced food is smaller than chopped food. Flavorful seasonings, such as garlic and fresh herbs, are often minced to distribute their flavor more evenly throughout a dish.

PORK AND RED CHILI STIR-FRY

FUKIEN RED-COOKED PORK

2 pounds boneless pork shoulder butt
5¼ cups plus 3 tablespoons water, divided
⅓ cup rice wine or dry sherry
⅓ cup soy sauce
¼ cup lightly packed light brown sugar
1 piece fresh ginger (about 1½ inches), peeled and cut into strips
3 cloves garlic, chopped
1 teaspoon anise seeds
½ head napa cabbage (about 1 pound)
1 pound carrots, peeled
2 tablespoons cornstarch
1 teaspoon sesame oil

Trim off excess fat from pork; discard. Cut meat into 1½-inch chunks. Place 4 cups water in wok; bring to a boil over high heat. Add pork chunks; return to a boil. Boil pork 2 minutes. Drain in colander; return pork to wok. Add remaining 1¼ cups water, wine, soy sauce, brown sugar, ginger, garlic and anise. Cover; bring mixture to a boil. Reduce heat to low and simmer 1¼ hours or until meat is almost tender, stirring occasionally.

Meanwhile, remove core from cabbage; discard. Cut cabbage crosswise into 1-inch-thick slices. Diagonally slice carrots. Stir remaining 3 tablespoons water into cornstarch in cup until smooth. Set aside.

Add carrots to pork; cover and cook 20 minutes or until pork and carrots are fork-tender. Transfer pork and carrots to serving bowl.

Add cabbage to liquid in wok. Cover and increase heat to medium-high. Cook cabbage about 2 minutes or until wilted. Stir cornstarch mixture until smooth; add to cabbage. Cook until sauce boils and thickens. Return pork and carrots to wok; add oil and mix well. Spoon mixture into serving bowl.   *Makes 4 to 5 servings*

NOTE: Red cooking is a Chinese cooking method where one braises meat or poultry in soy sauce giving the meat a deep color.

MONGOLIAN HOT POT

2 ounces bean threads
½ pound boneless beef top sirloin
  or tenderloin steaks
1 can (46 ounces) chicken broth
½ pound pork tenderloin, cut into
  ⅛-inch slices
½ pound medium raw shrimp,
  peeled and deveined
½ pound sea scallops, cut
  lengthwise into halves
½ pound small fresh mushrooms
  Dipping Sauce (recipe follows)
1 pound spinach leaves

1. Place bean threads in medium bowl; cover with warm water. Soak 15 minutes to soften; drain well. Cut bean threads into 1- to 2-inch lengths; set aside.

2. Cut beef lengthwise in half, then crosswise into ⅛-inch slices.

3. Heat broth in electric skillet to a simmer (or, heat half of broth in fondue pot, keeping remaining broth hot for replacement).

4. Arrange beef, pork, shrimp, scallops and mushrooms on large platter.

5. Prepare Dipping Sauce.

6. To serve, select food from platter and cook it in simmering broth until desired doneness, using chop sticks or long-handled fork. Dip into dipping sauce before eating.

7. After all food is cooked, stir spinach into broth and heat until wilted. (Cook spinach in two batches if using fondue pot.) Place bean threads in individual soup bowls. Ladle broth mixture into bowls. Season with dipping sauce, if desired.   *Makes 4 to 6 servings*

DIPPING SAUCE: Combine ½ cup light soy sauce, ¼ cup dry sherry and 1 tablespoon dark sesame oil in small bowl; divide into individual dipping bowls.

STIR-FRIED HAM AND PEA PODS

⅓ cup orange juice
3 tablespoons HOUSE OF TSANG®
  Teriyaki Stir-Fry Sauce
2 teaspoons cornstarch
1 teaspoon hot pepper sauce
1 tablespoon vegetable oil
3½ cups (1¼ pounds) CURE 81®
  ham, cut into strips
½ pound fresh pea pods, trimmed
3 green onions, cut into 1-inch
  pieces
½ cup unsalted roasted peanuts
4 cups hot cooked rice

In small bowl, combine orange juice, stir-fry sauce, cornstarch and hot sauce. Heat oil in wok or large skillet over high heat. Add ham and stir-fry 2 minutes or until browned; remove from wok and set aside. Add pea pods and green onions; stir-fry 1 to 2 minutes or until crisp-tender. Add orange juice mixture and ham to wok; cook until sauce thickens, stirring constantly. Stir in peanuts. Serve over rice. *Makes 4 to 6 servings*

Tip ▪▪▪

Choose small, plump pea pods that are firm, shiny and bright green. The pods should appear well filled. Avoid pods that are yellow, shriveled, limp or dry.

STIR-FRIED HAM AND PEA PODS

JAVANESE PORK SATÉ

1 pound boneless pork loin
½ cup minced onion
2 tablespoons peanut butter
2 tablespoons lemon juice
2 tablespoons soy sauce
1 tablespoon brown sugar
1 tablespoon vegetable oil
1 clove garlic, minced
  Dash hot pepper sauce

Cut pork into ½-inch cubes; place in shallow dish. In blender or food processor combine remaining ingredients. Blend until smooth. Pour over pork. Cover and marinate in refrigerator 10 minutes. Thread pork onto skewers (if using bamboo skewers, soak in water 1 hour to prevent burning.)

Grill or broil 10 to 12 minutes, turning occasionally, until done. Serve with hot cooked rice, if desired. *Makes 4 servings*

Favorite recipe from **National Pork Board**

LEMON-ORANGE GLAZED RIBS

2 whole slabs baby back pork ribs, cut into halves (about 3 pounds)
2 tablespoons soy sauce
2 tablespoons orange juice
2 tablespoons fresh lemon juice
2 cloves garlic, minced
¼ cup orange marmalade
1 tablespoon hoisin sauce

1. Place ribs in large plastic bag. Combine soy sauce, juices and garlic in small bowl; pour over ribs. Close bag securely; turn to coat. Marinate in refrigerator at least 4 hours or up to 24 hours, turning once.

2. Preheat oven to 350°F. Drain ribs; reserve marinade. Place ribs on rack in foil-lined, shallow roasting pan. Brush half of marinade evenly over ribs; bake 20 minutes. Turn ribs over; brush with remaining marinade. Bake 20 minutes.

3. Remove ribs from oven; pour off drippings. Combine marmalade and hoisin sauce in cup; brush half of mixture over ribs. Return to oven; bake 10 minutes or until glazed. Turn ribs over; brush with remaining marmalade mixture. Bake 10 minutes more or until ribs are browned and glazed. *Makes 4 servings*

JAVANESE PORK SATÉ

SAUCY TOMATO-PORK SKILLET

1 cup uncooked instant white rice
2/3 cup reduced-sodium or regular tomato juice
2 tablespoons reduced-sodium or regular soy sauce
1 tablespoon cornstarch
1/4 teaspoon paprika
3 boneless pork chops, cut 3/4 inch thick (about 3/4 pound)
1/4 teaspoon garlic salt
1/8 teaspoon red pepper flakes
2 slices uncooked bacon, chopped
3 medium tomatoes, chopped
2 green onions with tops, sliced diagonally

1. Prepare rice according to package directions; set aside.

2. Combine tomato juice, soy sauce, cornstarch and paprika in small bowl, stirring until cornstarch dissolves. Set aside.

3. Slice pork across grain into 1/4-inch slices; place in medium bowl. Sprinkle pork with garlic salt and pepper flakes; mix well.

4. Cook bacon in medium skillet over medium-high heat. Remove bacon from skillet using slotted spoon; set aside. Add pork, tomatoes and green onions to skillet; stir-fry over medium-high heat 3 minutes or until pork is barely pink in center. Stir in tomato juice mixture; cook, stirring constantly, 1 minute or until sauce thickens slightly. Remove from heat; stir in bacon.

5. Serve pork mixture over rice. *Makes 4 servings*

Prep and Cook Time: 28 minutes

SAUCY TOMATO-PORK SKILLET

STIR-FRIED PORK LO MEIN

Nonstick cooking spray
6 green onions, cut into 1-inch pieces
½ teaspoon garlic powder
½ teaspoon ground ginger
6 ounces pork loin roast, thinly sliced
3 cups shredded green cabbage
½ cup shredded carrots
½ cup trimmed snow peas
½ cup reduced-sodium chicken broth
2 teaspoons cornstarch
2 tablespoons hoisin sauce (optional)
1 tablespoon reduced-sodium soy sauce
8 ounces hot cooked linguine

1. Spray wok with cooking spray. Heat over medium heat until hot. Add onions, garlic powder and ginger; stir-fry 30 seconds. Add pork; stir-fry 2 minutes or until pork is no longer pink. Add vegetables; stir-fry 3 minutes or until vegetables are crisp-tender.

2. Blend chicken broth, cornstarch, hoisin sauce, if desired and soy sauce in small bowl. Add to wok. Cook and stir until mixture boils and thickens. Serve vegetables and sauce over linguine. *Makes 4 servings*

Tip ...

Green cabbage is the most common variety of cabbage found in the United States. It is round with tightly packed leaves ranging from light to dark green in color. It has a delicate flavor. Green cabbage can be used interchangeably with Savoy cabbage, which has a milder flavor and a less crisp, more tender texture.

STIR-FRIED PORK LO MEIN

Outstanding Beef

QUICK 'N' TANGY BEEF STIR-FRY

Sauce
- ½ cup *French's®* Worcestershire Sauce
- ½ cup water
- 2 tablespoons sugar
- 2 teaspoons cornstarch
- ½ teaspoon ground ginger
- ½ teaspoon garlic powder

Stir-Fry
- 1 pound thinly sliced beef steak
- 3 cups sliced bell peppers

1. Combine ingredients for sauce. Marinate beef in ¼ *cup* sauce 5 minutes. Heat *1 tablespoon oil* in large skillet or wok over high heat. Stir-fry beef in batches 5 minutes or until browned.

2. Add peppers; cook 2 minutes. Add remaining sauce; stir-fry until sauce thickens. Serve over hot cooked rice or ramen noodles, if desired.

Makes 4 servings

Prep Time: 10 minutes
Cook Time: about 10 minutes

QUICK 'N' TANGY BEEF STIR-FRY

GREEN DRAGON STIR-FRY

2 tablespoons vegetable oil, divided
1 pound beef flank steak, very
   thinly sliced
1 bunch asparagus *or* 8 ounces
   green beans, cut into 2-inch
   pieces
1 green bell pepper, cut into strips
1 cup julienned carrots
3 large green onions, sliced
1 tablespoon minced fresh ginger
1 clove garlic, minced
¼ cup water
1 tablespoon soy sauce
1 tablespoon TABASCO® brand
   Green Pepper Sauce
½ teaspoon salt
2 cups hot cooked rice (optional)

Heat 1 tablespoon oil in 12-inch skillet over medium-high heat. Add flank steak; cook until well browned on all sides, stirring frequently. Remove steak to plate with slotted spoon.

Heat remaining 1 tablespoon oil in skillet over medium heat. Add asparagus, green bell pepper, carrots, green onions, ginger and garlic; cook about 3 minutes, stirring frequently. Add water, soy sauce, TABASCO® Green Pepper Sauce, salt and steak; heat to boiling over high heat.

Reduce heat to low; simmer, uncovered, 3 minutes, stirring occasionally. Serve with rice, if desired.   *Makes 4 servings*

NOTE: Stir-fry is also delicious served over ramen or soba noodles.

BEEF FRIED RICE

¾ pound 90% lean ground beef
6 green onions, chopped
3 large ribs celery, chopped
8 ounces bean sprouts
½ cup sliced fresh mushrooms
½ cup finely chopped red bell
   pepper
1 teaspoon grated fresh ginger
3 cups cooked rice
2 tablespoons soy sauce
   Salt and black pepper

Brown beef in large skillet, stirring to separate meat. Drain. Stir in onions, celery, bean sprouts, mushrooms, bell pepper and ginger. Cook over medium-high heat 5 minutes or until vegetables are crisp-tender, stirring frequently. Stir in rice and soy sauce. Season with salt and black pepper to taste. Heat through, stirring occasionally.   *Makes 4 servings*

GREEN DRAGON STIR-FRY

SLOW-COOKED KOREAN BEEF SHORT RIBS

4 to 4½ pounds beef short ribs
¼ cup chopped green onions with
    tops
¼ cup tamari or soy sauce
¼ cup beef broth or water
1 tablespoon brown sugar
2 teaspoons minced fresh ginger
2 teaspoons minced garlic
½ teaspoon black pepper
2 teaspoons Asian sesame oil
    Hot cooked rice or linguini pasta
2 teaspoons sesame seeds, toasted

Slow Cooker Directions

1. Place ribs in slow cooker. Combine green onions, tamari, broth, brown sugar, ginger, garlic and pepper in medium bowl; mix well and pour over ribs. Cover; cook on LOW 7 to 8 hours or until ribs are fork tender.

2. Remove ribs from cooking liquid, cool slightly. Trim excess fat. Cut rib meat into bite-size pieces discarding bones and fat.

3. Let cooking liquid stand 5 minutes to allow fat to rise. Skim off fat.

4. Stir sesame oil into liquid. Return beef to slow cooker. Cover; cook on LOW 15 to 30 minutes or until mixture is hot.

5. Serve with rice or pasta; garnish with sesame seeds.

Makes 6 servings

VARIATION: Three pounds boneless short ribs may be substituted for beef short ribs.

Prep Time: 30 minutes
Cook Time: 7 to 8 hours

SLOW-COOKED KOREAN BEEF SHORT RIBS

ORIENTAL FLANK STEAK

¾ cup **WISH-BONE® Italian Dressing***
3 tablespoons soy sauce
3 tablespoons firmly packed brown sugar
½ teaspoon ground ginger (optional)
1 to 1½ pounds flank, top round or sirloin steak

Also terrific with Wish-Bone® Robusto Italian, Lite Italian or Red Wine Vinaigrette Dressing.

In small bowl, combine all ingredients except steak.

In large, shallow nonaluminum baking dish or plastic bag, pour ½ cup marinade over steak. Cover, or close bag, and marinate in refrigerator, turning occasionally, 3 to 24 hours. Refrigerate remaining marinade.

Remove steak from marinade, discarding marinade. Grill or broil steak, turning once and brushing frequently with reserved marinade, until steak is desired doneness. *Makes about 4 servings*

Prep Time: 5 minutes
Cook Time: 15 minutes
Marinate Time: 3 hours

DICED BEEF IN CHAR SIU SAUCE

9 ounces diced boneless beef steak
4 tablespoons **LEE KUM KEE® Char Siu Sauce, divided**
3 tablespoons vegetable oil, divided
½ teaspoon cornstarch
½ tablespoon **LEE KUM KEE® Minced Garlic**
6 Chinese dried mushrooms, soaked and diced
2 ounces diced red bell pepper
2 ounces diced green bell pepper

1. Marinate beef in 1 tablespoon Char Siu Sauce, 1 tablespoon oil and cornstarch 15 minutes.

2. Heat remaining 2 tablespoons oil in wok. Sauté garlic until fragrant. Add beef and stir-fry until cooked. Add mushrooms and bell peppers; stir-fry until crisp-tender.

3. Add remaining 3 tablespoons Char Siu Sauce and stir well.

Makes 4 servings

ORIENTAL FLANK STEAK

SZECHWAN BEEF LO MEIN

1 boneless beef top sirloin steak (about 1 pound)
4 cloves garlic, minced
2 teaspoons minced fresh ginger
¾ teaspoon red pepper flakes, divided
1 tablespoon vegetable oil
1 can (about 14 ounces) vegetable broth
1 cup water
2 tablespoons reduced-sodium soy sauce
1 package (8 ounces) frozen mixed vegetables for stir-fry
1 package (9 ounces) refrigerated angel hair pasta
¼ cup chopped fresh cilantro (optional)

1. Cut steak lengthwise in half, then crosswise into thin slices. Toss steak with garlic, ginger and ½ teaspoon red pepper flakes.

2. Heat oil in large nonstick skillet over medium-high heat. Add half of beef to skillet; stir-fry 2 minutes or until meat is barely pink in center. Remove from skillet; set aside. Repeat with remaining beef.

3. Add vegetable broth, water, soy sauce and remaining ¼ teaspoon red pepper flakes to skillet; bring to a boil over high heat. Add vegetables; return to a boil. Reduce heat to low; simmer, covered, 3 minutes or until vegetables are crisp-tender.

4. Uncover; stir in pasta. Return to a boil over high heat. Reduce heat to medium; simmer, uncovered, 2 minutes, separating pasta with two forks. Return steak and any accumulated juices to skillet; simmer 1 minute or until pasta is tender and steak is hot. Sprinkle with cilantro, if desired.

Makes 4 servings

BROCCOLI BEEF

2 tablespoons vegetable oil
1 teaspoon chopped shallots
10 ounces sliced boneless beef
6 tablespoons LEE KUM KEE® Stir-Fry Sauce, LEE KUM KEE® Spicy Stir-Fry Sauce or LEE KUM KEE® Stir-Fry Sauce Kung Pao, divided
1 cup cooked broccoli florets

Heat skillet over medium heat. Add oil. Sauté shallots. Add beef and 2 tablespoons Stir-Fry Sauce; stir-fry. When beef is half done, add broccoli and remaining 4 tablespoons Stir-Fry Sauce. Cook and stir until beef is done and broccoli is tender and heated through.

Makes 4 servings

SZECHWAN BEEF LO MEIN

TERIYAKI GLAZED BEEF KABOBS

1¼ to 1½ pounds beef top or bottom
   sirloin, cut into 1-inch cubes
½ cup bottled teriyaki sauce
1 teaspoon Oriental sesame oil
   (optional)
1 clove garlic, minced
8 to 12 green onions
1 or 2 plum tomatoes, cut into
   slices (optional)

Thread beef cubes onto metal or bamboo skewers. (Soak bamboo skewers in water for at least 20 minutes to keep them from burning.) Combine teriyaki sauce, sesame oil, if desired, and garlic in small bowl. Brush beef and onions with part of glaze, saving some for grilling; let beef stand 15 to 30 minutes.

Oil hot grid to help prevent sticking. Grill beef, on covered grill, over medium KINGSFORD® Briquets, 6 to 9 minutes for medium doneness, turning several times and brushing with glaze. Add onions and tomatoes, if desired, to grid 3 to 4 minutes after beef; grill until onions and tomatoes are tender. Remove from grill; brush skewers, onions and tomatoes with remaining glaze. *Makes 4 servings*

ORIENTAL BEEF WITH VEGETABLES

1 pound 90% lean ground beef or
   ground turkey
1 large onion, coarsely chopped
2 cloves garlic, minced
2½ cups (8 ounces) frozen mixed
   vegetable medley, such as
   carrots, broccoli and red
   peppers, thawed
½ cup stir-fry sauce
1 can (3 ounces) chow mein
   noodles

1. Cook beef and onion in wok or large skillet over medium heat until beef is no longer pink, stirring to separate meat. Drain.

2. Add garlic; stir-fry 1 minute. Add vegetables; stir-fry 2 minutes or until heated through.

3. Add stir-fry sauce; stir-fry 30 seconds or until hot. Serve over chow mein noodles. *Makes 4 servings*

TERIYAKI GLAZED BEEF KABOBS

SWEET AND SOUR BEEF

1 pound 90% lean ground beef
1 small onion, thinly sliced
2 teaspoons minced fresh ginger
1 package (16 ounces) frozen
    mixed vegetable medley, such
    as snap peas, carrots, water
    chestnuts, pineapple and red
    pepper)
6 to 8 tablespoons bottled sweet
    and sour sauce or sauce from
    vegetable mix
Cooked rice

1. Place meat, onion and ginger in large skillet; cook over high heat 6 to 8 minutes or until no longer pink, stirring to separate meat. Drain.

2. Stir in frozen vegetables and sauce. Cook, covered, 6 to 8 minutes, stirring every 2 minutes or until vegetables are heated through. Serve over rice. *Makes 4 servings*

SERVING SUGGESTION: Serve with sliced Asian pears.

Prep and Cook Time: 15 minutes

STIR-FRIED BEEF & SPINACH

Nonstick cooking spray
5 ounces fresh spinach leaves, torn
Dash salt
8 ounces boneless beef top sirloin
    steak, thinly sliced
¼ cup stir-fry sauce
1 teaspoon sugar
½ teaspoon curry powder
¼ teaspoon ground ginger

1. Coat large skillet or wok with cooking spray. Heat over high heat until hot. Add spinach; stir-fry 1 minute or until limp.

2. Remove skillet from heat; transfer spinach to serving platter, sprinkle with salt and cover to keep warm.

3. Wipe out skillet with paper towel. Coat skillet with cooking spray. Heat over high heat until hot. Add beef; stir-fry 2 minutes or until barely pink. Add sauce, sugar, curry powder and ginger; cook and stir 1½ minutes or until sauce thickens.

4. Spoon beef mixture over spinach. *Makes 2 servings*

SWEET AND SOUR BEEF

KOREAN BROILED BEEF (BULGOGI)

¼ cup soy sauce
2 tablespoons Sesame Salt
2 tablespoons rice wine, beef broth
    or water
1 tablespoon sugar
1 tablespoon sesame oil
¼ teaspoon black pepper
3 green onions, thinly sliced
2 cloves garlic, minced
1 boneless beef top sirloin steak
    (about 1½ pounds), cut into
    ⅛-inch-thick slices
  Leaf lettuce
  Cooked rice, roasted garlic,
    kimchee or Korean hot bean
    paste (optional)
  Carrot ribbon and additional
    green onion slices for garnish

½ cup sesame seeds
¼ teaspoon salt

1. Combine soy sauce, Sesame Salt, rice wine, sugar, sesame oil and pepper in large bowl. Add green onions, garlic and beef; toss to coat. Cover and refrigerate at least 30 minutes.

2. Preheat broiler. Spray broiler rack with nonstick cooking spray. Place strips of beef on broiler rack. Broil 4 inches from heat source 2 minutes; turn beef and broil 1 minute for medium or until desired doneness. (Beef can also be cooked to desired doneness on small hibachi.)

3. Line platter with leaf lettuce; arrange beef on top. Serve as is or use lettuce leaves to wrap beef with choice of accompaniments and eat burrito-style. Garnish, if desired.

Makes 4 servings

SESAME SALT

To toast sesame seeds, heat small skillet over medium heat. Add sesame seeds; cook and stir about 5 minutes or until seeds are golden. Cool. Crush sesame seeds and salt with mortar and pestle or process in clean coffee or spice grinder. Refrigerate in covered glass jar.

KOREAN BROILED BEEF (BULGOGI)

JAPANESE-STYLE STEAK WITH GARDEN SUNOMONO

Garden Sunomono
1 medium cucumber, peeled, seeded and thinly sliced
½ teaspoon salt
¼ cup rice wine vinegar
3 tablespoons sugar
1 cup thinly sliced radishes
½ cup carrot cut into matchsticks

Japanese-Style Steak
3 New York strip steaks, ¾ inch thick (8 ounces each)
¼ cup soy sauce
3 tablespoons dry sherry
1 teaspoon dark sesame oil
½ teaspoon ground ginger
1 large clove garlic, minced

1. For sunomono, place cucumber in colander; sprinkle with salt. Let stand 20 minutes. Squeeze out liquid; rinse with water and squeeze again.

2. Blend vinegar and sugar in medium bowl, stirring until sugar dissolves. Add cucumber, radishes and carrot. Cover; refrigerate 30 minutes to 2 hours, stirring occasionally.

3. Place steaks in shallow baking dish. Blend soy sauce, sherry, sesame oil, ginger and garlic in small bowl; pour over steaks. Cover; refrigerate 30 minutes to 2 hours, turning steaks occasionally.

4. Preheat broiler. Remove steaks from marinade; place on broiler pan rack. Discard marinade. Broil 2 to 3 inches from heat 5 to 6 minutes per side or until desired doneness.

5. Transfer steaks to cutting board; slice across grain into ½-inch slices. Serve with sunomono.

Makes 4 servings

JAPANESE-STYLE STEAK WITH GARDEN SUNOMONO

FIVE-SPICE BEEF
STIR-FRY

1 boneless beef top sirloin steak
   (about 1 pound)
2 tablespoons plus 1½ teaspoons
   cornstarch, divided
2 tablespoons light soy sauce
3 tablespoons walnut or vegetable
   oil, divided
4 medium carrots, cut into
   matchstick-size pieces (about
   2 cups)
1 red bell pepper, cut into chunks
1 yellow bell pepper, cut into
   chunks
1 cup chopped onion
¼ to ½ teaspoon red pepper flakes
1½ cups water
1 tablespoon plus 1½ teaspoons
   packed dark brown sugar
2 teaspoons beef bouillon granules
1 teaspoon Chinese five-spice
   powder
3 cups hot cooked rice
½ cup honey-roasted peanuts

1. Cut steak lengthwise in half, then crosswise into thin strips. Place beef in shallow glass baking dish. Combine 2 tablespoons cornstarch and soy sauce in small bowl. Pour soy sauce mixture over beef; toss to coat thoroughly. Set aside.

2. Meanwhile, heat 1 tablespoon oil 1 minute in large nonstick skillet or wok over high heat until hot. Add carrots. Stir-fry 3 to 4 minutes or until edges begin to brown. Remove carrots and set aside.

3. Reduce heat to medium-high. Add 1 tablespoon oil, bell peppers, onion and red pepper flakes; stir-fry 4 minutes or until onions are translucent. Remove vegetables and set aside separately from carrots.

4. Add remaining 1 tablespoon oil to skillet. Add half of beef; stir-fry 2 minutes until beef is barely pink in center. Remove beef to large bowl. Repeat with remaining beef.

5. Meanwhile, in small bowl, combine water, brown sugar, bouillon granules, five-spice powder and remaining 1½ teaspoons cornstarch; stir until smooth.

6. Add bouillon mixture, bell peppers and onions; bring to a boil. Cook and stir 2 to 3 minutes or until slightly thickened.

7. Toss rice with carrots; place on serving platter. Spoon beef mixture over rice and sprinkle peanuts over beef mixture. *Makes 4 servings*

FIVE-SPICE BEEF STIR-FRY

MALAYSIAN CURRIED BEEF

2 tablespoons vegetable oil
2 large yellow onions, chopped
1 piece fresh ginger (about 1-inch square), minced
2 tablespoons curry powder
2 cloves garlic, minced
1 teaspoon salt
2 large baking potatoes (1 pound), peeled and cut into chunks
1 cup beef broth
1 pound ground beef chuck
2 ripe tomatoes (12 ounces), peeled and cut into chunks
Hot cooked rice

1. Heat wok over medium-high heat 1 minute or until hot. Drizzle oil into wok and heat 30 seconds. Add onions and stir-fry 2 minutes. Add ginger, curry, garlic and salt to wok. Cook and stir about 1 minute or until fragrant. Add potatoes; cook and stir 2 to 3 minutes.

2. Add beef broth to potato mixture. Cover and bring to a boil. Reduce heat to low; simmer about 20 minutes or until potatoes are fork-tender.

3. Stir ground beef into potato mixture. Cook and stir about 5 minutes or until beef is browned and no pink remains; spoon off fat, if necessary.

4. Add tomato chunks; stir gently until thoroughly heated. Spoon beef mixture into serving dish. Top with rice. Garnish, if desired.

Makes 4 servings

TERIYAKI STEAK WITH ONIONS & MUSHROOMS

1 boneless sirloin steak, about 1 inch thick (1½ pounds)
¾ cup light teriyaki sauce, divided
1 tablespoon vegetable oil
1 can (8 ounces) sliced mushrooms, drained
1 small red or green bell pepper, cut into strips
1⅓ cups *French's*® French Fried Onions, divided

1. Brush each side of steak with 1 tablespoon teriyaki sauce. Heat oil in grill pan or heavy skillet over medium-high heat. Cook steak for 3 to 4 minutes per side or until desired doneness. Remove steak; keep warm.

2. Add mushrooms and bell pepper to pan; cook until pepper is crisp-tender. Stir in remaining teriyaki sauce and ⅔ *cup* French Fried Onions; heat through.

3. Serve mushroom mixture over steak. Sprinkle with remaining onions.

Makes 6 servings

Prep Time: 5 minutes
Cook Time: 15 minutes

MALAYSIAN CURRIED BEEF

APRICOT BEEF WITH SESAME NOODLES

1 beef top sirloin steak (about 1 pound)
3 tablespoons Dijon mustard
3 tablespoons soy sauce
2 packages (3 ounces each) uncooked ramen noodles
2 tablespoons vegetable oil
2 cups (6 ounces) snow peas
1 medium red bell pepper, cut into cubes
¾ cup apricot preserves
½ cup beef broth
3 tablespoons chopped green onions
2 tablespoons toasted sesame seeds,* divided

*Toast sesame seeds in a dry, heavy skillet over medium heat 2 minutes or until golden, stirring frequently.

1. Cut beef lengthwise in half, then crosswise into ¼-inch strips. Combine beef, mustard and soy sauce in medium resealable plastic food storage bag. Seal bag. Shake to evenly distribute marinade; refrigerate 4 hours or overnight.

2. Cook noodles according to package directions, omitting seasoning packets.

3. Heat oil in large skillet over medium-high heat until hot. Add half of beef with marinade; stir-fry 2 minutes. Remove to bowl. Repeat with remaining beef and marinade. Return beef to wok. Add snow peas and bell pepper; stir-fry 2 minutes. Add noodles, preserves, broth, onions and 1 tablespoon sesame seeds. Cook 1 minute or until heated through. Top with remaining sesame seeds before serving. *Makes 4 to 6 servings*

Tip ■ ■ ■

Today's beef is leaner than it used to be, with over 40% of beef cuts having no external fat at all. "Loin" or "round" in the name, such as sirloin, tenderloin or top round, are the leanest cuts of beef you will find.

APRICOT BEEF WITH SESAME NOODLES

BEEF WITH CASHEWS

1 beef top sirloin steak (about 1 pound)
4 tablespoons vegetable oil, divided
4 teaspoons cornstarch
½ cup water
4 teaspoons soy sauce
1 teaspoon dark sesame oil
1 teaspoon oyster sauce
1 teaspoon Chinese chili sauce
8 green onions with tops, cut into 1-inch pieces
1 piece fresh ginger (about 1-inch square), peeled and minced
2 cloves garlic, minced
⅔ cup unsalted roasted cashews (about 3 ounces)
Fresh carrot slices and thyme leaves for garnish

1. Cut beef lengthwise in half, then crosswise into ⅛-inch slices.

2. Heat 1 tablespoon vegetable oil in wok or large skillet over high heat. Add half of meat; stir-fry 3 to 5 minutes until browned. Remove from wok; set aside. Repeat with 1 tablespoon oil and remaining meat.

3. Combine cornstarch, water, soy sauce, sesame oil, oyster sauce and chili sauce in small bowl; mix well.

4. Heat remaining 2 tablespoons vegetable oil in wok or large skillet over high heat. Add green onions, ginger, garlic and cashews; stir-fry 1 minute. Stir cornstarch mixture; add to wok with meat. Cook and stir until sauce boils and thickens. Garnish, if desired.

Makes 4 servings

Tip ■ ■ ■

Cashews are the seeds of a tropical fruit called a cashew apple. The nut grows on the outside of the fruit at its base. This nut has a kidney-shaped shell which is highly toxic. The shell is removed commercially and the nut is cleaned before marketing. The nut itself is kidney-shaped with a sweet, buttery flavor and crunchy texture. Cashews are generally used for snacking and cooking, especially in Chinese stir-fries.

BEEF WITH CASHEWS

SATAY BEEF

1 pound beef tenderloin steaks
1 teaspoon cornstarch
5 tablespoons water, divided
3½ teaspoons soy sauce, divided
1 to 2 teaspoons dark sesame oil,
    or to taste
2 tablespoons vegetable oil
1 medium yellow onion, chopped
1 clove garlic, minced
1 tablespoon dry sherry
1 tablespoon satay sauce
1 teaspoon curry powder
½ teaspoon sugar
    Fresh chervil and carrot flowers*
    for garnish

*To make carrot garnish, cut carrot crosswise into thin slices; cut into desired shape with small decorative cutter or sharp knife.

1. Cut meat crosswise into thin slices; flatten each slice by pressing with fingers.

2. Combine cornstarch, 3 tablespoons water, 1½ teaspoons soy sauce and sesame oil; mix well. Add to meat in medium bowl; stir to coat well. Let stand 20 minutes.

3. Heat vegetable oil in wok or large skillet over high heat. Add ½ of meat, spreading out slices so they don't overlap.

4. Cook meat slices 2 to 3 minutes on each side or just until lightly browned. Remove from wok; set aside. Repeat with remaining meat slices.

5. Add onion and garlic to wok; stir-fry about 3 minutes or until tender.

6. Combine remaining 2 tablespoons water, 2 teaspoons soy sauce, sherry, satay sauce, curry powder and sugar in small cup. Add to wok; cook and stir until liquid boils. Return meat to wok; cook and stir until heated through. Garnish, if desired. *Makes 4 servings*

SATAY BEEF

ORIENTAL BEEF KABOBS

1 tablespoon olive oil
1 tablespoon seasoned rice vinegar
1 tablespoon soy sauce
4 purchased beef kabobs

1. Preheat broiler.

2. Whisk together oil, vinegar and soy sauce; brush on kabobs.

3. Arrange kabobs on broiler pan rack. Broil, 4 inches from heat source, 10 minutes or to desired doneness, turning after 5 minutes.

Makes 4 servings

SZECHWAN BEEF

1 pound ground beef
1 tablespoon vegetable oil
1 cup sliced carrots
1 cup frozen peas
⅓ cup water
3 tablespoons soy sauce
2 tablespoons cornstarch
¼ teaspoon ground ginger
1 jar (7 ounces) baby corn
1 medium onion, thinly sliced
  Sliced mushrooms and olives as
    desired
¼ cup shredded Cheddar cheese
1⅓ cups uncooked instant rice

1. In wok or large skillet, brown ground beef; remove from wok and set aside. Drain fat.

2. Add oil to wok or skillet and return to medium heat. Add carrots and peas and stir-fry about 3 minutes.

3. In small cup combine water and soy sauce with cornstarch and ginger. Add to vegetables in wok.

4. Return ground beef to wok along with baby corn, onion, mushrooms, olives and cheese. Cook over medium heat until all ingredients are heated through.

5. Prepare instant rice according to package directions. Serve beef and vegetables over rice.

Makes 4 to 5 servings

Favorite recipe from **North Dakota Beef Commission**

ORIENTAL BEEF KABOBS ON GREEN RICE (PAGE 116)

SHREDDED ORANGE BEEF

1 small beef flank steak (about
    1 pound)
2 tablespoons soy sauce, divided
3 teaspoons cornstarch, divided
1½ teaspoons dark sesame oil
1 egg white
1 tablespoon sugar
1 tablespoon dry sherry
1 tablespoon white vinegar
2 cups vegetable oil
4 medium carrots, cut into
    matchstick strips
2 tablespoons orange peel slivers
4 green onions with tops, cut into
    slivers
2 to 3 fresh red or green jalapeño
    peppers,* cut into strips
2 cloves garlic, minced
3 to 4 cups shredded lettuce
    (optional)

Jalapeño peppers can sting and irritate the skin; wear rubber gloves when handling peppers and do not touch eyes. Wash hands after handling.

1. Cut flank steak lengthwise in half, then crosswise into thin strips. Whisk together 1 tablespoon soy sauce, 1 teaspoon cornstarch, sesame oil and egg white in medium bowl. Add beef and toss to coat. Let beef marinate while preparing vegetables.

2. Combine sugar, sherry, vinegar, remaining 1 tablespoon soy sauce and 2 teaspoons cornstarch in small bowl; mix well. Set aside.

3. Heat vegetable oil in wok over medium-high heat until oil registers 375°F on deep-fry thermometer. Add carrots and fry about 3 minutes or until tender. Remove carrots with slotted spoon and place in large strainer set over medium bowl. Reheat oil and fry orange peel about 15 seconds or until fragrant. Remove to paper towels; drain.

4. To double-fry beef,** add beef to wok; fry about 1 minute or just until meat turns light in color. Remove beef to another strainer placed over large bowl. Reheat oil to 375°F. Place ⅓ of drained beef in oil; fry about 3 minutes or until browned. Transfer beef to strainer with carrots. Repeat with remaining beef in two batches, reheating oil to maintain temperature.

5. Pour off all oil from wok. Reheat wok over medium-high heat. Add onions, jalapeño peppers and garlic; stir-fry 30 seconds or until fragrant. Stir cornstarch mixture and add to wok. Cook and stir until sauce boils and thickens. Add beef, carrots and orange peel; stir-fry until thoroughly heated. Serve over lettuce on serving platter, if desired. Garnish, if desired. *Makes 4 main-dish servings*

***This technique helps keep the meat moist inside and crispy on the outside. The first frying "seals" in the juices while the second frying cooks the meat until crisp.*

SHREDDED ORANGE BEEF

KOREAN BEEF

1 beef flank steak (about 1 pound)
¼ cup reduced-sodium soy sauce
2 tablespoons sugar
1 tablespoon dark sesame oil
1 teaspoon ground ginger
¼ teaspoon red pepper flakes
¼ small head Napa cabbage
3 tablespoons vegetable oil
1 can (14½ ounces) beef broth
1 cup peeled baby carrots
2 cups frozen cauliflower florets,
    thawed
1 cup frozen green bean cuts,
    thawed
   Hot cooked rice noodles

1. Cut flank steak lengthwise in half, then crosswise into ¼-inch-thick slices. Combine soy sauce, sugar, sesame oil, ginger and pepper flakes in medium bowl. Add beef and toss to coat. Cut cabbage crosswise into 1-inch slices. Set aside.

2. Heat wok over high heat about 1 minute or until hot. Drizzle half of vegetable oil into wok and heat 30 seconds. Drain beef, reserving marinade. Add half of beef to wok; stir-fry until browned. Remove to large bowl. Repeat with remaining vegetable oil and beef.

3. Add reserved marinade and broth to wok. Cover; bring to a boil. Add carrots; cook, uncovered, 5 minutes or until crisp-tender. Stir in cabbage, cauliflower and beans; cook until tender. Return beef to wok; heat through. Serve over hot noodles in bowls. *Makes 4 servings*

Tip ■■■

Marinades add unique flavors to foods and help tenderize less-tender cuts of meat. Turn marinating foods occasionally to let the flavor infuse evenly. Heavy-duty plastic bags are great to hold foods as they marinate.

KOREAN BEEF

HOT GLAZED BEEF ON SAFFRON-ONION RICE

1½ **pounds boneless beef top sirloin steak, cut into thin strips**
½ **cup packed dark brown sugar**
½ **cup light soy sauce**
¼ **cup bourbon**
½ **teaspoon red pepper flakes**
1 **large package yellow Saffron rice**
2 **tablespoons vegetable oil, divided**
2 **cups chopped onions**
1 **cup chopped red bell pepper**
1 **can (8 ounces) sliced water chestnuts, drained**

1. Place beef in shallow glass baking dish.

2. Combine brown sugar, soy sauce, bourbon and pepper flakes in small bowl; whisk until sugar has dissolved completely. Pour over beef and marinate 15 minutes, stirring occasionally.

3. Cook rice according to package directions.

4. Meanwhile, add 1 tablespoon oil to large nonstick skillet or wok. Heat over medium-high heat 1 minute. Add onions; cook 15 minutes or until richly browned, stirring frequently. Remove from skillet and set aside.

5. Add remaining 1 tablespoon oil and bell pepper to skillet; stir-fry 3 minutes.

6. Toss cooked rice with bell pepper, water chestnuts and onions. Place on serving platter; keep warm.

7. Drain beef; reserve marinade. Increase heat to high, add half of beef. Stir-fry 4 minutes or just until all liquid has evaporated. Place beef on top of rice mixture and keep warm. Add remaining beef, repeat cooking procedure and place on serving platter.

8. Reduce heat to medium-high. Add reserved marinade, scraping bottom and side of skillet. Cook 4 minutes or until liquid is reduced to ⅓ cup. Drizzle cooked marinade over beef and serve immediately.

Makes 4 servings

HOT GLAZED BEEF ON SAFFRON-ONION RICE

STEAK STIR-FRY

1 beef top sirloin steak (about 1½ pounds)
1 package (8 ounces) dry rice stick noodles
¼ cup dry white wine
¼ cup soy sauce
1 tablespoon plus 1½ teaspoons cornstarch
1 tablespoon sugar
2 teaspoons finely chopped fresh ginger
2 tablespoons vegetable oil
2 teaspoons garlic, minced
2 cups sliced mushrooms
2 cups matchstick-size carrot strips
1 cup green bell pepper strips
½ cup sliced green onions
4 cups fresh spinach, trimmed, washed and drained

1. Cut beef lengthwise in half, then crosswise into ¼-inch strips. Set aside. Cook noodles according to package directions. Drain well. Set aside.

2. While noodles are cooking, combine wine, soy sauce, cornstarch, sugar and ginger in medium bowl; whisk to blend. Add beef strips; toss to coat well. Set aside.

3. Heat oil and garlic in large nonstick skillet or wok over high heat. Add mushrooms, carrots, bell peppers and green onions; stir-fry 4 minutes. Transfer vegetables to bowl. Cover and keep warm.

4. Add beef strips and marinade to wok; stir-fry 6 minutes. Return vegetables to wok; stir until blended.

5. Line serving platter with spinach leaves. Arrange noodles over spinach. Spoon beef mixture over noodles; serve immediately.

Makes 4 servings

NOTE: Stir-fry meat can be purchased presliced from the supermarket meat case.

Prep and Cook Time: 20 minutes

STEAK STIR-FRY

SESAME STEAK

Sauce
- ¼ cup LA CHOY® Soy Sauce
- ¼ cup BUTTERBALL® Chicken Broth
- 1½ tablespoons cornstarch
- 1 tablespoon dry sherry
- ¼ teaspoon Oriental sesame oil

Steak and Vegetables
- 2 tablespoons dry sherry
- 1 tablespoon LA CHOY® Soy Sauce
- 1 tablespoon cornstarch
- 1 pound round steak, sliced into thin 2-inch strips
- 4 tablespoons WESSON® Oil, divided
- 1 teaspoon *each:* minced fresh garlic and gingerroot
- 1 cup chopped red bell pepper
- 1 cup sliced fresh mushrooms
- 1 package (10 ounces) frozen French-cut green beans, thawed and drained
- 1 can (14 ounces) LA CHOY® Bean Sprouts, drained
- 1 can (8 ounces) LA CHOY® Sliced Water Chestnuts, drained
- ½ cup sliced green onions
- 2 tablespoons toasted sesame seeds

In small bowl, combine sauce ingredients; set aside. In medium bowl, combine sherry, soy sauce and cornstarch; mix well. Add steak; toss gently to coat. In large nonstick skillet or wok, heat 3 tablespoons oil. Add half of steak mixture; stir-fry until lightly browned. Remove steak from skillet; set aside. Repeat with remaining steak mixture. Heat remaining 1 tablespoon oil in same skillet. Add garlic and ginger; cook and stir 10 seconds. Add bell pepper; stir-fry 1 minute. Add mushrooms and green beans; stir-fry 1 minute. Stir sauce; add to skillet with bean sprouts and water chestnuts. Cook, stirring constantly, until sauce is thick and bubbly. Return steak to skillet; heat thoroughly, stirring occasionally. Sprinkle with green onions and sesame seeds. Garnish, if desired.

Makes 4 to 6 servings

Mincing or pressing garlic releases more of its essential oils, resulting in a stronger flavor than when garlic is sliced or whole. To add a mild garlic flavor to a dish, rub a crushed clove around the inside of a wooden salad bowl, skillet, baking dish or fondue pot.

SESAME STEAK

STIR-FRY TOMATO BEEF

1 cup uncooked long-grain white rice
1 pound flank steak
1 tablespoon cornstarch
1 tablespoon soy sauce
2 cloves garlic, minced
1 teaspoon minced gingerroot *or* **¼ teaspoon ground ginger**
1 tablespoon vegetable oil
1 can (14½ ounces) DEL MONTE® Stewed Tomatoes - Seasoned with Onions, Celery & Green Peppers

1. Cook rice according to package directions.

2. Meanwhile, cut meat in half lengthwise, then cut crosswise into thin slices.

3. Combine cornstarch, soy sauce, garlic and ginger in medium bowl. Add meat; toss to coat.

4. Heat oil in large skillet over high heat. Add meat; cook, stirring constantly, until browned. Add undrained tomatoes; cook until thickened, about 5 minutes, stirring frequently.

5. Serve meat mixture over hot cooked rice. Garnish, if desired.

Makes 4 to 6 servings

Prep Time: 10 minutes
Cook Time: 20 minutes

BLACK PEPPER BEEF SHORT RIBS

1 pound short ribs, cut into pieces
¾ cup plus 4 tablespoons LEE KUM KEE® Black Pepper Sauce, divided
Vegetable oil
1 ounce minced onion
1 ounce minced green bell pepper
1 ounce minced red bell pepper

Marinate short ribs in 4 tablespoons Black Pepper Sauce 10 minutes. Heat oil in wok. Pan-fry short ribs until cooked. Remove and drain. Sauté onion until fragrant. Add bell pepper and remaining ¾ cup Black Pepper Sauce. Bring to a boil and add short ribs. Stir well and serve.

Makes 4 to 6 servings

STIR-FRY TOMATO BEEF

BEEF WITH LEEKS AND TOFU

8 ounces boneless beef top sirloin, top loin strip or tenderloin steaks
2 cloves garlic, minced
8 ounces firm tofu, drained
¾ cup chicken broth
¼ cup soy sauce
1 tablespoon dry sherry
1 tablespoon cornstarch
4 teaspoons peanut or vegetable oil, divided
1 large *or* 2 medium leeks, sliced (white and light green portion)
1 large red bell pepper, cut into short, thin strips
1 tablespoon dark sesame oil (optional)
Hot cooked spaghetti (optional)

1. Cut beef lengthwise in half, then crosswise into ⅛-inch slices; cut each slice into 2-inch pieces. Toss beef with garlic in medium bowl. Press tofu lightly between paper towels; cut into ¾-inch triangles or squares.

2. Blend broth, soy sauce and sherry into cornstarch in small bowl until smooth.

3. Heat large, deep skillet over medium-high heat. Add 2 teaspoons peanut oil; heat until hot. Add half of beef mixture; stir-fry 2 minutes or until beef is barely pink in center. Remove to large bowl. Repeat with remaining beef. Remove and set aside.

4. Add remaining 2 teaspoons peanut oil to skillet. Add leek and bell pepper; stir-fry 3 minutes or until bell pepper is crisp-tender. Stir broth mixture; add to skillet with tofu. Stir-fry 2 minutes or until sauce boils and thickens and tofu is hot, stirring frequently.

5. Return beef along with any accumulated juices to skillet; heat through. Stir in sesame oil, if desired. Serve over spaghetti, if desired.

Makes 4 servings

BEEF WITH LEEKS AND TOFU

PEPPER BEEF

1 tablespoon soy sauce
2 cloves garlic, minced
¼ teaspoon red pepper flakes
1 pound boneless beef top sirloin steak, tenderloin or rib eye steaks
2 tablespoons peanut or vegetable oil, divided
1 small red bell pepper, cut into thin strips
1 small yellow or green bell pepper, cut into thin strips
1 small onion, cut into thin strips
¼ cup stir-fry sauce
2 tablespoons rice wine or dry white wine
¼ cup coarsely chopped fresh cilantro
  Hot cooked white rice or Chinese egg noodles (optional)

1. Combine soy sauce, garlic and pepper flakes in medium bowl. Cut beef lengthwise in half, then crosswise into thin slices. Toss beef with soy sauce mixture.

2. Heat wok or large skillet over medium-high heat. Add 1 tablespoon oil; heat until hot. Add half of beef mixture; stir-fry until beef is barely pink in center. Remove. Repeat with remaining beef mixture; remove and set aside.

3. Heat remaining 1 tablespoon oil in wok; add bell peppers and onion. Reduce heat to medium. Stir-fry 6 to 7 minutes until vegetables are crisp-tender. Add stir-fry sauce and wine; stir-fry 2 minutes or until heated through.

4. Return beef along with any accumulated juices to wok; heat through. Sprinkle with cilantro. Serve over rice, if desired. *Makes 4 servings*

PEPPER BEEF

STIR-FRIED BEEF AND VEGETABLES

⅔ cup beef broth or stock
2 tablespoons soy sauce
   Pinch of ground cinnamon
¼ teaspoon freshly ground black
   pepper
2 teaspoons cornstarch
2 tablespoons cold water
3 tablespoons CRISCO® Oil*
1 tablespoon chopped fresh ginger
2 teaspoons jarred minced garlic *or*
   1 large clove garlic, peeled and
   minced
1 pound lean beef, such as flank
   steak or boneless sirloin,
   trimmed and cut into ¼-inch-
   thick slices
1 carrot, peeled and thinly sliced
1 bunch scallions (or green onions),
   trimmed and cut into 1-inch
   pieces
¼ pound fresh snow peas, rinsed
   and stems removed

Use your favorite Crisco Oil product.

1. Combine broth, soy sauce, cinnamon and pepper in small bowl. Set aside. Combine cornstarch and water in small bowl. Stir to dissolve.

2. Heat oil in wok or large skillet on medium-high heat. Add ginger and garlic. Stir-fry 30 seconds. Add beef, carrot and scallions. Stir-fry 3 minutes or until beef is no longer red. Add broth mixture. Cook 2 minutes. Add snow peas. Cook 2 minutes, or until snow peas are bright green. Stir in cornstarch mixture. Cook 1 minute or until thickened. Serve immediately. *Makes 4 servings*

VARIATION: Other vegetables can be used in place of those specified. Broccoli flowerets or sliced celery can be used in place of the carrot. Cooking time will be the same. In place of scallions, 1 medium onion, peeled and sliced, can be substituted. Fresh or frozen green peas can be used in place of snow peas.

NOTE: If using canned broth, pour the remainder of the can into an ice cube tray and freeze. Once frozen, store the cubes in an air-tight plastic bag. That way you'll always have the few tablespoons of broth needed for many recipes.

Preparation Time: 25 minutes
Total Time: 35 minutes

MING DYNASTY BEEF STEW

2 pounds boneless beef chuck or veal shoulder, cut into 1½-inch pieces
1 teaspoon Chinese five-spice powder
½ teaspoon red pepper flakes
2 tablespoons peanut or vegetable oil, divided
1 large onion, coarsely chopped
2 cloves garlic, minced
1 cup beef broth
1 cup regular or light beer
2 tablespoons soy sauce
1 tablespoon cornstarch
Hot cooked Chinese Egg Noodles or Sesame Noodle Cake (recipes follow)

1. Sprinkle beef with five-spice powder and pepper flakes. Heat large saucepan or Dutch oven over medium-high heat. Add 1 tablespoon oil; heat until hot. Add half of beef; brown on all sides. Remove; set aside. Repeat with remaining oil and beef.

2. Add onion and garlic to saucepan; cook 3 minutes, stirring occasionally. Add broth and beer; bring to a boil. Reduce heat to medium-low. Return beef along with any accumulated juices to saucepan; cover and simmer 1 hour 15 minutes or until beef is fork tender.*

3. Blend soy sauce into cornstarch in cup until smooth. Stir into saucepan. Cook, uncovered, 2 minutes or until mixture thickens, stirring occasionally. Serve over noodles. Garnish as desired.   *Makes 6 to 8 servings*

*Stew may be oven-braised if saucepan or Dutch oven is ovenproof. Cover and bake in 350°F oven 1 hour 15 minutes or until beef is fork tender. Proceed as directed in step 3.

CHINESE EGG NOODLES

4 ounces Chinese egg or vermicelli noodles
1 tablespoon soy sauce

Cook noodles according to package directions; drain well. Place in large bowl. Toss with soy sauce until absorbed.   *Makes 4 servings*

SESAME NOODLE CAKE

1 tablespoon peanut or vegetable oil
½ teaspoon dark sesame oil

1. Prepare Chinese Egg Noodles. Heat large nonstick skillet over medium heat. Add peanut oil; heat until hot. Add noodle mixture; pat into an even layer with spatula.

2. Cook, uncovered, 6 minutes or until bottom is lightly browned. Invert onto plate, then slide back into skillet, browned side up. Cook 4 minutes or until bottom is well browned. Drizzle with sesame oil. Transfer to serving platter and cut into quarters.   *Makes 4 servings*

ORIENTAL STUFFED PEPPERS

½ **pound extra-lean ground beef**
2 **cups frozen Oriental vegetable combination**
1 **cup cooked white rice**
1 **jar (12 ounces) HEINZ® HomeStyle Brown Gravy**
2 **tablespoons low-sodium soy sauce**
½ **teaspoon ground ginger**
⅛ **teaspoon black pepper**
3 **medium green, red or yellow bell peppers, split lengthwise and seeded**

Brown beef in large skillet; drain, if necessary. Stir in vegetables and rice. Combine gravy, soy sauce, ginger and black pepper in small bowl; reserve ½ cup. Stir remaining gravy mixture into beef mixture. Place bell peppers in lightly greased 2-quart oblong baking dish. Fill bell peppers with beef mixture. Spoon reserved gravy mixture over bell peppers. Bake in 350°F oven 35 to 45 minutes or until hot. *Makes 6 servings*

TO MICROWAVE: Crumble beef into 2-quart microwave-safe casserole. Cover with lid or vented plastic wrap. Microwave at HIGH (100% power) 2½ to 3½ minutes or until meat is no longer pink, stirring once to break up meat. Drain. Stir in vegetables and rice. Combine gravy, soy sauce, ginger and black pepper in small bowl; reserve ½ cup. Stir remaining gravy mixture into beef mixture. Place bell peppers in 2-quart microwave-safe oblong baking dish. Fill bell peppers with beef mixture. Spoon reserved gravy mixture over bell peppers. Cover with vented plastic wrap. Microwave at HIGH 10 to 11 minutes or until bell peppers are tender-crisp and beef mixture is hot.

PAN-BROILED GARLIC STEAK

4 boneless beef top-loin steaks,
   ½ inch thick (about 6 ounces
   each)
¼ cup soy sauce
1 tablespoon plus 1½ teaspoons
   mirin* or sweet cooking rice
   wine
1 clove garlic, minced
¼ cup rice vinegar
1 tablespoon plus 1½ teaspoons
   sugar
6 ounces daikon, peeled and cut
   into matchstick strips
1 carrot, peeled and cut into
   matchstick strips
1 piece (1 inch) fresh ginger,
   peeled and cut into thin strips
1 tablespoon vegetable oil
¼ cup thinly sliced green onions
   (green part only)

*Mirin is a Japanese sweet wine available in
Japanese markets and the Asian section of large
supermarkets.*

1. Make several short, shallow cuts, against the grain, on each steak. Place steaks in large shallow glass dish. Combine soy sauce, mirin and garlic in small bowl; mix well. Pour soy sauce mixture over steaks; let steaks stand 20 minutes, turning occasionally. Drain.

2. Combine rice vinegar and sugar in small bowl; stir until sugar dissolves. Add daikon, carrot and ginger; let stand 5 minutes. Drain; squeeze lightly to remove excess moisture. Set aside.

3. Heat vegetable oil in large skillet over medium-high heat. Add steaks; cook about 3 minutes or until brown. Turn steaks; cook 3 to 5 minutes or until steaks are cooked to desired doneness.

4. Place steaks on individual serving plates; sprinkle each serving with 1 tablespoon green onion. Serve with daikon mixture.

Makes 4 servings

Tip ▪▪▪

Panbroiling is the technique used to cook meat or fish on the range top with little or no added fat. It is best suited for thin steaks, chops and fish fillets.

Seafood Treasures

TERIYAKI SALMON WITH ASIAN SLAW

4 tablespoons light teriyaki sauce, divided

2 (5 to 6 ounces each) boneless salmon fillets with skin (1 inch thick)

2½ cups packaged coleslaw mix

1 cup fresh or frozen snow peas, cut lengthwise into thin strips

½ cup thinly sliced radishes

2 tablespoons orange marmalade

1 teaspoon dark sesame oil

1. Preheat broiler or prepare grill for direct grilling. Spoon 2 tablespoons teriyaki sauce over meaty sides of salmon. Let stand while preparing vegetable mixture.

2. Combine coleslaw mix, snow peas and radishes in large bowl. Combine remaining 2 tablespoons teriyaki sauce, marmalade and sesame oil in small bowl. Add to cabbage mixture; toss well.

3. Broil salmon 4 to 5 inches from heat source or grill, flesh side down, over medium coals without turning 6 to 10 minutes until center is opaque.

4. Transfer coleslaw mixture to serving plates; top with salmon.

Makes 2 servings

TERIYAKI SALMON WITH ASIAN SLAW

ASIAN HONEY-TEA GRILLED PRAWNS

1½ pounds medium shrimp, peeled
    and deveined
Salt
2 green onions, thinly sliced

Marinade
1 cup brewed double-strength
    orange-spice tea, cooled
¼ cup honey
¼ cup rice vinegar
¼ cup soy sauce
1 tablespoon fresh ginger, peeled
    and finely chopped
½ teaspoon ground black pepper

In plastic bag, combine marinade ingredients. Remove ½ cup marinade; set aside for dipping sauce. Add shrimp to marinade in bag, turning to coat. Close bag securely and marinate in refrigerator 30 minutes or up to 12 hours.

Remove shrimp from marinade; discard marinade. Thread shrimp onto 8 skewers, dividing evenly. Grill over medium coals 4 to 6 minutes or until shrimp turn pink and are just firm to the touch, turning once. Season with salt, as desired.

Meanwhile prepare dipping sauce by placing reserved ½ cup marinade in small saucepan. Bring to a boil over medium-high heat. Boil 3 to 5 minutes or until slightly reduced. Stir in green onions.

Makes 4 servings

Favorite recipe from **National Honey Board**

ORIENTAL ROLL-UPS

1 package (9 ounces) uncooked
    BARILLA® lasagna
12 large shrimp, peeled, deveined,
    cooked and halved lengthwise
1 bunch watercress
¼ cup sliced baby carrots
1 avocado, peeled and sliced
Cilantro, for garnish
Soy sauce and/or peanut sauce
    for dipping

Bring large pot of water to boil. Add lasagna noodles; boil 8 to 9 minutes. Remove lasagna noodles to platter to cool.

To prepare roll-ups, place lasagna noodles on flat surface. Divide shrimp, watercress, carrots and avocado among lasagna noodles. Roll up each lasagna noodle, being careful to keep ingredients wrapped inside. Garnish with cilantro, if desired. Serve chilled or at room temperature with dipping sauce.

Makes 4 to 6 servings

ASIAN HONEY-TEA GRILLED PRAWNS

STIR-FRIED CATFISH WITH CUCUMBER RICE

1 seedless cucumber
1¼ cups water
½ cup uncooked rice
4 green onions, thinly sliced
½ teaspoon white pepper
2 teaspoons canola oil
1 pound catfish fillets, cut into
    1-inch chunks
1 teaspoon minced ginger
1 clove garlic, minced
¼ teaspoon dark sesame oil
2 packages (6 ounces each) snow
    peas
1 red bell pepper, seeded and diced
¼ cup white wine or water
1 tablespoon cornstarch

1. On medium side of grater, grate cucumber into colander set over bowl to drain.

2. Combine water, rice, cucumber, green onions and white pepper in medium saucepan. Bring to a boil over medium heat. Cover; reduce heat to low. Cook about 20 minutes or until rice is tender and liquid is absorbed.

3. Heat oil in 12-inch nonstick skillet over high heat. Add catfish, ginger, garlic and sesame oil. Stir-fry 4 to 5 minutes or until catfish is just cooked. Add snow peas and bell pepper. Cover and cook 4 minutes.

4. Combine wine and cornstarch in small bowl; stir. Pour mixture over catfish mixture; cook and stir about 2 minutes until sauce thickens. Serve over rice.

Makes 4 servings

SERVING SUGGESTION: Serve with Egg Drop Soup made by stirring beaten egg into simmering fat-free, low-sodium chicken broth seasoned with your favorite fresh chopped herbs, such as cilantro. Complete the meal with chilled fresh seasonal fruit cups or a scoop of lemon sorbet.

STIR-FRIED CATFISH WITH CUCUMBER RICE

RAINBOW STIR-FRIED FISH

Sauce
- ½ cup chicken broth
- 2 tablespoons LA CHOY® Soy Sauce
- 1 tablespoon cornstarch
- 1 teaspoon sugar
- ¼ teaspoon crushed red pepper (optional)

Fish and Vegetables
- 1 pound orange roughy filets,* cut into 1-inch chunks
- 1 tablespoon LA CHOY® Soy Sauce
- 3 tablespoons WESSON® Oil
- ½ cup julienne-cut carrots
- 1 teaspoon minced garlic
- 1 teaspoon minced fresh gingerroot
- 2 cups fresh broccoli flowerettes
- 1 can (8 ounces) LA CHOY® Sliced Water Chestnuts, drained
- 1 package (6 ounces) frozen pea pods, thawed and drained
- ½ cup diagonally sliced green onions

*Any firm-fleshed white fish can be substituted.

In small bowl, combine sauce ingredients; set aside. In medium bowl, combine fish and soy sauce; toss lightly to coat. In large nonstick skillet or wok, heat oil. Add fish mixture; stir-fry 2 to 3 minutes or until fish flakes easily with fork. Remove fish from skillet; drain. Set aside. Add carrots, garlic and ginger to same skillet; stir-fry 30 seconds. Add broccoli; stir-fry 1 minute. Add water chestnuts and pea pods; heat thoroughly, stirring occasionally. Return fish to skillet. Stir sauce; add to skillet. Heat, stirring gently, until sauce is thick and bubbly. Sprinkle with green onions. Garnish, if desired.

Makes 4 servings

Tip ...

Fresh fish filets and steaks should have moist flesh that is free from discoloration and skin that is shiny and resilient. If the filet or steak has a strong odor, it is not fresh.

RAINBOW STIR-FRIED FISH

TERIYAKI SCALLOPS

2 tablespoons soy sauce
1 tablespoon mirin* or sweet
    cooking rice wine
2 teaspoons sake or dry sherry
1 teaspoon sugar
1 pound large scallops
¼ teaspoon salt
8 ounces asparagus, diagonally
    sliced into 2-inch lengths
1 tablespoon vegetable oil

*Mirin is a Japanese sweet wine available in Japanese markets and the ethnic section of large supermarkets.

1. Combine soy sauce, mirin, sake and sugar in medium bowl; stir until sugar is dissolved. Add scallops; let stand 10 minutes, turning occasionally.

2. Meanwhile, bring 2½ cups water and salt to a boil in medium saucepan over high heat. Add asparagus; reduce heat to medium-high. Cook 3 to 5 minutes or until crisp-tender. Drain asparagus; keep warm.

3. Drain scallops, reserving marinade.

4. Preheat broiler. Line broiler pan with foil; brush broiler rack with vegetable oil. Place scallops on rack; brush lightly with marinade. Broil about 4 inches from heat source 4 to 5 minutes or until brown. Turn scallops with tongs; brush lightly with marinade. Broil 4 to 5 minutes or just until scallops are opaque in center. Serve immediately with asparagus. Garnish as desired. *Makes 4 servings*

BEIJING FILLET OF SOLE

2 tablespoons reduced-sodium soy
    sauce
2 teaspoons dark sesame oil
4 sole fillets (6 ounces each)
1¼ cups preshredded cabbage or
    coleslaw mix
½ cup crushed chow mein noodles
1 egg white, lightly beaten
2 teaspoons sesame seeds
1 package (10 ounces) frozen snow
    peas, cooked and drained

1. Preheat oven to 350°F. Combine soy sauce and oil in small bowl. Place sole in shallow dish. Lightly brush both sides of sole with soy mixture.

2. Combine cabbage, noodles, egg white and remaining soy mixture in small bowl. Spoon evenly over sole. Roll up each fillet and place, seam side down, in shallow foil-lined roasting pan.

3. Sprinkle rolls with sesame seeds. Bake 25 to 30 minutes or until fish flakes when tested with fork. Serve with snow peas. *Makes 4 servings*

TERIYAKI SCALLOPS

FISH ROLLS
WITH CRAB SAUCE

1 pound sole fillets, ¼ to ⅜ inch thick (about 4 ounces each)
1 tablespoon dry sherry
2 teaspoons dark sesame oil
1 green onion with top, finely chopped
1 teaspoon minced fresh ginger
½ teaspoon salt
  Dash white pepper

Crab Sauce
1½ tablespoons cornstarch
2 tablespoons water
1 tablespoon vegetable oil
1 teaspoon minced fresh ginger
6 ounces fresh crabmeat, flaked
2 green onions with tops, thinly sliced
1 tablespoon dry sherry
1¼ cups chicken broth
¼ cup milk
  Scored cucumber slices,* lemon wedges and fresh tarragon leaves for garnish

To score cucumber, run tines of fork lengthwise down all sides of cucumber before slicing.

1. If fillets are large, cut in half crosswise (each piece should be 5 to 6 inches long). Combine sherry, sesame oil, chopped green onion, 1 teaspoon ginger, salt and white pepper in small bowl. Brush each piece of fish with sherry mixture; let stand 30 minutes.

2. Fold fillets into thirds; place on rimmed heat-proof dish that will fit inside a steamer. Place dish on rack in steamer. Cover and steam 8 to 10 minutes, over boiling water until fish turns opaque and flakes easily with fork.

3. Meanwhile, prepare Crab Sauce. Blend cornstarch and water in small cup. Heat vegetable oil in medium saucepan over medium heat. Add 1 teaspoon ginger; cook and stir 10 seconds. Add crabmeat, green onions and sherry; stir-fry 1 minute. Add chicken broth and milk; bring to a boil. Stir cornstarch mixture; add to saucepan. Cook, stirring constantly, until sauce boils and thickens slightly.

4. Transfer fish to serving platter using slotted spoon; top with Crab Sauce. Garnish, if desired.

Makes 4 to 6 servings

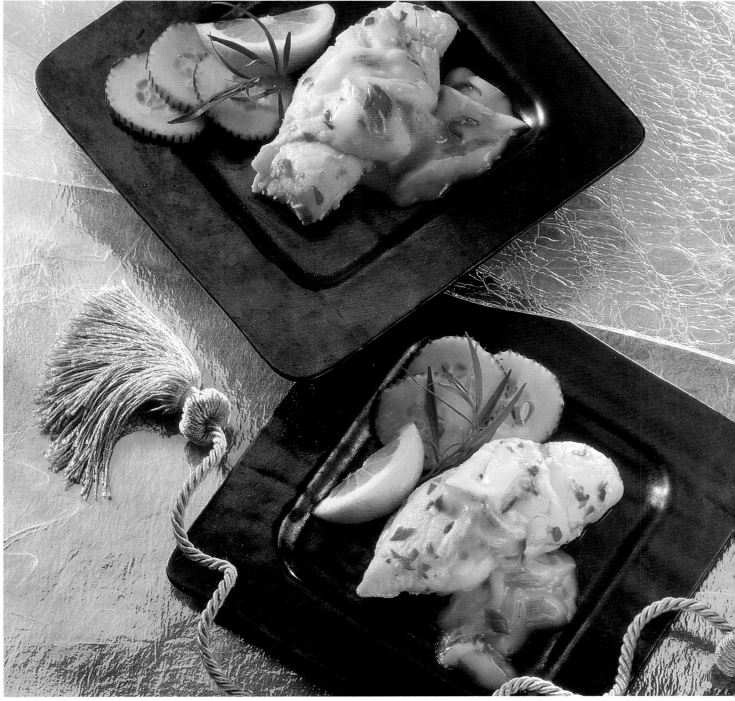

FISH ROLLS WITH CRAB SAUCE

STEAMED FISH
WITH BROCCOLI

2 (10- to 12-ounce) halibut steaks
    (1 inch thick), cut into halves*
3 tablespoons dry white wine
1 tablespoon rice vinegar or white
    vinegar
½ teaspoon salt, divided
⅛ teaspoon white pepper
1 tablespoon cornstarch
1 tablespoon oyster sauce
1 teaspoon sugar
1 teaspoon dark sesame oil
1 teaspoon soy sauce
3 cups broccoli florets
2 tablespoons vegetable oil, divided
2 teaspoons minced fresh ginger
1 clove garlic, minced
1 pound ripe tomatoes, cored and
    cut into ½-inch cubes, divided
Lemon wedges

*Or, substitute 4 catfish or mahi-mahi fillets
(about 7 ounces each), folded crosswise in half.

1. Rinse fish and drain on paper towels. Combine wine, vinegar, ¼ teaspoon salt and pepper in large glass bowl; mix well. Add fish; turn to coat. Let stand 30 minutes to marinate.

2. Meanwhile, combine cornstarch, oyster sauce, sugar, sesame oil and soy sauce in cup; mix well. Set aside.

3. Place broccoli in medium bowl. Add 1 tablespoon vegetable oil and sprinkle with remaining ¼ teaspoon salt; toss. Set aside.

4. To steam fish, place wire rack in wok. Add water to 1 inch below rack. (Water should not touch rack.) Cover wok; bring water to a boil over high heat. Drain fish and place on heat-proof plate. Arrange broccoli around fish. Place dish on rack. Cover and reduce heat to medium. Steam 8 to 10 minutes or until fish flakes easily when tested with fork. Carefully remove plate from wok; cover and keep warm.

5. Drain water from wok. Heat wok over high heat about 30 seconds or until dry and hot. Drizzle remaining 1 tablespoon vegetable oil into wok and heat 15 seconds. Add ginger and garlic; stir-fry 15 seconds. Add ½ of tomatoes. Stir-fry 1 minute; reduce heat to low. Cook 2 minutes or until tomatoes soften.

6. Stir cornstarch mixture; add to wok. Cook and stir until sauce boils and thickens. Stir in remaining tomatoes and cook until heated through.

7. Spoon some of tomato sauce over fish. Serve with remaining sauce and lemon wedges.
Makes 4 servings

STEAMED FISH WITH BROCCOLI

SWEET AND SOUR SHRIMP STIR-FRY

1 can (16 ounces) cling peach
    slices in syrup
½ cup stir-fry sauce
1 teaspoon arrowroot
2 tablespoons peanut oil
½ pound medium shrimp, peeled
    and deveined
2 cloves garlic, minced
4 ounces fresh snow peas, trimmed
1 cup cherry tomatoes, halved
¼ cup sliced green onions
⅔ cup large walnut pieces
    Hot cooked rice

Remove peaches from can, reserving ¼ cup syrup. Blend syrup, stir-fry sauce and arrowroot in small bowl; set aside.

Heat oil in wok or large skillet over medium heat. Add shrimp and garlic; stir-fry 1 to 2 minutes. Remove and set aside. Add snow peas; stir-fry 2 minutes. Remove and set aside. Add syrup mixture to wok; cook and stir until thickened. Add shrimp, snow peas, peaches, tomatoes and green onions. Stir-fry until shrimp become opaque and vegetables are heated through. Add walnuts. Serve over rice. *Makes 4 to 6 servings*

WASABI SALMON

2 tablespoons soy sauce
1½ teaspoons wasabi paste or
    powder, divided, plus more to
    taste
4 salmon fillets (6 ounces each),
    with skin
¼ cup mayonnaise

1. Preheat broiler. Combine soy sauce and ½ teaspoon wasabi paste; mix well. Spoon mixture over salmon. Place salmon, skin sides down, on rack of broiler pan. Broil 4 to 5 inches from heat source 8 minutes or until salmon is opaque in center.

2. Meanwhile, combine mayonnaise and remaining 1 teaspoon wasabi paste; mix well. Taste and add more wasabi, if desired. Transfer salmon to serving plates; top with mayonnaise mixture. *Makes 4 servings*

NOTE: For added flavor, marinate salmon in the soy sauce mixture 2 hours or overnight in the refrigerator before broiling.

SWEET AND SOUR SHRIMP STIR-FRY

GARLIC SHRIMP & VEGETABLES

2 tablespoons butter
1 tablespoon olive oil
1 bunch green onions, chopped
1 red bell pepper, diced
1 pound peeled, deveined large
    shrimp
2 cloves garlic, minced
    Juice of 1 lime
    Salt and black pepper
    Hot cooked spinach fettuccine
    (optional)

1. Heat butter and oil in medium skillet or wok over medium heat. Add onions and bell pepper. Stir-fry 2 minutes or until vegetables are crisp-tender.

2. Add shrimp and garlic; stir-fry 2 minutes or until shrimp turn pink.

3. Stir in lime juice. Season to taste with salt and black pepper. Serve over fettuccine, if desired. Garnish as desired.
Makes 4 servings

CURRIED TUNA SHELLS

1 to 2 tablespoons vegetable oil
½ cup chopped onion
½ cup chopped red bell pepper
1 medium zucchini, chopped
2 cups Quick White Sauce (recipe
    follows)
1½ teaspoons curry powder
1 (3-ounce) pouch of STARKIST®
    Premium Albacore or Chunk
    Light Tuna
6 ounces large pasta shells, cooked
    according to package
    directions

In large skillet, heat oil over medium-high heat; sauté onion and bell pepper until onion is soft. Add zucchini; sauté 2 more minutes. In large saucepan, combine white sauce with curry powder; blend well. Stir in tuna, cooked pasta and sautéed vegetables. Heat thoroughly; serve.
Makes 4 servings

QUICK WHITE SAUCE: In small saucepan, mix together 1 package (1.8 ounces) white sauce mix, 1½ cups milk or half & half and ¾ cup chicken broth. Bring to a boil over medium heat, stirring constantly. Reduce heat; cook 1 more minute, stirring constantly.

Prep Time: 20 minutes

GARLIC SHRIMP & VEGETABLES

GINGERED FISH WITH BOK CHOY

2 tablespoons sake or dry sherry
½ teaspoon salt, divided
¼ teaspoon black pepper
1¼ pounds skinless mahi-mahi fillets, cut into 1¼-inch-wide pieces, 1 inch thick
1 pound bok choy
¼ cup water
¼ cup teriyaki sauce
1 tablespoon cornstarch
¼ cup vegetable oil, divided
2 cloves garlic, minced
4 green onions with tops
1 piece fresh ginger (1 inch long), peeled and cut into thin strips
Hot cooked rice
Bok choy leaves and shredded red cabbage for garnish

1. Combine sake, ¼ teaspoon salt and black pepper in large bowl. Add fish and gently toss to coat; set aside.

2. Separate bok choy leaves from stems. Rinse and pat dry. Stack leaves and cut into 1-inch slices. Cut stems diagonally into ½-inch slices. Keep leaves and stems separate.

3. Stir water and teriyaki sauce into cornstarch in cup until smooth; set aside.

4. Heat wok over high heat about 1 minute or until hot. Drizzle 1 tablespoon oil into wok and heat 30 seconds. Add bok choy stems; stir-fry about 2 minutes or until crisp-tender. Add bok choy leaves and garlic; stir-fry until tender. Sprinkle with remaining ¼ teaspoon salt. Transfer to serving plate; cover and keep warm.

5. Drizzle remaining 3 tablespoons oil into wok and heat 30 seconds. Add fish mixture; stir-fry gently about 4 minutes or until fish is lightly browned and flakes easily when tested with fork. Place fish over bok choy.

6. Add onions and ginger to wok. Stir teriyaki mixture until smooth and add to wok. Stir-fry until sauce boils and thickens. Spoon sauce over fish. Serve with rice. Garnish, if desired. *Makes 4 servings*

GINGERED FISH WITH BOK CHOY

SEAFOOD & VEGETABLE STIR-FRY

2 teaspoons olive oil
½ medium red or yellow bell
    pepper, cut into strips
½ medium onion, cut into wedges
10 snow peas, trimmed and cut
    diagonally into halves
1 clove garlic, minced
6 ounces frozen cooked medium
    shrimp, thawed
2 tablespoons stir-fry sauce
1 cup hot cooked rice

1. Heat oil in large nonstick skillet over medium-high heat. Add vegetables; stir-fry 4 minutes. Add garlic; stir-fry 1 minute or until vegetables are crisp-tender.

2. Add shrimp and stir-fry sauce. Stir-fry 1 to 2 minutes or until hot. Serve over rice. *Makes 2 servings*

CLAMS IN BLACK BEAN SAUCE

24 small hard-shell clams
1½ tablespoons fermented, salted
    black beans
2 cloves garlic, minced
1 teaspoon minced fresh ginger
2 tablespoons vegetable oil
2 green onions, thinly sliced
1 cup chicken broth
2 tablespoons dry sherry
1 tablespoon soy sauce
1½ to 2 cups Chinese-style thin egg
    noodles, cooked and drained
3 tablespoons chopped fresh
    cilantro or parsley

1. Scrub clams under cold running water with stiff brush. (Discard any shells that refuse to close when tapped.)

2. Place black beans in sieve and rinse under cold running water. Coarsely chop beans. Combine beans with garlic and ginger; finely chop all three together.

3. Heat oil in 5-quart Dutch oven over medium heat. Add black bean mixture and onions; stir-fry 30 seconds. Add clams and stir to coat.

4. Add chicken broth, sherry and soy sauce to Dutch oven. Bring to a boil. Reduce heat; cover and simmer 5 to 8 minutes until clams shells open. (Discard any clams that do not open.)

5. To serve, arrange clams on noodles. Ladle broth over clams. Garnish with cilantro. *Makes 4 servings*

SEAFOOD & VEGETABLE STIR-FRY

STEAMED FISH FILLETS IN FRESH CILANTRO CHUTNEY

½ **cup green onions, cut into ½-inch lengths**
1 **to 2 hot green chili peppers,* seeded and coarsely chopped**
2 **tablespoons chopped fresh ginger**
2 **cloves garlic, peeled**
1 **cup cilantro leaves**
2 **tablespoons vegetable oil**
2 **tablespoons lime juice**
1 **teaspoon salt**
1 **teaspoon sugar**
¼ **teaspoon ground cumin**
8 **large romaine lettuce leaves**
4 **tilapia or orange roughy fillets (about 1 to 1¼ pounds)**

*Chili peppers can sting and irritate the skin; wear rubber gloves when handling peppers and do not touch eyes. Wash hands after handling.

1. To prepare chutney, drop green onions, chilies, ginger and garlic through feed tube of food processor with motor running. Stop machine and add cilantro, oil, lime juice, salt, sugar and cumin; process until cilantro is finely chopped. Set aside.

2. Trim 1 inch from base of each lettuce leaf; discard. Blanch lettuce leaves in large saucepan of boiling water 30 seconds; remove and drain.

3. Place 2 leaves flat on cutting board, overlapping slightly. Lay one fillet horizontally in center of leaves.

4. Coat fillet with ¼ of chutney. Fold ends of leaves over fillet; fold top and bottom of leaves over fillet to cover completely. Repeat procedure with remaining lettuce, fillets and chutney.

5. To steam fish, place 12-inch bamboo steamer in wok. Add water to 1 inch below steamer. (Water should not touch steamer.) Remove steamer. Cover wok; bring water to a boil over high heat.

6. Place wrapped fillets in steamer; place steamer in wok. Reduce heat to medium. Cover and steam fish 10 minutes per inch of thickness of fish or until fish turns opaque and flakes easily when tested with fork. Carefully remove fish from steamer. Serve immediately. Garnish as desired.

Makes 4 servings

STEAMED FISH FILLETS IN FRESH CILANTRO CHUTNEY

SEAFOOD COMBINATION

Fried Noodles (recipe follows)
½ cup water
1 tablespoon soy sauce
2 teaspoons cornstarch
2 teaspoons dry sherry
1 teaspoon instant chicken bouillon
    granules
4 tablespoons vegetable oil, divided
8 green onions with tops,
    diagonally cut into thin slices
3 ribs celery, diagonally cut into
    thin slices
1 can (8 ounces) water chestnuts,
    drained and cut into halves
1 can (8 ounces) sliced bamboo
    shoots, drained
8 ounces fresh or thawed frozen
    shrimp, peeled and deveined
8 ounces fresh or thawed frozen
    fish fillets, skin removed and
    cut into 1½-inch pieces
8 ounces fresh or thawed frozen
    sea scallops, cut into quarters

8 ounces Chinese rice vermicelli or
    bean threads
Vegetable oil for frying

1. Prepare Fried Noodles; set aside.

2. Combine water, soy sauce, cornstarch, sherry and bouillon granules in small bowl; mix well. Set aside.

3. Heat 2 tablespoons oil in wok or large skillet over high heat. Add green onions, celery, water chestnuts and bamboo shoots; stir-fry about 2 minutes or until crisp-tender. Remove from wok; set aside.

4. Heat remaining 2 tablespoons oil in wok over high heat. Add shrimp, fish pieces and scallops; stir-fry about 3 minutes or until all fish turns opaque and is cooked through.

5. Stir cornstarch mixture; add to wok. Cook and stir until liquid boils. Return vegetables to wok; cook and stir 2 minutes. Serve over Fried Noodles.

Makes 6 servings

FRIED NOODLES

1. Cut bundle of vermicelli in half. Gently pull each half apart into small bunches.

2. Heat oil in wok or large skillet over medium-high heat to 375°F. Using slotted spoon or tongs, lower small bunch of vermicelli into hot oil. Cook until vermicelli rises to top, 3 to 5 seconds; remove immediately. Drain vermicelli on paper towels. Repeat with remaining bunches.

Makes about 4 servings

SEAFOOD COMBINATION

SHRIMP IN MOCK LOBSTER SAUCE

½ cup fat-free reduced-sodium beef or chicken broth
¼ cup oyster sauce
1 tablespoon cornstarch
1 egg
1 egg white
1 tablespoon peanut or vegetable oil
¾ pound raw medium or large shrimp, peeled and deveined
2 cloves garlic, minced
3 green onions with tops, cut into ½-inch pieces
2 cups hot cooked Chinese egg noodles

1. Stir broth and oyster sauce into cornstarch in small bowl until smooth. Beat egg with egg white in separate small bowl. Set aside.

2. Heat wok over medium-high heat 1 minute or until hot. Drizzle oil into wok and heat 30 seconds. Add shrimp and garlic; stir-fry 3 to 5 minutes or until shrimp turn pink and opaque.

3. Stir broth mixture; add to wok. Add onions; stir-fry 1 minute or until sauce boils and thickens.

4. Stir eggs into wok; stir-fry 1 minute or just until eggs are set. Serve over noodles. *Makes 4 servings*

ASIAN SALMON STEAKS

3 tablespoons reduced-sodium soy sauce
3 tablespoons lime juice
1 tablespoon honey
½ teaspoon ground ginger
2 cloves garlic, pressed through garlic press
4 salmon steaks
Minced fresh cilantro, for garnish

Combine soy sauce, lime juice, honey, ginger and garlic in jar with tight-fitting lid. Cover and shake well. Place salmon steaks in glass dish; spoon about 1 tablespoon marinade over each salmon steak. Refrigerate 10 to 30 minutes.

Remove salmon from marinade; discard marinade. Place salmon on lightly greased broiler pan. Brush fish with some marinade from jar. Broil 10 minutes for each inch of thickness of fish, turning and basting once. Serve garnished with minced cilantro. *Makes 4 servings*

Favorite recipe from **National Fisheries Institute**

VEGGIE AND SCALLOP STIR-FRY

1 tablespoon vegetable oil
1 bag (16 ounces) BIRDS EYE®
    frozen Farm Fresh Mixtures
    Pepper Stir-Fry vegetables
½ pound small sea scallops
1 small onion, chopped *or* 3 green
    onions, sliced
1 tablespoon light soy sauce
1 tablespoon Oriental salad
    dressing
⅛ teaspoon ground ginger
    Garlic powder
    Salt and black pepper
    Hot cooked rice (optional)

- In wok or large skillet, heat oil over medium heat.

- Add vegetables; cover and cook 3 to 5 minutes or until crisp-tender.

- Uncover; add scallops and onion. Stir-fry 2 minutes.

- Stir in soy sauce and Oriental salad dressing.

- Reduce heat to low; simmer 3 to 5 minutes or until some liquid is absorbed.

- Stir in ginger, garlic powder and salt and pepper to taste; increase heat to medium-high. Stir-fry until all liquid is absorbed and scallops turn opaque and begin to brown.

- Serve over rice, if desired.

Makes 4 servings

Prep Time: 3 minutes
Cook Time: 10 to 12 minutes

ORIENTAL BAKED COD

2 tablespoons reduced-sodium soy sauce
2 tablespoons apple juice
1 tablespoon finely chopped fresh ginger
2 cloves garlic, minced
1 teaspoon crushed Szechwan peppercorns
4 cod fillets (about 1 pound)
4 green onions, thinly sliced

1. Preheat oven to 375°F. Spray roasting pan with nonstick cooking spray; set aside.

2. Combine soy sauce, apple juice, ginger, garlic and peppercorns in small bowl; mix well.

3. Place cod fillets in prepared pan; pour soy sauce mixture over fish. Bake about 10 minutes or until fish is opaque and flakes easily when tested with fork.

4. Transfer fish to serving dish; pour pan juices over fish and sprinkle with green onions. Garnish, if desired. *Makes 4 servings*

SHANGHAI STEAMED FISH

1 cleaned whole sea bass, red snapper, carp or grouper (about 1½ pounds)
¼ cup teriyaki sauce
2 teaspoons grated fresh ginger
2 green onions, cut into 4-inch pieces
1 teaspoon dark sesame oil (optional)
Bell pepper strips (optional)
Green onions (optional)

1. Sprinkle inside cavity of fish with teriyaki sauce and ginger. Place onions in cavity in single layer.

2. Place steaming rack in wok. Pour enough water into wok so that water is just below steaming rack. (Water should not touch rack.) Bring water to a boil in wok. Reduce heat to medium-low to maintain a simmer. Place fish on steaming rack in wok. Cover and steam fish about 10 minutes per inch of thickness measured at thickest part. Fish is done when it flakes easily when tested with fork.

3. Carefully remove fish; discard onions. Cut fish into 4 portions. Sprinkle with sesame oil and garnish with pepper strips and green onions, if desired. *Makes 4 servings*

ORIENTAL BAKED COD

STIR-FRIED CORKSCREW SHRIMP WITH VEGETABLES

Sauce
- ¼ cup LA CHOY® Soy Sauce
- ¼ cup BUTTERBALL® Chicken Broth
- 3 tablespoons dry sherry
- 1 tablespoon cornstarch
- 1 teaspoon sugar
- ¼ teaspoon *each:* black pepper and Oriental sesame oil

Shrimp and Vegetables
- 1 egg white
- 1 tablespoon cornstarch
- 1 pound shrimp, peeled, deveined and cut in half lengthwise
- 3 tablespoons WESSON® Oil, divided
- 1 cup sliced onion
- 1 tablespoon minced fresh garlic
- 1½ teaspoons minced gingerroot
- 1 cup sliced fresh mushrooms
- ½ cup thinly sliced carrots
- 1 can (14 ounces) LA CHOY® Bean Sprouts, well drained
- 1 can (8 ounces) LA CHOY® Sliced Water Chestnuts, drained
- 1 package (6 ounces) frozen pea pods, thawed

In small bowl, combine sauce ingredients; set aside. In medium bowl, beat together egg white and cornstarch until well blended. Add shrimp; toss gently to coat. In large nonstick skillet or wok, heat 2 tablespoons oil. Add shrimp mixture; stir-fry until shrimp curl and turn pink. Remove shrimp from skillet; drain. Heat remaining 1 tablespoon oil in same skillet. Add onion, garlic and ginger; stir-fry 30 seconds. Add mushrooms and carrots; stir-fry 1 to 2 minutes or until carrots are crisp-tender. Stir sauce; add to skillet. Cook, stirring constantly, until sauce is thick and bubbly. Return shrimp to skillet with bean sprouts, water chestnuts and pea pods; heat thoroughly, stirring occasionally. Garnish, if desired.

Makes 4 to 6 servings

Tip ▪▪▪

A sauce is generally defined as a thickened, seasoned liquid that is served with a food to add flavor and moisture and to enhance its appearance. It can be thick or thin, hot or cold, savory or sweet.

STIR-FRIED CORKSCREW SHRIMP WITH VEGETABLES

ALBACORE STIR-FRY

3 tablespoons vegetable oil
½ cup sliced onion
1 clove garlic, minced or pressed
1 bag (16 ounces) frozen Oriental
    vegetables, thawed and
    drained*
1 (7-ounce) pouch of STARKIST®
    Premium Albacore Tuna
3 tablespoons soy sauce
1 tablespoon lemon juice
1 tablespoon water
1 teaspoon sugar
2 cups hot cooked rice

*You can use 4 cups fresh vegetables, such as carrots, pea pods, broccoli, bell peppers, mushrooms, celery and bean sprouts instead of the frozen vegetables.

In wok or large skillet, heat oil over medium-high heat; sauté onion and garlic until onion is soft. Add vegetables; cook about 3 to 4 minutes or until vegetables are crisp-tender. Add tuna, soy sauce, lemon juice, water and sugar. Cook 1 more minute; serve over rice. *Makes 4 servings*

SWEET & SOUR SEAFOOD SAUTÉ

1 tablespoon vegetable oil
12 ounces raw sea scallops or
    shrimp, peeled and deveined
1 cup bell pepper strips
1 cup unsweetened pineapple
    chunks
½ cup canned bamboo shoots,
    drained
½ cup sweet and sour sauce
    Hot cooked rice

Heat oil in wok or large nonstick skillet; add scallops and bell pepper. Sauté 3 to 5 minutes or until scallops are opaque (or shrimp is pink). Add pineapple, bamboo shoots and sweet and sour sauce; cook 3 to 5 minutes or until heated through. Serve over hot rice. *Makes 4 servings*

*Favorite recipe from **National Fisheries Institute***

ALBACORE STIR-FRY

PACIFIC RIM HONEY-BARBECUED FISH

¼ cup honey
¼ cup chopped onion
2 tablespoons lime juice
2 tablespoons soy sauce
2 tablespoons hoisin sauce
2 cloves garlic, minced
1 jalapeño pepper, seeded and
    minced
1 teaspoon minced fresh gingerroot
4 swordfish steaks or other firm
    white fish (4 ounces each)

Combine all ingredients except swordfish in small bowl; mix well. Place fish in shallow baking dish; pour marinade over fish. Cover and refrigerate 1 hour. Remove fish from marinade. Grill over medium-hot coals or broil fish about 10 minutes per inch of thickness or until fish turns opaque and flakes easily when tested with fork. *Makes 4 servings*

Favorite recipe from **National Honey Board**

SZECHUAN TUNA STEAKS

4 tuna steaks (6 ounces each), cut
    1 inch thick
¼ cup dry sherry or sake
¼ cup soy sauce
1 tablespoon dark sesame oil
1 teaspoon hot chili oil *or*
    ¼ teaspoon red pepper flakes
1 clove garlic, minced
3 tablespoons chopped fresh
    cilantro

Place tuna in single layer in large shallow glass dish. Combine sherry, soy sauce, sesame oil, hot chili oil and garlic in small bowl. Reserve ¼ cup soy sauce mixture at room temperature. Pour remaining soy sauce mixture over tuna. Cover and marinate in refrigerator 40 minutes, turning once.

Prepare grill. Drain tuna, discarding marinade. Place tuna on grid. Grill, uncovered, over medium-hot coals 6 minutes or until tuna is opaque, but still feels somewhat soft in center,* turning halfway through grilling time. Transfer tuna to carving board. Cut each tuna steak into thin slices; fan out slices onto serving plates. Drizzle tuna slices with reserved soy sauce mixture; sprinkle with cilantro. *Makes 4 servings*

*Tuna becomes dry and tough if overcooked. Cook it as if it were beef.

PACIFIC RIM HONEY-BARBECUED FISH

SHRIMP STIR-FRY

1 bag SUCCESS® Brown Rice
   Vegetable cooking spray
1 tablespoon cornstarch
2 tablespoons reduced-sodium soy
   sauce
3 medium carrots, sliced
1 medium yellow bell pepper, cut
   into strips
¾ pound cleaned, cooked shrimp
   (or any other cooked meat)
½ pound snow pea pods, trimmed
¾ cup plain nonfat yogurt

Prepare rice according to package directions.

Spray skillet or wok with cooking spray. Combine cornstarch and soy sauce in small bowl; mix well. Set aside. Add carrots and bell pepper to hot skillet; stir-fry until crisp-tender. Stir cornstarch mixture. Add to vegetable mixture; cook and stir until sauce is thickened. Remove from heat. Stir in shrimp, pea pods and yogurt; heat thoroughly, stirring occasionally, about 5 minutes. Serve over hot rice. Garnish, if desired.

Makes 6 servings

BAKED FISH

1½ pounds firm-fleshed fish fillets (such
   as swordfish, tuna or seabass),
   cut into serving-sized pieces
½ cup SMUCKER'S® Plum Preserves
1 tablespoon soy sauce
1 teaspoon cornstarch
½ teaspoon ginger
2 cloves garlic, finely minced
   Salt and pepper

Plum Sauce
½ cup SMUCKER'S® Plum Preserves
1 clove garlic, finely minced
2 teaspoons soy sauce
¼ teaspoon pepper

Rinse fish and pat dry. Place in 9-inch baking dish coated with nonstick cooking spray.

Combine preserves, soy sauce, cornstarch, ginger, garlic and salt and pepper. Mix well. Pour over fish. Bake, uncovered, at 350°F for 20 minutes or until the thickest pieces of fish flake with a fork. *Do not overbake.*

Meanwhile, in small saucepan, combine all ingredients for plum sauce and cook over low heat, stirring occasionally for 3 minutes. Serve with fish.

Makes 4 servings

SHRIMP STIR-FRY

TANDOORI-STYLE SEAFOOD KABOBS

½ **pound each salmon fillet, tuna steak and swordfish steak***
1 **teaspoon salt**
1 **teaspoon ground cumin**
¼ **teaspoon black pepper**
  Dash ground cinnamon
  Dash ground cloves
  Dash ground nutmeg
  Dash ground cardamom (optional)
½ **cup plain low-fat yogurt**
¼ **cup lemon juice**
1 **piece (1-inch cube) peeled fresh ginger, minced**
1 **tablespoon olive oil**
2 **cloves garlic, minced**
½ **jalapeño pepper, seeded and minced**
½ **pound large shrimp, shelled with tails intact, deveined**
1 **each red and green bell pepper, cut into bite-size pieces**
  Fresh parsley sprigs
  Fresh chives

Any firm fish can be substituted for any fish listed above.

Cut fish into 1½-inch cubes; cover and refrigerate. Heat salt and spices in small skillet over medium heat until fragrant (or spices may be added to marinade without heating); place spices in 2-quart glass dish. Add yogurt, lemon juice, ginger, oil, garlic and jalapeño pepper; mix well. Add fish and shrimp; turn to coat. Cover and refrigerate at least 1 hour but no longer than 2 hours. Thread a variety of seafood onto each metal or wooden skewer, alternating with bell peppers. (Soak wooden skewers in hot water 30 minutes to prevent burning.) Grill kabobs over medium-hot KINGSFORD® Briquets about 2 minutes per side until fish flakes easily when tested with fork and shrimp are pink and opaque. Remove seafood and peppers from skewers. Garnish with parsley and chives.

Makes 4 servings

Tip

Jalapeño peppers are small, dark green chilies, normally 2 to 3 inches long and about ¾ of an inch wide with a blunt or slightly tapered end. Their flavor varies from hot to very hot. Ripe jalapeño peppers are red and sweeter than the green jalapeño. They are also sold canned or pickled.

TANDOORI-STYLE SEAFOOD KABOB

ORIENTAL BAKED SEAFOOD

¼ **cup chopped California Almonds**
2 **cups water**
½ **teaspoon salt**
1 **cup long-grain white rice**
1 **tablespoon grated fresh ginger**
1 **tablespoon sesame oil**
1 **teaspoon grated lemon peel**
1 **pound halibut**
½ **pound large scallops**
¼ **pound medium shrimp, shelled and deveined**
1 **clove garlic, minced**
1 **tablespoon light soy sauce**
½ **cup slivered green onions**

Preheat oven to 350°F. Spread almonds in shallow baking pan. Toast in oven 5 to 8 minutes until lightly browned, stirring occasionally; cool. Bring water and salt to a boil in medium saucepan. Stir in rice, ginger, sesame oil and lemon peel. Bring to a boil; cover and reduce heat to low. Simmer 20 to 25 minutes or until water is absorbed. Meanwhile, preheat oven to 400°F or preheat broiler or grill. Remove skin and bones from halibut; cut into large pieces. Cut 4 (12-inch) squares of foil. Divide halibut, scallops and shrimp among foil. Sprinkle seafood with garlic and soy sauce; seal squares tightly. Bake 12 minutes or broil or grill 4 inches from heat 15 minutes, turning once. Stir almonds into rice. Pour seafood mixture and juices over rice. Sprinkle with green onions. *Makes 4 servings*

MICROWAVE DIRECTIONS: Spread almonds in shallow pan. Cook at HIGH (100% power) 2 minutes, stirring often; cool. Combine water, salt, rice, ginger, sesame oil and lemon peel in 3-quart microwave-safe dish. Cover with plastic wrap. Cook at HIGH (100% power) 12 minutes, stirring halfway through. Let stand 10 minutes. Prepare fish packets as above using parchment paper instead of foil. Bring edges up and seal with rubber band. Place packets in microwave-safe baking dish. Cook at HIGH (100% power) 5 minutes, rotating dish. Serve as directed.

Favorite recipe from **Almond Board of California**

ORIENTAL BAKED SEAFOOD

ORIENTAL FISH STEW

8 to 10 dried shiitake mushrooms
¼ cup reduced-sodium soy sauce
2 tablespoons Chinese rice wine
1 teaspoon chopped fresh ginger
  Black pepper to taste
½ pound medium shrimp, peeled and deveined
½ pound halibut, cubed
1 tablespoon vegetable oil
2 cloves garlic, chopped
2 cups diagonally sliced bok choy
1½ cups diagonally sliced napa cabbage
1 cup broccoli florets
2 cubes vegetable bouillon dissolved in 2 cups hot water
½ cup bottled clam juice or water
2 tablespoons cold water
2 tablespoons cornstarch
¼ pound pea pods, stems removed
2 green onions with tops, sliced
  Hot cooked rice (optional)

Soften mushrooms in bowl of warm water 15 minutes. Drain; squeeze out excess water. Discard stems; slice caps. Set aside.

Combine soy sauce, rice wine, ginger and pepper in small bowl. Add shrimp and halibut; marinate at room temperature 10 minutes.

Meanwhile, heat oil in 5-quart Dutch oven over medium-high heat. Cook and stir garlic in hot oil 3 to 5 minutes until soft. Stir in bok choy, napa cabbage and broccoli.

Drain seafood, reserving marinade. Add dissolved vegetable bouillon, clam juice and seafood marinade to Dutch oven. Bring to a boil over high heat. Reduce heat to low. Simmer 5 to 10 minutes until vegetables are crisp-tender. Add seafood and mushrooms. Simmer 3 to 5 minutes until shrimp are opaque and fish flakes easily when tested with a fork.

Blend water into cornstarch until smooth; stir into fish stew. Cook and stir until stew boils and thickens slightly. Remove from heat; stir in pea pods and green onions. Serve over rice, if desired. *Makes 4 to 6 servings*

ACKNOWLEDGMENTS

The publisher would like to thank the companies and organizations listed below
for the use of their recipes and photographs in this publication.

Almond Board of California

American Italian Pasta Company-Pasta LaBella

Barilla America, Inc.

Birds Eye®

Bob Evans®

Campbell Soup Company

Colorado Potato Administrative Committee

ConAgra Foods®

Delmarva Poultry Industry, Inc.

Del Monte Corporation

Dole Food Company, Inc.

Fleischmann's® Margarines and Spreads

The Golden Grain Company®

Grandma's® is a registered trademark of Mott's, Inc.

Guiltless Gourmet®

Heinz North America

Hillshire Farm®

Hormel Foods, LLC

The Kingsford Products Company

Lawry's® Foods

Lee Kum Kee (USA) Inc.

McIlhenny Company (TABASCO® brand Pepper Sauce)

Mrs. T's Pierogies

National Fisheries Institute

National Honey Board

National Pork Board

National Turkey Federation

North Dakota Beef Commission

Peanut Advisory Board

Pear Bureau Northwest

Plochman, Inc.

The Quaker® Oatmeal Kitchens

Reckitt Benckiser Inc.

Riviana Foods Inc.

The J.M. Smucker Company

Splenda® is a registered trademark of McNeil Nutritionals

StarKist® Seafood Company

The Sugar Association, Inc.

Texas Peanut Producers Board

Unilever Bestfoods North America

USA Rice Federation

Walnut Marketing Board

INDEX

METRIC CONVERSION CHART

VOLUME MEASUREMENTS (dry)

⅛ teaspoon = 0.5 mL
¼ teaspoon = 1 mL
½ teaspoon = 2 mL
¾ teaspoon = 4 mL
1 teaspoon = 5 mL
1 tablespoon = 15 mL
2 tablespoons = 30 mL
¼ cup = 60 mL
⅓ cup = 75 mL
½ cup = 125 mL
⅔ cup = 150 mL
¾ cup = 175 mL
1 cup = 250 mL
2 cups = 1 pint = 500 mL
3 cups = 750 mL
4 cups = 1 quart = 1 L

VOLUME MEASUREMENTS (fluid)

1 fluid ounce (2 tablespoons) = 30 mL
4 fluid ounces (½ cup) = 125 mL
8 fluid ounces (1 cup) = 250 mL
12 fluid ounces (1½ cups) = 375 mL
16 fluid ounces (2 cups) = 500 mL

WEIGHTS (mass)

½ ounce = 15 g
1 ounce = 30 g
3 ounces = 90 g
4 ounces = 120 g
8 ounces = 225 g
10 ounces = 285 g
12 ounces = 360 g
16 ounces = 1 pound = 450 g

DIMENSIONS

¹⁄₁₆ inch = 2 mm
⅛ inch = 3 mm
¼ inch = 6 mm
½ inch = 1.5 cm
¾ inch = 2 cm
1 inch = 2.5 cm

OVEN TEMPERATURES

250°F = 120°C
275°F = 140°C
300°F = 150°C
325°F = 160°C
350°F = 180°C
375°F = 190°C
400°F = 200°C
425°F = 220°C
450°F = 230°C

BAKING PAN SIZES

Utensil	Size in Inches/Quarts	Metric Volume	Size in Centimeters
Baking or Cake Pan (square or rectangular)	8 × 8 × 2	2 L	20 × 20 × 5
	9 × 9 × 2	2.5 L	23 × 23 × 5
	12 × 8 × 2	3 L	30 × 20 × 5
	13 × 9 × 2	3.5 L	33 × 23 × 5
Loaf Pan	8 × 4 × 3	1.5 L	20 × 10 × 7
	9 × 5 × 3	2 L	23 × 13 × 7
Round Layer Cake Pan	8 × 1½	1.2 L	20 × 4
	9 × 1½	1.5 L	23 × 4
Pie Plate	8 × 1¼	750 mL	20 × 3
	9 × 1¼	1 L	23 × 3
Baking Dish or Casserole	1 quart	1 L	—
	1½ quart	1.5 L	—
	2 quart	2 L	—